THOMAS EDMONDSON AND T

# THOMAS EDMONDSON
## *and*
# THE DUBLIN LAUNDRY

*A Quaker Businessman,
1837–1908*

MONA HEARN

IRISH ACADEMIC PRESS
DUBLIN • PORTLAND, OR

First published in 2004 by
IRISH ACADEMIC PRESS
44 Northumberland Road, Dublin 4, Ireland

*and in the United States of America by*
IRISH ACADEMIC PRESS
c/o ISBS, Suite 300
920 NE 58th Avenue
Portland, Oregon 97213-3644

*Website*: www.iap.ie

British Library Cataloguing in Publication Data

A catalogue record of this book is available from the British Library.

ISBN 0–7165–2769–3 (cloth)
0–7165–2770–7

Library of Congress Cataloging-in-Publication Data

A catalog record of this book is availabe from the Library of Congress.

Typeset by
Carrigboy Typesetting Services, County Cork.
Printed by
ColourBooks Ltd, Dublin.

*In memory of G.L.A.*

# Contents

# *Illustrations*

## *List of Tables*

## *A Note on Money*

All references to money in the book are in the old British, pre-decimal currency of pounds ($\pounds$), shillings (s.) and pence (d.), in which 12d. = 1s. and 240d. = 20s. = $\pounds$1.

The $\pounds$ in 1900 was the equivalent of $\pounds$73 in early February 2003, or €106; a few conversions are given below:

$$1^1/_2\text{d.} = €0.66 \text{ euros}$$
$$2\text{s.}6\text{d.} = €13.25 \text{ euros}$$
$$\pounds1.15\text{s.} = €185.5 \text{ euros}$$

# Acknowledgements

I WOULD LIKE to thank Brian Donnelly of the National Archives of Ireland for his assistance in researching the Dublin Laundry Papers, an invaluable source. David and David Benson generously granted me lengthy interviews, and David put his extensive collection of photographs at my disposal.

M.H.
December 2003

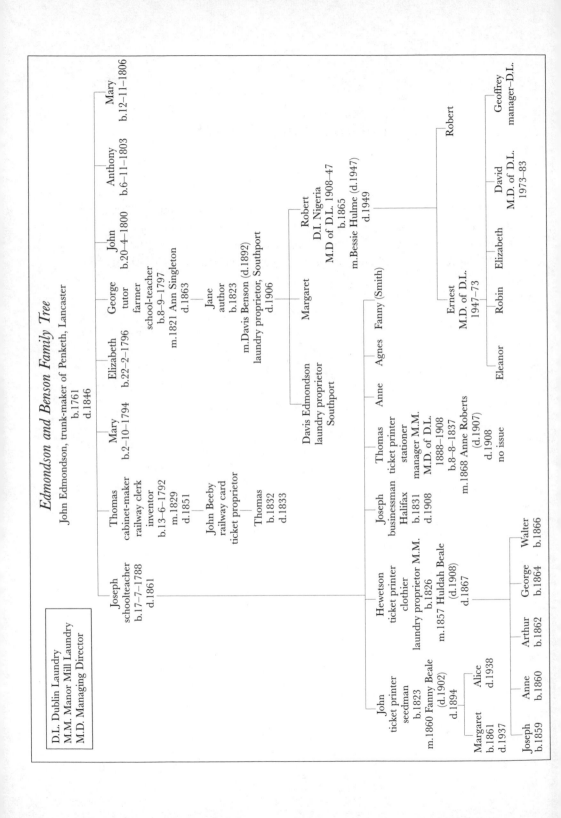

*Edmondson and Benson Family Tree*

John Edmondson, trunk-maker of Penketh, Lancaster
b.1761
d.1846

D.L. Dublin Laundry
M.M. Manor Mill Laundry
M.D. Managing Director

# Introduction

WHEN THOMAS EDMONDSON decided to start a new laundry in 1887, the time was ripe for such an enterprise, though the circumstances which gave rise to its foundation were unusual and came about unexpectedly. The second half of the nineteenth century was the heyday of the laundry trade, though the expansion continued well into the twentieth century. There were 197 laundries in London in 1882, 421 in 1892 and 624 in 1913.[1] Many of these were small, private laundries, probably run by one laundress and her family, but the expansion in numbers was dramatic. In 1861, 167,607 people were employed as laundry workers in England and Wales. The number in the trade rose over the rest of the century reaching a high of 205,015 in 1901. In 1861 laundry work ranked eleventh in a table of the principal occupations in England and Wales. The percentage of women and girls employed in the trade in England and Wales was 99 in 1861 and this fell to 91 in 1911.[2] It was always a predominantly female occupation. In Dublin the growth of the trade was much slower. There were three laundrykeepers named in *Thom's Directory* when the trade was listed for the first time in 1865. The number of laundries became seven when Edmondson's laundry, The Dublin Laundry, joined the list in 1888; there were thirteen in 1905 and this rose to sixteen in 1919.[3]

The expansion of the trade from the 1860s onwards was due to the growth of the middle classes and the move to the suburbs initiated by its most prosperous members.[4] People were taking a new pride in their homes on which they were prepared to lavish money. When there was a rise in income it was found that it was immediately followed by a disproportionately large increase in the expenditure on washing and mangling. The wearing of 'frequently and perfectly pressed linen' was, according to one writer on the trade in Victorian England, part of the 'paraphernalia of gentility' and was essential for those aspiring to upward mobility. Demand for laundry work was particularly heavy in London, with its high concentration of wealthy households, lodgers and

1

large institutions.[5] To a lesser extent, the same was true of Dublin. There was an increase in the size and the number of institutions such as boarding schools, hospitals, hotels and clubs. Edmondson assiduously sought their custom when starting his business, because, of course, they could be counted on to supply regular and large amounts of laundry, and, it was hoped, pay their bills regularly.

Increased spending on the house and its inhabitants was not just a feature of life for the upper classes. The improving economy in Ireland increased investment in household goods. Retail sales of furniture boomed from the 1890s: between 1904 and 1911 the value of imports of carpets and matting increased by 36 per cent[6]—extra bed linen, table coverings and curtains were needed. Men and women, to an increasing extent, bought their clothes from drapers or travelling dealers, and they were prepared to spend large sums on their 'Sunday best'.[7] Not only had people more clothes, they washed them more frequently, made aware, by the emphasis at the time on hygiene, of the need for cleanliness of the person and of the home. As commercial laundries were located in cities and large towns, a large proportion of the population had to continue to do their own increased washing at home, and were encouraged to do so by women columnists who maintained that the machines in laundries tore the clothes and that communal washing spread disease.[8] To help the housewives, the Congested District Board pioneered domestic classes in 1898 at which women were taught cookery, laundry work and housewifery.[9] Later, the Department of Agriculture and Technical Instruction started rural and urban schemes and laundry work was always a major subject on these courses.[10] The importance given to the home, clothes and sanitary matters helped commercial laundries by raising public awareness of the importance of clean, properly laundered linen.

From the earliest times the washing of clothes was an essential domestic chore; women used nearby streams and rivers, a method still used in undeveloped countries. Edmondson, holidaying on the Continent, mentions women washing on the bed of a stream at Nice; another 'pounding away at the linen' before her in a barge on the river Rhone and rinsing in the river; groups washing in nooks on the banks of streams at San Remo, and women washing in a constant stream of water flowing through a stone trough in the market square there; they stood on either side, rubbing the linen on the stone coping and on boards, and rinsing in the trough water, those at the end of the line getting, as he pointed out, the benefit of the others' soap, but also the

1. Women washing in a barge on the Rhône and rinsing in the river. Photograph taken by Thomas Edmondson.

dirtiest water. 'What a very conspicuous part the laundress does play upon the stage of Continental travel!', he declared.[11] Edmondson's keen laundryman's eye seeing, no doubt, what other travellers would have failed to notice. Much nearer home, popular names given to certain areas in Dublin reflect this important activity; Beaver Row, on the banks of the Dodder in Donnybrook, was known as Sudsy Row.[12] There was a washerwoman's lane in St. Catherine's parish,[13] and Glasnevin Hill was known as Washerwoman's Hill, because the Tolka was used for laundry.[14] The Banks of Pimlico was the place in the Liberties where the women did their washing in the river Poddle.[15]

The laundering of clothes was also a thoroughly disliked chore. In houses where there was no running water available, it was sheer drudgery. In evidence to the commissioners appointed to inquire into the working of the Factory and Workshop Acts in 1875, Dr Edward Dillon Mapother, consulting sanitary officer to the Public Health Committee of Dublin Corporation, spoke of 'the wretched tenement accommodation' in Dublin. Dublin had a large number of tenement houses in proportion to its population—9,300 out of a total of 24,000.[16] Many tenements were in what had been fine Georgian houses abandoned by prominent citizens after the Act of Union in 1801. One of these tenements could house a dozen families. A primitive toilet and a single tap in the backyard had to serve all the inhabitants.[17] On washday every drop of water had to be carried up the stairs, heated, perhaps on an open fire and the dirty water carried down again. Clothes were dried in a one- or two-roomed flat or, perhaps, hung out in the smoky, dirt-laden air of inner Dublin, on what was known as a 'line pole' shoved out the window.

In an effort to alleviate this hardship, the Bath and Wash-house Act of 1846 authorised any town to establish baths and wash-houses out of the rates. The Corporation of Liverpool had opened baths and wash-houses in 1842 where, for a penny, a tub and hot water were provided.[18] The first public baths and wash-house in Dublin were not provided by the corporation, but by the Mendicity Institution. It was opened on 16 February 1852 at Usher's Island and had ten baths for male and eight for female bathers. The wash-house was considered the province of the women and had forty stalls each partitioned off 'so one female cannot look at another's clothes'. The wash-house had a machine for extracting water, a drying closet, a mangle, smoothing tables and irons. Since most poor people had only one set of clothing, each woman was given a loose shift to wear while washing and drying her own clothes. She could then take a bath before going home. The managing committee saw their future clientele as not only the poor in the Institution and surrounding neighbourhood, but also the working class throughout the city. The baths immediately became very popular, 'being universally adopted by the various classes of society'; the wash-house was not as popular. The committee hoped that the working classes, for whom it was intended, would learn to appreciate it, as workers in England had done.[19] When, in 1881, Dublin Corporation decided to provide public baths and a wash-house, they considered taking over those provided by the Mendicity Institution. The terms offered by the governors of the Institution were not acceptable to the Corporation and the idea was abandoned. Portobello Basin on the Grand Canal was then considered as a site for the new baths. This was rejected as being too large, and, more importantly, too far from the city centre where most of those who might use the baths lived.[20] In 1882 the Corporation acquired a site at the corner of Poolbeg Street and Shoe-lane, which had formerly been occupied by Messrs Tedcastles, the coal merchants. The new building was to have ten reclining baths, one swimming bath and toilet facilities for men. The women's department would have its own entrance, five reclining baths, swimming bath and toilets; in addition, there would be a wash-house, measuring 40ft long by 25ft wide and containing twenty wash tubs with drying house and ironing tables. A report from Charles A. Cameron, the superintendent medical officer of health and city analyst, pointed out that there were three public baths and wash-houses in Manchester and eight in Liverpool.[21] The' first stone' of the baths and wash-house was laid by the Lord Mayor, William Meagher, on 17 April 1884. On the same day a new street, Tara Street, which gave its name to the building, was opened.[22] The Tara Street baths and wash-house were opened on 1 June 1885.[23] It cost 1d. an hour to use the wash-house, this included the use of trough, steam, hot and cold water. No charge was made for wringing, drying or mangling clothes.[24] It was calculated that the average washer spent two and three-quarters hours at the trough, for which she paid 2¾d.[25] In 1890 15,410 washers used Tara St.[26] In spite of recommendations by the Municipal Council of Dublin in 1900, 1905 and 1914, that more wash-houses, baths and swimming pools should be erected in different parts of the city, nothing further was done to alleviate the hardship of washday for the poor of Dublin.[27] Of course, the development of commercial laundries was of no use to the poor, and were probably also too expensive for the lower middle classes.

Even in homes in the fashionable squares of the city centre and the new suburbs, washday presented difficulties, though, as always, the problems of the well-to-do were of a different order from those of the poor. All the processes associated with laundering clothes—drawing cold water from a scullery or backyard tap, heating water and boiling clothes on the kitchen range, steeping, washing, rinsing, blueing whites and starching when necessary, even drying the clothes when the weather was wet—had to be done in the scullery and kitchen. This completely disrupted the normal running of the household, and family meals were planned to take account of the extra turmoil. Even Samuel Pepys in the seventeenth century was discommoded by this weekly activity: 'Home, and being washing-day, dined upon cold meat.'[28] Apart from the absence of machinery and modern detergents, all clothes and household linens were made entirely from natural fabrics which required to be handled with great care. Woollens and flannels had to be washed carefully in warm water to prevent shrinkage. Coloured garments, which could and usually did run, were also washed separately, and kept well away from the other clothes. Clothes worn in the 1850s exacerbated the ordeal of washday. Increasing prosperity brought an increasing elaboration of dress. Skirts continued to expand, and for the first half of the decade the desired effect was obtained by wearing a larger number of petticoats underneath. When the weight of these finally became intolerable, they were replaced by a 'cage crinoline', flexible steel hoops hung by tapes from the waist or sewn into a petticoat.[29] Not only were skirts enormous and often flounced, garments were trimmed with ribbon and lace which had to be removed and sewn on again every time the article was washed. Men's clothes presented different problems. Collars, cuffs and shirt fronts had to be starched stiffly and polished using a glossing iron, a tedious process, and one which continued well into the twentieth century. Ironing was a difficult chore, and everything had to be ironed. All cottons and linen articles were sprinkled with water and rolled up tightly to give an even dampness, so that a smooth surface would be obtained when they were ironed. Flat irons, which were available in different sizes—heavier ones for flat work, small ones for tiny gathers and fiddly parts—were usually used. They were heated on top of the range, and great care had to be taken to ensure that smuts did not ruin the clean linen. When the iron cooled, it was replaced by another hot iron. It is not surprising that washday was considered the hardest day's work of all.[30]

In addition there were staff problems, whether servants were expected or not expected to do the laundry was often a bone of contention between the mistress and servant. Indeed, many felt it necessary to make the matter clear in their advertisements for servants or situations by indicating that a charwoman was employed, or a servant might say that she was willing or unwilling to do the washing.[31] Many mistresses with two or three live-in servants had the services of a charwoman on washday, and housewives who could not afford a servant employed a charwoman for a day or a half-day a week to do the washing. Some washerwomen took the dirty linen to their own homes or the public wash-house and brought it back clean and ironed. Commercial laundries were therefore a boon for those who could afford them as it removed this most troublesome chore from the home altogether. There were, as has have seen, reservations about commercial laundries: Mrs Beeton said that the mechanical and chemical processes were supposed to injure the fabric of the linen, and 'in many families the fine linen, cottons and muslins, are washed and got up at home, even where the bulk of the washing is given out'.[32] In a later book, Beeton says that 'it is so customary to quote the reasons against home washing that we often lose sight of its real advantage'. The greatest saving was not the laundry bill but the wear and tear on clothes. Children's 'little garments carefully washed at home will last twice the time they would if sent to a laundry'.[33]

From the end of the eighteenth and the beginning of the nineteenth century, Dubliners had a laundry service supplied by religious and philanthropic bodies which used the labour of inmates to partly, or sometimes almost completely, defray the running costs of their establishments. Laundry work was the single most effective way of utilising the unskilled labour of women and supplying what was a growing need. These institutions varied in size and in importance as public laundries. While their aims and policies differed somewhat, they were, broadly speaking, committed to the rescue and reform of so-called 'fallen' women and girls.

The Magdalen Asylum at 8 Lower Leeson Street was founded in 1767, by Lady Arabella Denny, well known in Dublin for her charitable activities. It was the first of its kind in Ireland, although a similar institution in London had been started a few years earlier. At that time many charitable institutions had chapels attached to them, and it was largely from the collections at special charity sermons and those at the regular weekly services that costs were met. The collection on the opening day of the Magdalen Chapel in Leeson Street, 31 January, 1768, yielded £153.19s.8d.[34] The asylum was for Protestant young women after a first 'fall' and for those who were about to become mothers; 'those hardened in vice' were not admitted. The girls were trained as servants, and were expected to stay for two years. The laundry earned £135.7s.3d in 1899, a modest sum.[35] Dublin by Lamplight, founded in 1856, took inmates from all parts of the country. Those who remained for two years were placed in 'situations' or sent to America. The laundry was the chief support of the institution, described in 1899 as one of the largest in the city with good drying grounds.[36] The Dublin Female Penitentiary on the North Circular Road was founded in 1812 and was under trustees and a committee. Its admission policy made no distinction on religious grounds and its income depended on laundry-work and subscriptions. The Asylum for Penitent Females in Upper Baggot Street was founded in 1835 in association with the Episcopal Chapel. Again, it was managed by trustees, committee and a ladies committee. It had many Roman Catholic inmates. The income from the laundry, £1,180 in 1899, seems a large sum as there were only thirty-five inmates that year. Receipts from washing formed 'a considerable item in support of the institution', and the committee solicited orders from the public.[37]

The Dublin Roman Catholic Discharged Female Prisoners' Aid Society at 10 Henrietta Street was to help discharged Catholics who were just 'commencing a life of crime'. It was run by the Sisters of St.

Vincent de Paul; they were helped by a ladies' committee who visited the prisons but took only those they considered suitable and likely to reform. Income in 1899 was £1,683, £952 of which came from the laundry; the remainder was from subscriptions and other sources.[38] St. Mary Magdalen Asylum for Female Penitents, Donnybrook, was founded in 1798 by Mrs Ryan at 91 Townsend Street. It was later taken over by the sisters of charity and moved to Donnybrook in 1837. It had a hundred penitents, who 'contribute to their support by washing and needlework'.[39] The taking over of a magdalen asylum, which had been under lay management, by a religious order was not unusual. Two Catholic congregations brought into Ireland around the middle of the nineteenth century, the Sisters of Our Lady of Charity of the Refuge and Our Lady of Charity of the Good Shepherds of Angers, popularly known as the Good Shepherds, had the running of magdalen homes as their primary objective. The Irish Sisters of Charity and Sisters of Mercy also began to run these institutions in this period.[40]

There was continual antagonism between these laundries and the commercial laundries during the second half of the nineteenth century, and this extended well into the next. Commercial laundries accused the institution laundries of undercutting their prices; they also resented the fact that the institution laundries remained for years outside the ambit of the Factory Acts. During his long life as a laundryman, Edmondson never ceased to be annoyed by what he considered the unfair trading methods of the institution laundries.

Owners of country houses were in the happy position of being able to afford the space for their own private laundries and the specialised staff to run them: laundry-maids had been working in country houses for many centuries before housekeepers and housemaids were employed. Laundries were usually found on the periphery of the house, near the drying ground and in a position where the steam and smells could not penetrate into the kitchen and living quarters. The laundry department had a wash-room, drying room and an ironing room and, when machinery became available, they were mechanised.[41] Well-planned laundries were found, among others, in Pakenhall Hall,[42] Castleward,[43] and Humewood, Co. Wicklow.[44]

The laundry trade was a latecomer to the technical and organisational revolution in industry. The development of mechanised laundries did not, on the whole, occur until the 1860s at the earliest; the extensive establishment of steam laundries was a development of the period from the 1890s to the First World War.[45] This was another reason for the rapid

2. Women doing their laundry at a washing trough in San Remo. Photograph taken by Thomas Edmondson.

growth in the laundry business at that time: laundries were becoming much larger and more efficient. The trade entered a new phase, the factory stage, with a high initial expenditure being undertaken in order subsequently to save on time and labour in dealing with large quantities of work. Water power, gas engines and electric motors were all used for driving laundry machinery, but the steam engine was the one most generally favoured.[46] When Hewetson Edmondson, Edmondson's brother, started the first steam laundry in Ireland at Dundrum, County Dublin, in 1863, he was bringing the very latest in laundry technology to the country.[47]

With the coming of larger laundries and mechanised laundries, the trade came within the field of regulation and legislation by the state. From the beginning of the nineteenth century, it was clear that state intervention was necessary to regulate the enormous growth in manufacturing and trade engendered by the industrial revolution. Factory reform was a slow and painful process extending well into the twentieth century. It began in England with the cotton mills, taking nearly fifty years to attain a nominal ten-hour working day. Partial regulation had spread to other textile industries by 1833, but it was not until 1861 that further trades were included. From the beginning many manufacturers opposed factory legislation on the grounds, first, that it would increase costs and endanger British competitiveness with other countries, and, secondly, that it was an unwarrantable interference with private property.[48] The Factory Act of 1867 made a substantial advance in bringing within the scope of the law all premises in which fifty or more persons were engaged in a manufacturing process. The complementary Workshops Regulation Act brought under control all premises in which fewer than fifty persons were employed, defining 'employed' as occupied with or without wages, thus including home industry. Neither Act was effective in operation:[49] as far as the laundry business was concerned, it was totally ineffectual, allowing that trade to remain outside the control of the law for almost another thirty years (see ch.6). Factory inspectors had power over factories, but not workshops: these could be referred to the local authority, if conditions warranted intervention.[50]

Factory and workshop law was very complicated at this time, and an effort was made to simplify and unify the whole body of factory legislation. The Factory Acts of 1864 and 1867 and the Workshops Regulation Act of 1867 were repealed and a consolidating Factories and Workshop Act became law in 1878. This Act abolished the old distinction between factory and workshop, based on the number of persons employed, and decreed that a workplace using mechanical power was a factory; one not using mechanical power was a workshop.[51] The Factory Acts of the nineteenth century dealt only with the working conditions of children, young persons and women; the hours of adult males were usually indirectly regulated by the hours of females and young persons.[52]

CHAPTER ONE

# *The Founding of the Dublin Laundry*

THOMAS EDMONDSON, founder of the Dublin Laundry, was born in Great Bolton on 8 August 1837, the fourth and youngest son of a school teacher, Joseph Edmondson and his wife Anne. He came from a Yorkshire family which belonged to the Society of Friends, a fact which greatly affected their personal, social and business lives. Thomas's grandfather John was a trunk-maker in Lancaster. He and his wife Jane had eight children, five sons and three daughters: Joseph, Thomas, Mary, Elizabeth, George, John, Anthony and Mary.[1] One of his sons, George, who was reputed to have a gift for mechanical invention, was educated at Ackworth, Yorkshire, a famous Quaker school, where he was taught agriculture by Daniel Wheeler. He left at the age of fourteen as he wanted to be a teacher and was apprenticed to William Singleton, the reading master at Ackworth, who had started a boarding school at Broomhall, a suburb of Sheffield; George was to marry Singleton's daughter. In 1814 Alexander I of Russia visited England and was much impressed by the Quakers. In 1817 he invited Wheeler to superintend the reclamation of waste crown lands aroundSt. Petersburg: George, on Singleton's recommendation, joined Wheeler and his family as tutor to Wheeler's children and assistant in the work. The party left for Russia on 22 June 1818, when George was twenty years old. He came back to England in 1820 to marry Anne Singleton, and the young couple returned to Okta, near St. Petersburg. They were living there during severe flooding in 1824, described as 'the most awful visitation that has ever occurred within the memory of the oldest person living', which threatened the complete destruction of the city and suburbs They returned finally to England in 1825, George declaring that the winter was a very trying time for his wife and that the state of her health made the move necessary. They had a two-year-old daughter Jane at the time.[2]

11

Jane was to marry Davis Benson, described as a sugar refiner, who later started a successful steam laundry on Sussex Road, Southport. They had three children: Davis Edmondson Benson, the D.E. with whom Thomas Edmondson was in constant correspondence, a daughter Margaret, and Robert, the youngest, who was to become a future managing director of the Dublin Laundry. Jane wrote two books: *Quaker Pioneers in Russia*, which described their time in that country, and *From the Lune to the Neva*.[3] The latter was an account of Ackworth and Quaker life: fictional names were used, but it was no secret that Daniel Brady was Wheeler and John Skelton, his friend and tutor to his family, George Edmondson, Jane's father.[4] George went into education and ended his career as principal of Queenwood College in Hampshire. At Queenwood he was able to add agriculture to the subjects taught, and achieved his aim of establishing a science and technical school.[5] A reviewer of *Quaker Pioneers in Russia* expressed interest in the attraction which the Quakers seemed to have for the Russian Emperor, 'so emphatically contrasted with all their aspirations and ideas', and concluded that 'it may have been the fascination of the unlike'. As the Emperor had failed to get the work done by Russians, due to their 'incapacity and corruption', he, like more humble people everywhere, was probably attracted by the Quakers' industry and honesty.[6] In 1902 Jane was to consult her cousin Thomas Edmondson about the terms offered by Headley Brothers, when publishing *Quaker Pioneers*. It was brought out at the most favourable time of the year for Quaker publications, before the Yearly Meeting. It does not appear to have been too successful; Headleys were not satisfied with the sales of Friends books at that Yearly Meeting and criticised the 'plethora' of meetings which kept Friends so busy that they 'could not spend time among the books'. They also said that there would have been much more demand for the book if it had been published twenty years earlier. 'The dates to which it refers are not recent enough to interest keenly present-day readers.' A letter from Headleys in November 1903 admitted that sales were better than expected, and they agreed to Jane Benson's suggestion that they would issue a four-page leaflet of favourable press notices. A copy of the book was sent to the Tsar, and the authoress received gracious thanks on behalf of Nicholas II, from the *Ministre de la Court Impériale de Russie*.[7]

George's older brother Thomas, who in his youth also displayed an aptitude for mechanical invention, was later to become famous as the inventor of the card ticket system for railways. He is depicted in *From the Lune to the Neva* as the 'young pickle' who was taught knitting to keep him out of mischief.[8] He began his career as a journeyman cabinetmaker, and during that time made several improvements in cabinetmaking implements. Then he entered business in Carlisle, but the firm in which he was a partner went bankrupt. A biographer, in a revealing statement about Quakers in business, said: 'though a Friend, he was not successful'.[9] He was bankrupt, maintaining himself as a railway clerk in a small station on the Newcastle–Carlisle line, where one of his chores was to fill up paper tickets for each passenger; this he found both irksome and slow. It occurred to him that the work might be done by a machine, and tickets printed giving the name of the station, the class of carriage, dates of the month, the number of the ticket, and that all companies, from end to end of the kingdom, might be on one, uniform system. This was a much more significant invention than it might appear at first sight, because out of it grew the railway clearing house. Before that, in the course of a journey, travellers might have to move themselves and their luggage a number of times, buy new tickets and wait while they were filled up, wait, as a contemporary writer said 'at almost every joint of the journey, and having to do with diverse Companies who had nothing to do with each other but to find fault and be jealous'. Under the new arrangement, companies came together 'to carry a passenger and his carpet-bag as far as he wanted to go, and save him the trouble of dividing the fare among them by doing it themselves'. This was done in the clearing house at Euston Square Station. Here 200 clerks computed the charges of each company, an extremely complicated task involving examining and recording the business of thousands of stations.

Thomas Edmondson was responsible for replacing the paper ticket, filled in by hand with pen and ink, by a little cardboard ticket 'which gentlemen stick in their hats and ladies carry in their gloves'. There were six different, coloured tickets, which were printed in, to modern eyes, a very simple piece of apparatus. The type was inked by a saturated ribbon which travelled over a wheel; a feeder withdrew the blank tickets one by one from the bottom of a pile and passed them under the form of type, which was pressed down upon each by a lever: the ticket proceeded face upwards towards the opening, where the printer could check that it was correct before it fell into a receptacle below. Many companies had a logo, what they called a 'device', also printed on their tickets as a distinguishing mark. These could be chosen from a pattern book supplied by the patentee; these devices entailed extra work for the printer, such as double printing. The process was faster than might be thought, as one man could print 200 tickets per minute. Edmondson also invented a checking machine to verify the numbering of the tickets. The dating press, the machine into which the clerk pushed the end of the ticket he was selling and from which it came out dated, was also Edmondson's work. Blaylock, a Dublin watchmaker, helped to carry out Edmondson's idea.[10]

The Manchester and Leeds Railway first adopted Edmondson's invention and employed him at Oldham Road station for a time. He took out a patent and let it out on profitable terms, 10s. per mile per annum, a railway 30 miles long thus paid £15 a year for a licence to print tickets. He then devoted himself to perfecting details of his invention and providing tickets. When he began to make a profit, the first thing he did was to pay all his creditors what was due to them including the interest.[11] His nephew Thomas was able to recount that it took him twenty years to do so, Thomas junior, who was then short of money himself and was trying to pay off debts, seemed to take some consolation from this.[12] Edmondson was forty-six years of age when he got his great idea but lived only a further twelve years to enjoy the fruits of his invention. The clearing house was of inestimable advantage to the railways in saving time and money. A contemporary said: 'It is not an exaggeration to contribute a considerable proportion of the existing passenger traffic to the skilful administration of tickets', the present number of passengers could not have been 'forwarded' if tickets had still been filled in by hand.[13]

John, eldest son of Joseph and brother of Thomas, the future laundryman, went to Ireland from Yorkshire to print tickets for the Irish railway on behalf of his uncle. For many years he and one assistant supplied all the railways in the country. He carried on the business under his uncle's name, described in *Thom's Directory* of 1850, as 'patentee of railway ticket apparatus' at 31 Pill Lane, moving in 1852 to 61 Dame Street.[14] When Thomas died in 1851 the business was run under the name of his son John Beeby Edmondson. John was helped by his brother Heweton, until Hewetson went to Cork. In 1852 Harriet Martineau, the English tract-writer and novelist, described a visit to the 'moderate-sized' apartment where 'the passports of all Ireland' were produced and 'Two neatly-dressed, cheerful-faced, kind-spoken Friends—young brothers, who quietly work out here the invention of their honoured relative.'[15] John was twenty-nine at that time and Hewetson twenty six.

In 1858 John was joined by his youngest brother Thomas. A letter from the Hardshaw East Monthly Meeting of Friends, held at Manchester in September 1858, introduced Thomas Edmondson, a member of this meeting, who 'has removed to Dublin' to the Dublin Monthly Meeting of Friends. It informed the Dublin Friends that enquiry into his conduct and 'respecting debts' did not uncover any reason for not issuing a certificate on his behalf, and 'we recommend him to your Christian care'.[16] Thomas helped his brother in the railway ticket business, but, as the Edmondson patent was taken up by printing firms, John established a seed business in Dublin;[17] in 1862 John Edmondson and Brothers had a seed warehouse at 10 Dame Street.[18] Thomas's name appeared for the first time in *Thom's Directory* in 1866, when he was described as 'a stationer, printer, engraver and account book manufacturer', working at 9 Dame Street, premises previously held by Shannon and Co., wholesale stationer and printer. Perhaps his experience as a ticket printer stimulated an interest in printing, which he decided to become involved in when a suitable opportunity arose.

Hewetson, who went to Dublin in 1849, was also vouched for, first, by the Hardshaw West Monthly Meeting,[19] and three years later, when he moved to Cork, by the Dublin Monthly Meeting.[20] The certificates issued by the monthly meetings provided character testimonials and introductions to Friends in a new town or country and were of inestimable value to the young emigrant. Even if Thomas had not had two brothers living in Ireland when he arrived, he would have been welcomed into a comparatively small, prosperous community, committed to looking after the welfare of their members. This close-knit community resulted from the small number of Quakers in Ireland, their fraternal concern for one another and their discouragement of 'mixed marriages'. Every effort was made to prevent 'marrying out', even though there was no complete ban provided that the marriage took place in the meeting.[21] Those who married before a priest were certainly disowned.[22] The three Edmondson brothers all married Quakers. Thomas married Anne Roberts of Mountmellick on 19 August 1868. Anne was the ninth in a family of eleven children, six sons and five daughters. Thomas Edmondson thus gained a large, extended family and maintained close contact with many of them over the years. Thomas and Anne had no children,[23] a fact which was to influence the conduct of his laundry business. After his marriage he and his wife went to live in Millmount, Dundrum.[24]

On 12 November 1857 Hewetson married Huldah, daughter of George and Anne Beale, of Cork and also a member of a large family. He was working in Cork as a clothier.[25] Later, on 28 June 1860 John married Huldah's sister Fanny.[26] Publication of the intention of John Edmondson and Fanny Beale to marry had been made at the close of a meeting for worship in Cork on 13 May 1860. It was reported at that meeting that a 'man Friend' and two 'women Friends' had had an interview with Fanny; she had 'declared herself clear of any other marriage'; 'advice to Friends intending to marriage was read to the parties jointly'. Nothing had arisen to 'obstruct', and a certificate of 'clearings' having been received from the Dublin Monthly Meeting on behalf of John, the pair were at liberty to wed.[27] By the 1860s the Edmondson brothers had established a niche for themselves within the Quakers and the business community in Dublin, reinforced by what would have been regarded as eminently suitable marriages.

As has been said, membership of the Society of Friends influenced all aspects of the lives of its members. The Society differed from other sects, having no formula of beliefs such as a creed, no liturgy, no priesthood and no sacraments.[28] Quakers believed that the Spirit was available to everyone who turned to it genuinely, it was this 'Light of Christ' that informed and guided. Christ came to teach his people himself, not only in the present, but from the beginning of the world. As a direct consequence, no one should stand between the individual and God, neither priest nor presbyter.[29] Fearful lest they should limit the working of the Holy Spirit, the Inward Light, in each person, they had no set programme of readings, prayers or hymns; they met in silence so that the service might depend on spiritual guidance. Anyone who felt called to do so might read a passage of scripture or pray aloud. Friends refused to pay tithes, saying that the Gospel should be free, and that no one should earn money by preaching.[30]

The revelation of the spirit must be treated with absolute honesty as must everyday life. Such honesty was a condition of spiritual growth, as was the love of God and neighbour emphasised in the Gospels.[31] George Fox, the founder of the Society of Friends, believe that Friends must act faithfully in two ways, inward to God and outward to man.[32] Customs for which Quakers were noted stemmed direct from their beliefs. Where there is religious and civil liberty, and equality for all men and women, there is no place for titles or marks of servility or superiority. Weapons should not be used even on behalf of lawful authority; oaths are not necessary for those who always tell the truth, honesty in business and simplicity in lifestyle are enjoined on all. They also rejected the usual names of the days and months, as these were old pagan names, which neither their Christianity nor their simplicity would accept, thus Sunday was plain First Day and February, Second Month. They used the plain 'thee' and 'thou' instead of the more polite 'you'.[33] The name 'Quakers' was applied as early as 1647, first in derision, as the bodies of some fervent members shook and trembled with emotion while at prayer.[34]

Some members of the Society of Friends suffered persecution for their beliefs, all suffered certain restrictions on their freedom. Oaths were required for entry into university, and, as the Quakers would not take an oath, this closed many professions to their members. Later they were allowed to affirm or promise instead of swearing.[35] The army was also ruled out as they would not bear arms nor go to war. This meant that many Quakers turned to trade and industry, in which they were very successful. This was due, in no small measure, to the fact that people trusted them to be honourable and honest in their dealings.[36] Quakers helped one another, lent capital to start businesses and supported each other's businesses, as Thomas Edmondson did all his life. Edmondson was very annoyed with a Friend who had obtained loans from his fellow Quakers under what Thomas called 'false pretences', saying: 'Your letters dwell pretty entirely on the money question, and ignore the moral aspect of it.'[37] The love of neighbour led to the just and humane treatment of employees, and this had beneficial business effects which were little understood by the majority of employers at the end of the nineteenth century. At a time when being in business was looked down upon by a class-conscious society, Quakers seemed to be supremely confident in their role; they were, for the most part, successful, leading comfortable, upper-middle-class lives, and enjoying the respect of the community. It has been said that a child born into a Quaker home could feel a degree of security and know that he or she had a very definite place in the world.[38] Research into entrepreneurial success by minority or marginalised groups has shown that many of the factors affecting Quakers noted here, such as relative social blocking, the undervaluing of trade and commerce by the wider society, allied to a positive attitude towards it within the group and a high degree of group solidarity and cohesion, have been present. Other characteristics identified as leading to success have been the self-confidence of the group, the tendency to recruit and reward from within the group, the provision of mutual assistance, at least some degree of social integration, and an organised set of beliefs regarding the nature of the world.[39] It was pointed out that, while many successful business men were too snobbish to pay attention to their trade and made professional men of their sons, Quaker businesses tended to endure.[40]

The Society was organised by monthly meetings, quarterly meetings and a yearly meeting, held in the spring. Monthly meetings consisted of all members living within 'their limits'. They were attended, at first by invitation of well-established Quakers and later by all those 'in unity'. The monthly meetings, and indeed the other meetings, were very influential, any of those present could speak if he or she so desired on subjects both practical and religious. A clerk was appointed to record decisions and the records were agreed without voting.[41] The young Edmondsons were introduced to the Dublin and Cork Friends by their own monthly meetings in England. Thomas Edmondson attended the little meeting of Friends at Churchtown, Dundrum. At a preparatory meeting held there on the first of the second month 1891, he and Elizabeth Greene were appointed to the monthly meeting in Dublin. They were to report on 'the state of our meeting', bible classes and home mission work.[42] Representatives were appointed to the quarterly meetings by the monthly meetings. At the quarterly meetings ministers and elders met on the Seventh Day, meetings for worship were held on the First Day, meetings for discipline commenced on the Second Day and a concluding meeting for worship was then held at a time appointed by the quarterly meeting. The yearly meeting consisted of all Friends who were members of any monthly meeting within that jurisdiction. However, to ensure attendance, each quarterly meeting appointed representatives.[43]

Monthly meetings could appoint Friends to visit the Quaker families in its area. These visitors were called elders and had particular responsibility for the spiritual condition of the meetings which they served. Appointments were mostly for a limited period. It was believed that ministers were called to serve God and acted upon it: this was realised by others who could feel this power in them. The ministers were then 'recorded', that is recognised as being ministers and generally remained in that position for life.[44] Thomas Edmondson was a minister, as was his brother Joseph who lived in Halifax and was reputed to have a deeply-rooted faith.[45]

In 1871 Thomas Edmondson moved his stationers business to 11 Dame Street, when numbers 7, 8 and 9 Dame Street were taken over for the rebuilding of the Munster Bank.[46] At this stage he had become involved in the laundry business, to which he was to dedicate the remainder of his life. His brother Hewetson, who had started the steam laundry at Dundrum, Co. Dublin, near Dundrum Castle, known as the Manor Mill Laundry, had died at the age of forty-one, leaving a widow and five children, four sons and a daughter, the eldest of whom was seven.[47] Shortly afterwards, Thomas entered into a partnership arrangement with Huldah under which they shared the profits equally, while Thomas managed the laundry and received a salary; this was £200 a year in 1880. The laundry, of course, belonged to Huldah and her family.[48] Edmondson spent the next twenty years running this laundry, although he continued his involvement in the printing business. By the late 1870s he had left Dame Street.[49] No doubt he found that he was unable to run two businesses, and the laundry was absorbing all his energies. At about that time he put money into a printing business at 97 Middle Abbey Street. It was run by Thomas Moore and printed the *Gardener's Record* and the *Irish Farmer's Newspaper*. This proved an unfortunate investment and was to cause Thomas much trouble and financial loss (see below, p.000).

Letters written by Thomas between 1880 and 1883, when he was at the Manor Mill Laundry thirteen to fifteen years, show a man who was interested and happy in his work and was actively involved in plans to expand the laundry. He was pleased with the progress of the business which produced a net profit of £867 in 1880, about £21 better than in any previous year. He was not slow to point out to his sister-in-law his contribution to this satisfactory state: 'It has however only been by close watching that the hands help our work up so well.'[50] This improvement continued over the next few years, a net profit of £1,069 was recorded in 1882.[51] Relations between Huldah and her brother-in-law appear to have been extremely cordial. On 14 June 1882 Thomas said that he and his wife would be glad to see George, Huldah's son, to dinner on Saturday or any other time that suited him.[52] In August 1883 he discussed with Huldah the possibility of involving George in the business but thought that it was perhaps premature to talk to him about this;[53] George was just nineteen at the time. Again, on 27 September 1882 he invited Huldah to dinner to discuss business.[54] Edmondson, however, seemed to take the major decisions. He told the postmistress that all letters addressed to any person whatsoever at the Manor Mill were to be left at his private house, Lyndon, to which he had moved in 1880.[55] In November 1882 he informed Huldah that he was getting a town office as an advertisement and as a convenient way of receiving and distributing laundry, and that ultimately it would be connected by telephone with the Manor Mill.[56]

In 1880 Thomas was thinking of moving the laundry to a new site at Dartry Mills in Upper Rathmines, because the lease of the Dundrum premises was short and renewal uncertain.[57] Dartry Mills was an old ruin which was formerly a paint mill.[58] In August 1881 he wrote to a Mr Blandford in Manchester telling him that he had procured a splendid site nearer Dublin, but still in the country, and asking him to come over and give some rough plans and suggestions to his builder and architect:

he said: 'I intend to make it a really model concern.'[59] In August 1883 he told Huldah that he had to look ahead to the building of Dartry Mills and that he hoped to be able soon to 'put before thee my ideas'.[60] These plans, in spite of Edmondson's obvious enthusiasm for the project, did not materalise, and the Manor Mill Laundry remained in Dundrum. Business discussions with Huldah seemed to be opportunities for Thomas to inform her of his plans for the business and to explain decisions already taken. This somewhat high-handed approach to a business which belonged, after all, to Huldah and her family, may have contributed in no small measure to the final split between the two families.

During these years Edmondson had experienced severe financial problems with the printing and publishing business, the Abbey Publishing Works in Middle Abbey Street.[61] He told a friend in January 1882, 'I have a large sum so locked up that I cannot realise it for several months and in the meantime am worse off than yourself probably'.[62] In September 1881 Edmondson had turned down completely a plan of Thomas Moore's to start a new paper, saying that he, Edmondson, had already put £706.10s.0d, a considerable sum at the time, into the business since the previous January, and could not be expected to find new capital; he added that Moore had enough to do to look after the business, and to get in 'what is due to us'. He told Moore, unequivocally, that he would have from this time on to get in enough money to pay current expenses 'as I can furnish no more'.[63] Things did not improve, and by the end of November 1881 Edmondson had decided to dispose of 97 Middle Abbey Street as a going concern.[64] He assured Moore that he was willing 'to pay you whatever is honestly due', and to leave it to arbitration, 'I know of no better way of settling such differences, if each party concerned is really desirous of only getting what is fairly due him'; he concluded: 'I am, I imagine, a just man'.[65] In suggesting arbitration, Thomas was following the Quaker method of settling disputes through discussion or arbitration. Friends were required not to go to law, though it was acknowledged that this was not always an attainable ideal.[66]

Finally, Edmondson decided to settle with Moore, and to pay him a lump sum, and 'be done with all his claims'.[67] He undertook to pay bills totalling £500 due to the Munster Bank. He also gave notice to two employees.[68] In spite of his bruising experiences with Moore, Edmondson agreed in March 1882 to rent him the front and back offices on the ground floor for a rent of £50 per annum, and gave Moore the right, by a separate agreement, to publish *The Irish Farmers' Newspaper*.[69] By July 1882 Edmondson had to threaten to use the law against Moore for non-payment of rent and had to disclaim liability for two bills.[70] Recourse was not made to the law, only because Edmondson paid Moore a good deal more than that to which he was entitled.[71] Edmondson did not finally get possession of his offices from Moore until early 1883,[72] though his involvement with the man probably went on longer. The whole affair took a lot of Thomas's time and caused him much worry and trouble, not to mention financial embarrassment. He complained many times during these years of being in need of money.[73] While he lost money on the venture, he was, he maintained, the only loser.[74]

It is clear from correspondence that he envisaged spending the remainder of his working life at the Manor Mill Laundry, and taking George, Huldah's son, into the business, probably, in time, to become an active partner. These expectations, however, were dashed when the happy relationship between Edmondson and Huldah's family ended abruptly in 1887. A legal flaw was discovered in his partnership arrangement of twenty years previously, which was, in Thomas's own words, 'taken advantage of by my nephew to deprive me of all my interest in the business';[75] he was, he said, turned out penniless.[76] Thomas was, understandably, very bitter about this, especially having spent so long 'working it up'.[77] He left the Manor Mill making a handsome profit,[78] 1886 was, in fact, a particularly good year.[79] He made no secret of his anger and told former business associates and friends exactly what had happened. Manor Mill accounts sent to Edmondson at this time were returned forthwith accompanied by a letter stating that he had no connection with the Manor Mill Laundry, and advising that they be sent to 'The Proprietors, Manor Mill Laundry'.[80] He, in turn, advised the Surveyor of Taxes that the assessment for the Manor Mill should, he supposed, be in the name of George B. Edmondson, 'who appears to be acting for the present possessors of that concern'.[81]

Thomas Edmondson did not spend too long wallowing in self-pity and recriminations. Even before he left the Manor Mill he started to build a new future for himself and his wife within the laundry industry. In March 1887 he sought quotations for equipment from Thos. Bradford and Co., Manchester, which, he said, was not for the Manor Mill but to fill an order he hoped to secure.[82] In the same month he was in touch with Robert Gibney, of the Maltings, Maryboro, to know whether his mill was on the market, again pretending that it was for another 'party': he wanted to know so that he 'may include it (or otherwise) in a list of similar concerns for my "client" '.[83] It had been acquired by Gibney in 1856 and run as a flour mill in conjunction with a bakery in Patrick

Street, Dublin. It was situated on the Milltown side of the Nine Arches, on the right-hand side of the road when going from Rathmines to Milltown; the chimney, the only remaining part of the laundry, can still be seen today. While Edmondson entered into negotiations with Capt Percy Harvey about Londers Park Mills,[84] he was obviously keen from the beginning to get the Gibney mill. Several months were to pass before the matter was finally settled. Robert Gibney was slow to quote terms and those he proposed initially were unacceptable.[85] Then there was great difficulty about signing the lease. Edmondson stated in September that he had been waiting six weeks for a 'party', in fact the head landlord, to come home from the Continent whose signature 'is needful on the lease'.[86] Though it is clear that he felt he had secured the premises he wanted in Milltown in June, he was discussing alterations to the mill with W. and A. Roberts, the builders of Grand Canal Street, his brother-in-law,[87] matters were not finally resolved until October: Edmondson paid Gibney £500 purchase money and an annual rent of £75.[88] The premises extended from the old bridge of Milltown to the railway viaduct; it was bounded on the north by the Milltown Road, on the south by the river Dodder, on the east by Milltown and on the west by the 'holding' of the railway company.[89] On 21 October 1887 Edmondson announced that at last they were in possession of their premises, that about thirty men were at work putting them in order, which he expected would take from six to seven weeks.[90] The engineering work was done by J.F. Roberts, another brother-in-law. The renovations took almost four months.[91]

'We are glad indeed that we have got the Milltown place', Thomas told a relative, adding that it was 'without doubt' the best position in Co. Dublin.[92] It is probable that his requirements were those he enunciated in 1880 when he contemplated moving the Manor Mill to Dartry. Fresh country air was seen as essential in competition with the 'institution laundries', which preoccupied him for most of his working life as a laundryman. He also listed water supply, an obvious necessity, main drainage and water power, if possible. He indicated that he wished to stay on the south side and not too far from Kingstown. Lastly, he mentioned the need for a supply of 'hands'. In 1880 he said that Dartry was near enough to Dundrum to enable them to keep nearly all the Manor Mill workers, if they moved the laundry.[93] When he started his own laundry at Milltown, which was nearer to Dundrum than Dartry, he brought most of his admittedly small starting staff with him from the Manor Mill; many others followed. This availability of trained staff was obviously a factor in Edmondson's plans, though it must have caused enormous difficulties for the Manor Mill. In December 1887 Edmondson told a friend, possibly with a certain amount of satisfaction, 'things are not going very smoothly at the "old shop", I would not much wonder if Mrs. H. and family are already sorry . . . The pond overflowed and flooded their sitting room lately and damaged the new carpet.'[94]

The equipment for a modern steam laundry was expensive. In August, when he had left the Manor Mill, he said that he intended spending over £1,000 immediately on machinery and £500 on the premises.[95] It was estimated by professionals in 1909 that £500 capital was required to start a laundry with a turnover of £40 to £50 a week, £395 for machinery and equipment, including engine and boiler, and £100 for working capital.[96] Of course, labour and machinery would have been slightly cheaper in 1887.[97] Thomas Edmondson was aiming for a turnover of at least a £100 per week. From the end of March onwards he was engaged in obtaining estimates and placing orders for this machinery— he told suppliers that he was fitting out a large steam laundry, without divulging that it was his own.[98] In August 1887 Edmondson undertook the work of remodelling a large hospital laundry in Cork Street,[99] which put him in the happy position of being able to bargain effectively with laundry suppliers anxious to do business with a man dispensing so much largess. Quakers were involved in the Cork Street Fever Hospital from its foundation in 1804,[100] and Edmondson was probably considered an obvious choice for this job. He had, between the two concerns, about £2,000 worth of fittings to order,[101] and he exploited this situation to the full. On 16 September 1887 he ordered £208.2s.6d of equipment for the Cork Street hospital and £253.14s.0d worth for the Dublin Laundry, on condition that Bradford and Co. gave 15 per cent discount, 'guarantee complete success in working of the two Crescent Ironers', and delivered all carriage and packaging free to the North Wall.[102] He ordered a water heater at £25 less 20 per cent discount—'I suppose you will deliver free for Cork Street?'; he added that he would probably want another for the Dublin Laundry if the price were satisfactory.[103] Thomas's third brother, Joseph, helped him in purchasing machinery locally, in Halifax. Many of the English firms from whom Edmondson bought equipment were those to whom he was well known from his time at the Manor Mill—firms such as: James Armstrong and Co., 13 Fore Street, London EC, Thomas Bradford and Co., Salford and Thomas Broadbent and Sons, Huddersfield. When asked to furnish references by an iron works in Huddersfield, Edmondson said he could give any number of Dublin ones, but gave his brother Joseph, who was 'well-known' in Halifax and can satisfy you as to 'my *bone fides*'.[104] He also used James Armstrong, of London, with whom he seemed to be very friendly, as a referee.[105]

While the Manor Mill Laundry was privately owned by Huldah Edmondson and her family,[106] Thomas Edmondson had to form a limited company to start the Milltown laundry. He reckoned that the outlay of £1,500 would be sufficient to fit out the premises as a 'first-class Steam Laundry, on the most approved modern principles'. At the time of his writing that, 6 June 1887, on the occasion of forming the company, negotiations for the acquisition of premises were not, as has been seen, completed (see above). The proposed directors of the company were Henry J. Allen and John Edmondson, the managing director was Thomas Edmondson. Share capital of £1,750 was to be raised, in 1,000 ordinary shares of £1 each and £750 in 6 per cent preference shares of £1 each. Of the ordinary shares, £750 were taken up by Edmondson's wife, who had money of her own, and it was decided that the remaining £250 would not be offered at that time. The 6 per cent preference shares were allocated to the owners of £750 then invested in the Manor Mill, members of well-known Quaker families, such as the Bewleys, Goodbodys and Pims, which would be withdrawn as soon as possible by the owners, and all, or the bulk of it, invested in the Dublin Laundry Co. Ltd. As there might be some delay in realising that sum and to provide sufficient surplus capital for contingencies, it was decided to raise £750 in 6 per cent debentures of £50 each (redeemable at par by the company upon giving six months' notice after three years from the date of the debentures). As the debentures were the first charge on the business, this was considered ample security. It was pointed out that steam laundries, when properly managed, were good paying concerns. Figures were quoted for three English and Scottish laundries to prove this point, and it was stated that the Manor Mill, worked on a small capital, showed much better results. In short, Edmondson, with his previous experience and large personal connections, was convinced that the Dublin Laundry would prove a success, and he therefore felt confident in asking his friends to take up the debentures.[107]

Huldah and her family were, indeed, abandoned by those who might have been expected to give support. John Edmondson, married to Huldah's sister, immediately became a director of the new company. Quaker investors were willing to withdraw their money and reinvest it in the new laundry. These happenings might be explained by the fact that Huldah left the Society of Friends a year after her husband's death.

In a letter to the monthly meeting of Women Friends held at Eustace Street in May 1868, Huldah resigned, 'I have for so long seen differently from you'; she stated her case at great length. She said that within the preceding two years the Lord had shown her plainly by his spirit and his written word what He would have her do. 'I have waited upon Him and prayerfully considered the subject and believe the time has now come . . .'. Friends visited her and had 'a very free and open interview'. 'There appearing to be no prospect of Huldah Edmondson altering her present decision', the monthly meeting held in Dublin on 12 August 1868 accepted her resignation, and said that they could 'no longer consider her to be a member of our Religious Society'. Huldah was aware that this would upset friends and family. 'To cause dear relatives any regret is hard, but Jesus said "He that loveth Father or Mother more than me, is not worthy of me".'[108] There was a hint that Hewetson 'ceased to be a Friend', but he was buried in the Friends' Burial Ground, Temple Hill on 24 April 1867.[109] Also, it must be remembered that Hewetson ran the Manor Mill Laundry for four years; Thomas ran it for twenty. Most of the Quaker money, especially in view of Huldah's defection, was probably attracted to the business by Thomas. He was identified as the power behind the enterprise, a position he took every opportunity to enhance. Many shrewd Quaker businessmen might have been anxious to withdraw their money as soon as possible from what was seen as a rudderless ship and to pledge their support to the erstwhile captain in his new venture. Anyway, sympathy in the feud seemed to be with Thomas, and he was initially the bigger loser.

Later, in June, Edmondson decided that he would require additional money as £500 was invested in the Milltown property, and so he got friends to take £250 more preference shares, and this enabled him to issue £250 more in debentures without affecting the security offered to holders.[110] The seven original members of the company were: John Edmondson, 10 Dame Street, seed merchant; Henry J. Allen, 28 Lower Sackville Street, merchant; Francis Roberts, Seapoint Villas, Monkstown, gentleman; Frederick W. Wood, Larchfield, Dundrum, merchant; William F. Webb, 47 Lower Sackville Street, solicitor; William C. Roberts, 7 Grand Canal Street, builder; Thomas Edmondson, Lynton, Dundrum, steam laundry manager. The memorandum of association of the new company was signed on 12 August 1887.[111] In October Thomas Edmondson was writing to investors, calling in the capital, as he required the money urgently to pay the bills.[112] He asked Fred Wood, who had promised to take three £50 debenture shares, whether he would mind taking £50 of it in 6 per cent preference shares. He agreed that debentures offered the best security, but said that he believed the preference shares were perfectly safe, and, of course, gave a voice in management. Edmondson said that all the debentures were taken up and he would like some to offer with preference shares.[113] Wood agreed to this.[114] The ease with which Edmondson obtained capital is a measure of the confidence that business people had in him and of the solidarity of the Quaker community. He himself appeared to have little money at this time; this was due to the troubles he had at 97 Middle Abbey Street. He told the surveyor of taxes in March 1887, that, since he left 11 Dame Street, he was not liable for taxes due to his heavy losses in other concerns—until 1886, which was an exceptionally good year at the Manor Mill.[115] When he left there in July 1887 he had no income;[116] he and his wife had money invested in the Manor Mill to which he was unable to get access.[117] Since he had left the stationery business, he and his wife were assessed separately for income tax purposes.[118]

Edmondson was extremely busy during this time with building work, purchasing equipment and the myriad other tasks necessary before the laundry could open, which he hoped would be before Christmas.[119] All the old flour machinery and a large waterwheel, which was not required, had to be removed. Floors were taken out to give sufficient height and ventilation, new window frames and sashes were fitted, and other extensive repairs and alterations were carried out. The steam boiler, shafting and machinery had to be installed.[120] In August he asked the Alliance Gas Co. of D'Olier Street to have the gas reconnected to Gibney's Mill and charged to their account.[121] In October he protested that the price was too high and that the extent to which they would use gas, for heating especially, would depend on the price.[122] He was negotiating with Thomas Heiton and Co., Westmoreland Street in November about the cost of carriage of coal to Milltown.[123] Advice was sought on softening and filtering the water, and whether the hardness of the water would justify the expense; filtering, he considered essential, as the stream became muddy in rainy weather.[124] The county engineer was approached about the serious pollution of the Dodder, which had 'ashes and all sorts of refuse thrown into it'.[125] Signs were ordered for the laundry from an enamel company in Wolverhampton, about 25ft long with 'The Dublin Laundry Co. (Limited)', written in 18in high letters, and smaller signs, giving the address of the laundry and the name of the managing director, for erection at railway stations.[126] Lighting, painting, flooring, new ceilings[127]—all received minute attention from

Edmondson. He ordered stationery from his friend Frederick Wood of Wexford.[128] In reply to a request for a price list in September, Edmondson said that he would send one when printed, and that it would not vary much from the Manor Mill list. By mid-November he was soliciting the laundry-work from the director of the new Central Hotel, saying that he felt sure that the Dublin Laundry could do better for the hotel than if the hotel had its own laundry. He quoted prices for the usual range of articles sent by hotels—tablecloths cost from 1d each, napkins 9d a dozen, sheets (all sizes) 1s. a dozen, shirts 3d each, cuffs 1d a pair, collars $^{1}/_{2}$d each.[129] In that month also, he asked the United Telephone Co. to quote for a line from the laundry to the Central Exchange;[130] in December he told them that he considered the price too high,[131] and did not install the telephone until March 1890.[132] Edmondson wrote to Messrs. A. Thom and Co. Ltd, asking them to put the Dublin Laundry's name in the 1888 *Directory*, and to remove his name wherever it appeared in connection with the Manor Mill.[133]

Edmondson surrendered Lyndon on 31 December 1887 at the end of a seven-year tenancy.[134] He intended moving to Shanagarry (the old garden), a manager's house on the laundry grounds. Shanagarry was, in fact, two back-to-back houses, Thomas's had a front garden, while the other, occupied by the manageress, faced the laundry entrance.[135] Thomas had refurbishment work done on his part of the house. With his usual attention to detail, he was arranging early in November to have the rest of the border for the dado sent out so that all might be finished. He and his wife moved in on 10 November 1887,[136] to what he himself described as, 'a comfortable home'.[137] He paid a firm at 30 South Anne Street £2.9s.6d for removing his furniture, having deducted 6d for the telegram sent because the proprietor's sons arrived one and half hours late.[138]

The hiring of staff is an essential task when starting a new enterprise, yet it was one singularly absent from mention in Edmondson's correspondence at this time. The reason was that the staff, a modest number to begin with, were mainly coming from the Manor Mill. This is hinted at in a reference written by Edmondson for the forewoman in the wash house in May, when he suggested that one of the reasons why she left the Manor Mill was the impending retirement of the writer, himself, and others with whom she was long associated.[139] Mrs Walsh, who became manageress of the new laundry, had been, in Edmondson's words 'my right-hand woman for fifteen years in Dundrum'.[140] Those who applied for a job at this time were told, by Thomas, that he had no vacancy, but that when work began he might have 'something'.[141] During the first year of its operation, Edmondson said that some of the best hands from the Manor Mill were employed in the Dublin Laundry.[142]

During these months before the opening of the Dublin Laundry, Edmondson was absolutely confident of the success of the venture. He wrote to a Quaker friend in Cardiff in September: 'We have no doubt of our success if health be given us'.[143] Later that month he told James Armstrong: 'We shall have a splendid concern at Milltown, nearer to Dublin than this [Dundrum], with splendid water power, and an abundance of space for expansion.'[144] He said that they were very cheerful about their business prospects and felt sure of doing a paying trade at once.[145] He believed that they would have the best equipped public laundry in Ireland.[146] No doubt Edmondson had grounds for optimism—he knew the laundry business, had successfully managed a steam laundry for twenty years, and had seen growth in the years from 1877 onwards.[147] There was expansion in the commercial laundry trade in Great Britain (see above), and he obviously that felt the business was also ripe for expansion in Ireland. Edmondson had had an unfortunate experience with his printing business, and the question could be asked whether he should have seen the flaw in his contract with his sister-in-law; however, in view of the usual strong familial bonds and loyalties among Quakers, he could be forgiven for not anticipating subsequent developments. In spite of these mishaps, he had the support of the Quakers and of the business community.

By the end of November Edmondson was trying to hurry up the refurbishment. He told the builders that it was vitally important that the laundry should start work as soon as possible, and that they would have to try working longer hours or putting in one or two extra men.[148] Arrangements were made with Alliance Gas for temporary gas fittings so that carpenters could work till seven or eight in the evening.[149] In spite of this, by early December Edmondson was resigned to the fact that it would be at least four weeks before they would be ready for the public opening.[150] At Christmas he was forecasting the opening for the middle of January. They were doing a little work as they had obtained the contract for the Central Hotel and were afraid of missing it if they could not start at once.[151] This might have been a mistake, because, at the beginning of February, Edmondson had to beg Mrs Mayhew, the manageress, for another chance, explaining that they really had no opportunity of doing themselves justice hitherto.[152] Advertisements for the Dublin Laundry appeared on the front pages of both the *Freeman's Journal* and the *Daily Express* at the end of December.[153]

This was a worrying time for Edmondson. He told a friend in December that they were as yet earning nothing and spending thousands.[154] In January he told the builders that expenditure on the laundry had gone so far beyond his expectations that he would have to look for a considerable addition to their capital.[155] The matter was discussed two days later, at the general meeting of shareholders held at Milltown on 12 January 1888, with Thomas in the chair and Francis Roberts, Fred Wood, John Edmondson and Anne Edmondson present. No conclusion was reached, and it was left to the managing director to make the best arrangements possible. That meeting also fixed Edmondson's salary at £52 per annum, with free house, coals, gas, vegetables and washing.[156] In order to get the additional money needed, Edmondson tried to raise capital by mortgaging his wife's property, but found that there were difficulties in doing this. He was advised to issue further debentures instead.[157] He asked his family to invest in the new 6.5 per cent debenture issue; one of those approached was his mother-in-law,[158] and he also contacted his friends Fred Wood, Thomas Rhodes and Henry John Williams and others.[159] He successfully raised the £1,000 in this way. The capital of the company was largely in the hands of Edmondson and his wife, family members and Quaker friends. Nannie, his wife, owned £750 ordinary shares (the seven people involved in the formation of the company had one ordinary share each[160]). Edmondson was depending on the dividend from these to supplement his annual salary.

# CHAPTER TWO

# *The Early Days at the Dublin Laundry*

THE DUBLIN LAUNDRY was officially opened on 30 January 1888.[1] Work began with a total staff of sixteen,[2] most if not all of whom appear to have been former employees of the Manor Mill. A picture of the laundry as it was at that time appears as Plate 4; the old flour mill had, in the words of Thomas Edmondson, been 'transformed',[3] though the outer appearance remained virtually unchanged. The machinery was worked by a waterwheel; two vans collected the linen. In addition to the normal requirements of a laundry, wash house, sorting and packing room, ironing room and office, there was, from the beginning, a mess room;[4] this was quite unusual at the time, though it was a feature of many Quaker enterprises. Edmondson was intensely proud of the new laundry and, in March, he told Henry Goodbody that 'he would be glad if you, or any other of our shareholders called to see the place.'[5] However, he was not willing to show a 'professional' around the laundry as he feared that he might have been commissioned by his opponents to 'spy out the land'.[6]

From the beginning the venture was successful. Receipts went up steadily from £8:17s.3d for the first week to £42.5s.0d for the thirteenth.[7] Early in March Edmondson reported that 'there had been a large increase in business'.[8] He told his cousin that they had undoubtedly the finest concern in Dublin. They were all working very hard; it was a pleasure to be earning again after a long time 'not of idleness but of no income'.[9] The first week's work in April 1888 far exceeded any previous week and Thomas had no doubt of the concern being a financial success;[10] business came in so fast that they were hardly able to keep pace with it.[11] At the end of that month, he wrote to a Quaker friend, 'It is indeed wonderful how we have been helped "in all our difficulties"'. He decided that for the first year he would give up almost everything outside business, this included the yearly meeting; he

30

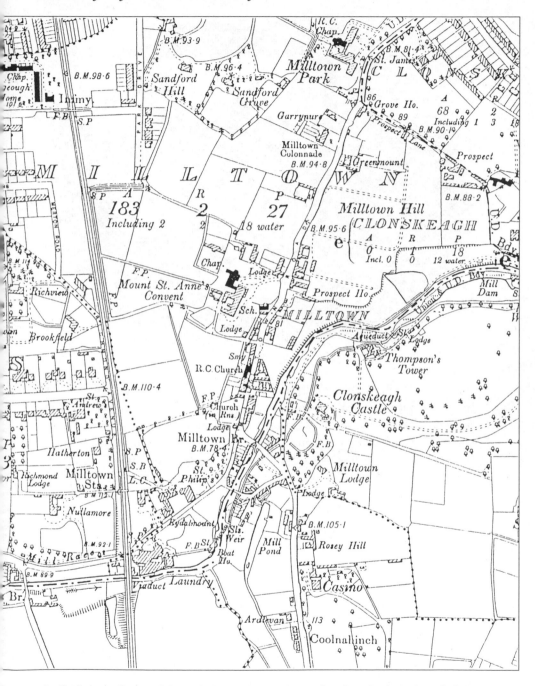

3. Ordnance Survey Map of the Milltown Area, showing the laundry, viaduct and the Milltown road.

4. Sketch of the Dublin Laundry in 1888.

said, 'I dont expect to be at many or any of the sittings'; he saw this as his 'clear duty'.[12] That this conscientious and dedicated member of the Society of Friends should curtail his attendance at the most important event of the Quaker year shows a concept of duty that afforded high status in life to business and is indicative of the close link which Quakers held between religion and everyday life.[13]

Edmondson told a customer in May, 'We believe that, on the whole, we are now doing our work about the best of any laundry in Dublin'; they had forty hands employed. 'Business is flourishing beyond our most sanguine expectation', he said at the end of June.[14] A week in mid-August was 'their heaviest week yet', when they made £65 profit, even though many of their best customers were away. Thomas hoped this would almost reach £100 by the end of the year.[15] On 30 January 1889 he proudly proclaimed that the Dublin Laundry Company was just one year old, and that they had seventy-five people employed.[16]

Of course, every effort had been made to secure additional business. From 1888 daily advertisements for the laundry were appearing in the *Irish Times*, Edmondson requesting that they be placed directly under the advertisements for the Manor Mill Laundry.[17] A new advertisement was substituted in April for the one placed in February; in his covering letter Edmondson underlined that it was to be in 'the same relative position'.[18] Whether his reason was to embarrass the Manor Mill, which it must have, or to show that there were now two different laundries in the Dundrum/Milltown area, is not clear. Certainly there was some confusion about the two. '"Much Pleased" I am indeed much pleased with the way my clothes are washed and done up' reads an advertisement inserted about this time, purporting to be a letter from 'A Lady in Bray' to the Dublin Laundry; 'the lady' going on to urge her friends to give their custom to that laundry.[19] Advertisements were also placed in the professional press, such as *The Laundry Journal* and the *Laundry News*: Edmondson told the editors that he would be glad of 'friendly notices of our circular in your column'.[20]

In March 1888 thousands of circulars were sent out and temporary staff engaged to address the envelopes,[21] 5,000 additional copies of each of the three circulars were ordered from Fred Wood in April. These included information on the success of the laundry since it opened.[22] Show cards were also used to advertise the laundry, and in May 1888 Edmondson asked Ward and Co., Royal Ulster Works, Belfast, to quote for various quantities, from 500 to 10,000. He pointed out that the design was their own and could not be used by the printers for anyone else. Edmondson was about to offer them, however, to successful laundries in England.[23] Early in 1890 the Dublin Laundry was using the Advertising Company Ltd, D'Olier Street, to look after this part of the business, and instructing them to send out circulars at the rate of about 2,000 per week, beginning with the city and finishing with the more distant suburbs.[24] Edmondson believed in advertising his laundry by taking part in the Spring Show. In 1890 the Dublin Laundry won the silver medal for the 'Van and Horse' competition at Ballsbridge.[25] In 1896 he took space to erect a small tent for the Dartry Dye Works at the Horse Show.[26]

Besides advertising, new customers were sought by letter and by personal contact. Mrs Spencer from Southport, obviously previously known to Thomas Edmondson, was brought over for a few weeks to call on prospective customers, and this started before the laundry opened. Her second-class return fare was paid, she had full board and lodgings in the Edmondson home, and she was paid £1 a week for the two or three weeks for which her services were required.[27] Mrs Walsh, the manageress, was sent to seek orders before Christmas, armed with a letter of introduction from Edmondson and a price list.[28] Thomas himself was busy writing to potentially remunerative customers, such as hotels and large institutions; some of these were followed by a visit from Mrs Walsh. At the time it was usual for the staff in large drapery stores to live in, so in May 1888 Thomas wrote to Messrs Todd Burns and Co., Mary Street, asking for a trial 'if they were thinking of making a change in their laundry', and saying that they were now returning the sheets of hotels and large houses, such as yours, 'most thoroughly aired'; they were able to do this 'having a splendid machine for the purpose';[29] Arnotts was also approached.[30] Returning sheets ready for immediate use was a feature much stressed at this time by Thomas, it was obviously something which he felt would give them an advantage over their competitors; it was also a boon not offered to private houses. In the same month, Edmondson heard that the management of the Shelbourne Hotel was contemplating alterations to the laundry; many hotels had their own. He immediately wrote to the manageress offering to undertake the hotel washing during the building period. 'We have facilities such as no other Laundry in Ireland possesses for turning out large quantities of work with rapidity and excellence.'[31] This was followed by a letter to the man likely to get the job of refurbishment, asking him to put in 'a good word' for the Dublin Laundry. Edmondson then pointed out that he had noticed a lot of smoke coming from the Shelbourne chimney, showing 'something defective in their consumption of coal'; he offered to go over the laundry with the builder and give his advice; the only fee he would expect would be the builder's intercession 'on behalf of this concern as opportunity offers.'[32] This shows that Edmondson set about acquiring contracts in a methodical manner using, in his own words, every opportunity that arose. He wrote to the Revd S. Tomlinson seeking the contract for washing the surplices of St. Patrick's Cathedral Choir— saying that he understood that Tomlinson was contemplating a change. Edmondson said that his manageress Mrs Walsh would call on Monday morning, 'in the hope of her coming to some definite arrangement'.[33] This was followed by a letter to the Revd J. Bewley, asking him to intervene on their behalf, and saying 'it amounts to a good sum and we are anxious to secure it'.[34]

Edmondson also turned his attention to the nobility, and did not confine his focus to Ireland. He wrote to a Mr Davis at 5 Grosvenor Place, London, enclosing a circular and saying, that he believed Lord Edward was acquainted with his brother in Dame Street, and adding that he himself was well known to Lord Ardilaun. He said that his company was doing work for The Royal Irish Yacht Club, The Absolute Club and the new Central Hotel, and 'I may say giving satisfaction to all'.[35] He was later to seek the contract for the United Service Club.[36] He solicited work from Lady Cloncurry, telling her that he had managed the Manor Mill for twenty years and enclosing a printed explanation of why he had left.[37]

He also approached the President of the Officers' Mess in the Curragh Camp, telling him that the Dublin Laundry was doing work for the 4th King's Own, Royal Barrack; he said 'no laundry in Ireland can do as well. We have every appliance.' A month later, when Capt Campbell, 93rd Highlanders, Curragh Camp, expressed satisfaction with the laundry, Edmondson wrote immediately for a letter to that effect so that he could show it to other officers.[38] He continued to seek military contracts and in December 1889 solicited the mess laundry for the 3rd Grenadier Guards, Richmond Barracks.[39] By this time he was experiencing difficulty in obtaining payment from a number of officers. He wrote to Capt Somerville, Skibereen, saying, 'we really had so much money due from officers in your and other regiments, that we could not continue to give credit. Many took not the smallest notice of our application.'[40] Thomas was clearly exasperated by the cavalier approach of the officers to paying their accounts, an attitude completely foreign to one brought up in the Quaker tradition. In January 1890 he wrote to the President, Officers' Mess, 4th King's Own, Ballsbridge:

> we expected one or two of your officers to pay us what we believe to be honestly due to us. We ask you, Sir, as 'an officer and a gentleman', if you think it fair to treat us so? . . . it was only when we had many such accounts, a very long time due to us from your officers, that we pressed for settlement. Several of them still owe us accounts, and neither pay nor take any notice of our letters.[41]

Thomas did not get any satisfaction from the officer on this occasion. In February he wrote to the Commander-in-Chief, Horse Guards, London, about the conduct of Lt Willmott of the 5th Dragoon Guards. Having failed, after many attempts, to get Willmott to pay his bills, the Dublin Laundry management decided to hold his linen; Willmott sent a telegram saying he would pay when he got his laundry; a van man went with linen and bill, the lieutenant, 'with curses, mounted into the van and forcibly took the linen out', and did not pay.[42] Thomas trusted that the Commander-in-Chief would take some notice of it, which does not appear to have happened, as the matter had to be put into the hands of a solicitor.[43] The Dublin Laundry finally got a cheque from Willmott, which Edmondson hoped would be honoured.[44] When writing to London, he took the opportunity to talk of 'an increased tendency on the part of many officers to neglect these small accounts, and as it is not to the credit of the service, I call it to your attention.'

The assiduous seeking of new business was certainly successful, but the rapid growth in customers from the day the Dublin Laundry opened, brought its own problems. More hands were required, more machinery was needed; this put strains on financial resources. In April Thomas Edmondson said that he was just lodging cheques in the Royal Bank in time to meet the builders' bills.[45] He told the First Annual General Meeting in February 1889, that 'the continued and unprecedented increase of business compelled further outlay, chiefly for a second Ironing Machine and Improved Drying Apparatus'. Special arrangements were made for deferring payment for some of the larger items, but he did not think it necessary to seek additional capital. A Tyler ironer and another hydraulic washer were bought from James Armstrong on the understanding that Edmondson might not be able to pay for them for six months.[46] In January 1889 he put a fourth van on the road, which was to be used solely for hotel work.[47] He apologised for the late payment of a bill, saying that they had been 'a little light of cash' because trade increased so rapidly, which involved large expenditures for additional machinery.[48]

Perhaps the biggest problem for Edmondson was the need to recruit more staff rapidly. 'We make our place as perfect as possible as to machinery and appliances, but we still have to depend on fallible helpers, and find it impossible to get hands sufficient, of such a class as we should prefer to have and are willing to pay.'[49] While declaring in March that the laundry was in 'perfect working order', he said it was easier to buy 'new brooms' than to get people to use them 'with brains'.[50] By April and May 1888 staff were required urgently and a number of girls were called to interview early the following day and told to bring their testimonials with them; he admitted to making a couple of appointments 'in a great hurry'.[51] He sought temporary assistance for a few days from a friend, saying that they were very busy and needed help, chiefly in the office.[52] In spite of his dire need for staff, he explained to a friend, who was seeking a job for a girl, that he could not find a 'corner' for her. 'We seem to find it needful to employ married hands in preference and plenty of such have offered.'[53] He did not explain why, but he probably considered them less flighty and easier to manage than young, single girls; the ability 'to keep order among a lot of hands' was always stressed when selecting a forewoman. Also, there was a tradition of employing married women in British laundries which probably had an influence. In a letter to a friend in June 1889, he admitted that they had found it difficult to organise a good staff of hands fast enough to cope with the work, but he said they would improve in that and other points.[54] He also said at that time, that 'it taxed all our energies to get together in 8 months the staff for such a business.'[55] In February 1889 they had a 'lot of trouble' with staff which lasted for a few weeks.[56] The cause of the trouble was not given, perhaps hasty recruitment had led to less careful selection than was to be used in the future. At the time staff were working long hours, from 8 a.m. until 9 p.m., except on Saturday, when they finished at 7.30 p.m.—some finishing earlier—this may have contributed to the unrest. The high morale generated by a small staff, well-known to the Edmondsons, working together to launch a new enterprise, would have made long hours acceptable. A year later a much larger new staff without the same commitment would have been much less willing to accept those hours. On the other hand, hours of work may not have been the issue. In the days before legislation was introduced, other laundries worked even longer hours.

In the first year Edmondson spent much time trying to recruit supervisory staff, a task to which he always devoted the utmost care and attention. He was much aware of the crucial role they played in the success of the business. A Quaker friend who wrote to him on behalf of a girl seeking work—this was common at the time when young people felt they needed an influential sponsor, and also may have had difficulty in writing the necessary letters—was asked whether the girl was a Protestant and whether she would be able 'to oversee' staff.[57] While it was never stated that religion was important when selecting managerial and supervisory staff, applicants were asked to state their religious affiliation, and the vast majority of those in positions of authority belonged to the Church of Ireland or the Church of England. Edmondson asked another sponsor about an applicant for a position as sorter and packer: 'Is she a Protestant, about what age. Is she a steady, dependable girl?' He then added: 'I am always afraid of people who have been to America and returned. They are so often unsettled in habits.'[58] In 1882, when managing the Manor Mill laundry, Edmondson sent a list of questions to a married woman who had applied for an outdoor job in the laundry. These included ones about her husband and his occupation, her children, previous work experience, references available, salary expected, and whether she was 'perfectly strong and healthy and able for constant work?' On receipt of her replies, he wrote that he should require 'thoroughly satisfactory references, both as to your own and your husband's characters, for altho he would not be employed by me, I should be just as particular as to his character, as if he were.' He asked whether her husband was also a Protestant, and whether she were Church of Ireland or Lutheran.[59] Besides a probable bias for Protestants, many of those in positions of authority were recruited in England and were likely to be Anglicans. Quakers were, of course, particularly welcome. A girl from Enniscorthy, who was considered for a supervisory post was told: 'whether to live in our house or not would depend on circumstances, but if we engaged a "Friend", we should be glad to have her with us. In that case we should commence at £25 per annum with, of course, full board and washing.'[60] A competent woman was sought to take 'partial oversight' of the wash house where about twenty women were employed.[61] In April 1889 Thomas decided to employ a permanent man in the wash house, and asked James Armstrong if he knew 'a likely man'. In May he went over to interview six men who answered an advertisement for the post. The interviews were held in Armstrong's office in London and he was asked to include also any 'likely men' who did not write.[62] This set a pattern which Thomas was to follow throughout the remainder of his working career; he frequently went to England to interview job applicants using facilities provided by family, friends or business colleagues. On these occasions he might ask his cousins in Southport to interview or shortlist applicants for him. In April 1889 Edmondson offered a job to Martha Haughton from Ferns, a Quaker, suggesting that she come for a month to see how it 'suits us both', and then they would see what post she would best fill. The salary to begin with was £20, but, if she 'proved able', she would get more responsibility and a higher salary.[63] Religion, age, education, previous knowledge of the applicant or of the applicant's family and ability to control staff were the most important factors; previous knowledge of the laundry business was considered desirable but not essential. This co-operation with his cousins in Southport was not all one way; they often sought Thomas's advice and help. In 1895 he sent Robert Benson 'a batch of replies to various advertisements to see if any would suit him.'[64] He employed 'lady clerks' in the office, when it was by no means a common practice.[65]

When the laundry opened Mrs Edmondson took charge of the sorting and packing room. By the end of April, Thomas was seeking an 'active, young, clever woman' to relieve his wife in this job.[66] He admitted that sorting and checking soiled linen was not very pleasant, but it had to be done and done carefully.[67] It was, in fact, probably the hardest and most distasteful job in a laundry, where work generally was hard and conditions difficult (see Chapter 4). Mrs Edmondson obviously did not shirk hard and unpleasant work, and this, no doubt, was a good example for the staff. By August she had some help and was not quite as busy.[68] However, her husband was still seeking a competent person for the sorting and packing department in January 1889; he wanted someone 'able in every way to represent my wife in her absence'. The Edmondsons thought that anyone under thirty would not suit the position 'as being not sufficiently removed in point of age from those under her'. Otherwise, he told Josephine Walpole, from Ballycastle, Queen's Co., they would have been glad for her sake and her family's 'to have had you with us'. They gave the job to a thirty-year-old with business experience.[69]

At the end of March the search was still going on for someone to relieve his wife as much as possible.[70] In May an advertisement was placed in *The Friend* for a capable woman to take 'oversight of sorting and packing rooms where about ten others are engaged'; business experience, not necessarily in the same line, was required. 'Anyone thoroughly equal to the requirements of that position would be liberally dealt with and have a comfortable home'.[71] In his reply to the Quaker sponsor of an English applicant, Edmondson said: 'the vacant post is one that could be suitably filled by an educated lady. It is, however, very different from teaching or from almost any other business . . . an arduous post'. He said that the work consisted of overseeing the checking in of soiled linen, marking it if necessary, pricing and looking after the packing of clean linen. He added that, 'Of course the more menial (for want of a better word) parts are done by subordinates, but anyone in the room should be willing "to give a hand" in emergency.' He was looking for someone who, in time, would take the weight of the whole department from his wife's shoulders, someone who was not afraid of a little hard work, and who would 'settle down with the view of making it worth our while to keep her!' He said that, although the laundry was a limited company, he and his wife had much the largest interest in it, and 'can do as we like'; he went on to say that, as they had no children, there was 'a better opening for 'an "outsider" to make a good place for herself'. This is a theme to which Edmondson returned on a number of occasions about this time. He was over fifty, had no family and wanted to recruit people who would take over responsibilities from himself and his wife, and were more likely to do this if they had, or hoped to have, some vested interest in the business. He suggested that his friend's protégé could call on his cousin Jane Benson at the steam laundry on Sussex Road, Southport: Jane would tell her more about the Dublin Laundry and the duties of the post.[72] That letter was written on 13 June 1889, six days later he received letters from Jane Benson, approving of the girl and from the applicant herself. He offered her a starting salary of £40 which would go up to £50 at the end of one year, if she were satisfactory, and it might even go beyond that. This was a very good salary at that time. He explained that he could not give more than ten days of holidays, only one or two people had two weeks. The hours were long, but he said there was one advantage not usually found in a boarding school—her laundry would be free. He asked her to telegraph her reply and said that, if she were interested, he would go over at the end of the week to see her.[73] The teacher does not appear to have taken the post, possibly she considered the holidays too short, because Edmondson offered two weeks to his next applicant.

In June Edmondson wrote to a Miss Baker, who, he had just discovered was 'one of us', to check on a woman working in a laundry owned by Quakers in England, where Baker had also been employed.[74] The Friends had an active network which they used extensively for business purposes. At the same time, he was negotiating with another woman, Miss Alice Dixon, a Quaker, in Yorkshire. He offered her a starting salary of £30 a year with full board in his own house and free washing. If she were 'thoroughly efficient', they would be quite willing and desirous to give a very liberal salary'. As before, he said that the prospects in the Laundry could be very good, and that they were anxious 'to get as much relief as possible from the weight of the business'.[75] A few days later he engaged Dixon, and promised her two weeks' holidays. He told her that she would have to share a bedroom with one or possibly two others, but that they were pleasant girls and the room was large and airy. He then told her that they had engaged another woman, with similar experience, who lived in the neighbourhood: they were going to divide the job: one person was to have oversight of the packing and one of the receiving. Edmondson thought that the work would be better done and that there would be less strain; he hastened to reassure Miss Dixon that this would not affect her salary or prospects.[76]

Less than six months later, on 1 January 1890, Edmondson was still seeking a head for the sorting and packing department; whether this person was to be over Dixon and her colleague is not known. Dixon

5. The Dublin Laundry in 1900.

remained in the Laundry until 1891, but the other woman may have left. Edmondson had recourse to his friend James Armstrong, asking him whether he knew of a 'tip top head for sorting and packing', and requesting him to put an enclosed advertisement in the 'most likely papers' and send the replies to him: 'Steam Laundry, Sorting and Packing Rooms. Wanted a competent person to take entire charge of these Departments, in large successful Steam Laundry, with prospects of an interest in business to thoroughly conscientious and experienced person.'[77]

The saga of replacing Mrs Edmondson in the packing and sorting department shows the extreme care with which Edmondson chose staff for managerial roles; he considered the filling of the place 'rightly is very important'.[78] In April 1890 he was looking for a 'thoroughly good couple' to help them with the management of the laundry. It was so successful—they were 'doing' £134 a week, and expected this to rise to £150 before the busy season—that he and his wife were finding it too much for them. They were willing to make generous arrangements; again he repeats that 'altho' a limited company, it is practically our own, and as we have no children to succeed us, it will be a really good opening for some one or other'. They were looking for a suitable married couple of thirty to forty-five years-of-age, well educated and with business expe-

6. Laundry office, with loading shed and manageress's house on the left.

"Shanagarry"

7. The managing director's residence in the laundry grounds, where the Edmondsons lived from 1887 to 1898.

rience. The man would take 'general oversight of the concern'; the woman would assist the present manageress in the practical working of the laundry departments. He was also willing to consider separate applications for the two positions.[79] Two years after starting the Laundry Edmondson was looking for help in the management and supervision of the business and, indeed, promising a possible share in it to a suitable person.

Between 1888 and 1900 enormous improvements were made to the building, changes made necessary by the rapid increase in the business (Plate 5). By 1894, when most of the building was done, the laundry was a very different place from what it had been in 1888. On entering it from the main gate on Milltown Road, the office was straight ahead with the loading shed beside it and the manageress's house to the left. This was the other half of Shanagarry, and was called Tinnamullen (the house by the mill) (Plate 6). Shanagarry itself, the managing director's residence, had recently been remodelled, (Plate 7). In the office building there was a visitors' room to the left, and this was where the telephone was kept; this was, in 1894, a sign that the company was 'up to date'. Then there was the managing director's office and the general office, which, in Edmondson's words, was a 'spacious, light and airy room'.

8. Office with women clerks.

Four or five women worked there and a shorthand clerk and 'type-writer' had an office to herself (Plate 8).[80]

The baskets and bundles of dirty linen, (at the time the word was used to cover personal clothes as well as tablecloths and bed clothes, because underclothing was made of linen or cotton) were brought from the vans into the receiving room (Plate 9). Here, at the beginning of the week, the whole staff of, in 1894, twenty sorters and packers compared the contents with the lists attached.[81] The linen was then sorted into several washing classifications: whites, coloureds, woollens and silks; these could be further broken down into table linen, bed linen, handkerchiefs, shirts, socks and so on. In small laundries sorting and packing were done in the same room, which was fitted for packing. It was strongly recommended at the time that the two departments should be kept separate.[82] The Dublin Laundry, which was not of course a small laundry, had a separate packing room.

The receiving room led into the large wash house, which measured 40ft × 30ft. In 1894 this contained nine modern washing machines (Plate 10). From the washing machines, the clothes were taken to the hydro extractors (Plate 11).[83] Wash houses were usually built on the ground

9. Receiving room.

10. Wash-house, showing wooden washing machines; mangle in right-hand corner.

floor, this was obviously the easiest place in which to locate them. They were blamed for much of the unhealthiness of laundry workers since the steam from them tended to percolate to the departments overhead. The health of workers in all parts of the building, it was said, was dependent on the location, drainage, provision for the escape of steam and the forced ventilation of the wash house.[84] It was recommended, therefore, that the wash house should be built above the other departments, though only two laundries out of twenty-eight in a study of laundries in Pittsburgh in 1909 had wash houses at a higher level.[85] The wash house in the Dublin Laundry was on the ground floor of a three-storey building, but there was never any indication that it posed problems for other departments. The linen was then hung out to dry on lines on the drying ground, if the weather were fine, or brought to the drying rooms. These were on three floors, one above the other; the air was heated by steam pipes on the lowest floor, and, by the use of fans, a constant current was kept circulating upwards from floor to floor; the water-laden air was discharged at the top of the building.[86]

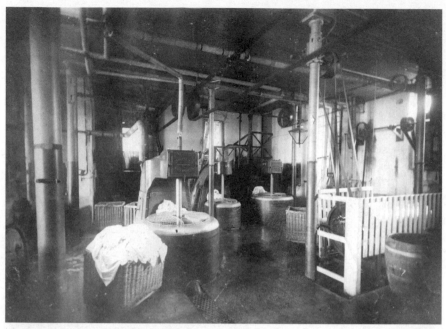

11. Hydro-extractors.

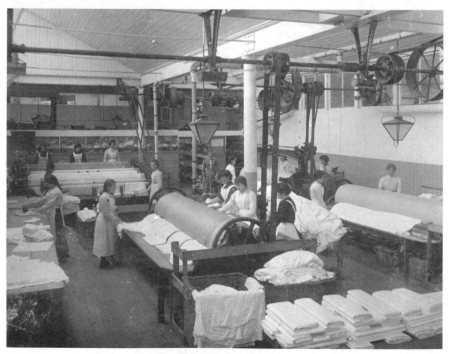

12. Flat work room, showing single and multi-roll (back of picture) calendars.

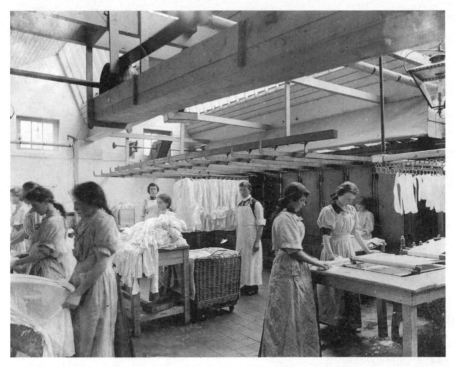

13. Ironing dress shirts; girl at left polishing the front of a shirt on a machine.

There were three ironing rooms, the first a large room about 90ft long on the ground floor where table linen and bed linen were ironed. It contained three 108in ironing machines, known as calenders, one used principally for sheets, one for tablecloths and the third for table napkins, pillow slips and other small items (Plate 12). Edmondson observed, that though he inspected new machinery regularly, he had never seen any ironing machines which he considered superior. In these machines the linen was fed between a blanket-covered roller and a polished, steam-heated, concave base. At one end of this room, special machinery for finishing collars was located; men at the time wore detached collars which were stiffly starched and polished. The second ironing room, which was on the next floor, was used for the mangling, folding and ironing of body-linen; in 1894 this department employed thirty hands. The ironing room on the top floor was devoted to the starching and ironing of shirts. Women ironed the fronts and bodices of shirts, then gave them to girls who polished the fronts and cuffs on a special glossing machine and then handed them back to the same women to finish them off and fold them and put them to air (Plate 13).[87]

14. Packing room.

Finally, the linen went to the packing room on the ground floor. Here it was sorted and checked and put into baskets or bags by some of the sorting and packing staff (Plate 14). At the end of the week, the whole of the staff would be involved in this room, whereas they would all be busy in the receiving room on Mondays. The packages then went to the loading dock where they were placed on the vans ready for the return journey to the customers. At this time the Laundry had a harness room, a ten-stall stable, van yard and shed.[88] The refreshment bar or mess room was situated on the ground floor. Here staff could buy a large cup of tea with milk and sugar for $\frac{1}{2}$d, a bowl of soup for 1d penny or a plate of meat (2oz), with potatoes and vegetables, for $1\frac{1}{2}$d (66 cents today). The service was subsidised, but Edmondson said that even at these rates, and after paying for fuel and the cook's wages, the total loss did not exceed a pound or two per annum.[89]

There were different types of laundry work. First, there was family work, which was the backbone of the trade done by the commercial laundries. This was usually collected on a Monday or a Tuesday and returned on Friday or Saturday. This work was mixed, consisting of personal clothing, bed linen and table linen. Much of this was described as flat work, that is, linen that was mangled, not ironed. Secondly, there was contract work, which was the washing taken from institutions such as schools, hotels, restaurants, clubs and barracks; here bed linen and table linen often predominated over body linen. Thirdly, there was new work or shop work. This was the laundering of manufactured articles such as shirts, cloths and fancy work, before sale. Laundry proprietors were advised, when equipping a new business, to keep the type of work they intended to do in mind. Of course, most laundries did some of each,[90] but it was wise to remember the line of business which might predominate.

Edmondson did what he described as a high-class family business; in addition, he sought, as has been seen, as much contract work as possible. He would not take hospital washing, explaining to Miss Knight of the Adelaide Hospital that their work was for 'high class private families, hotels and clubs', and for that reason he should not like to take hospital work.[91] Many people were prejudiced against commercial laundries because they felt that their linen might be contaminated from the dirt and disease of others. This was the reason that Edmondson eschewed hospital washing, and stressed the 'high class' nature of the family work. He would also have been worried about the health of the work force, as he made clear to a customer whose laundry he had refused to take, because she had a case of an infectious disease in her house. 'Bear in mind that your linen has to pass thro' the hands of perhaps half a dozen young people in our sorting room, and you will see we could not act otherwise.'[92] All customers were notified of the policy of not receiving washing from homes where there was infectious disease, and Edmondson enforced this as strictly as possible. It was, of course, a policy which would have been held by all reputable laundries. Likewise Edmondson did not do shop work saying that, if he were to take any trade work, this would 'put our whole place under the Factory Act which would be highly inconvenient.'[93]

In the second annual report of the Laundry, 1889 was declared a prosperous year with the anticipated continued expansion in the business confirmed. The average weekly turnover was £101. The net profit, after payment of interest on debentures and loans, was £1049.11s.5d. This was used to pay £425 to suppliers of machinery; the MD got an additional salary of £148, making it £200 a year; the manageress received a bonus of £25. The dividend on 6 per cent preference shares came to £58.16s.0d, and a 50 per cent dividend, amounting to £378.10s.0d, was paid on ordinary shares.[94] The situation of Edmondson and his wife had greatly improved; after two years on a low salary, Thomas was now earning £200 a year, the amount he was getting at the Manor Mill after twenty years, and his wife earned an excellent return on the ordinary shares held by her. On 1 January 1890 Edmondson took up the remaining 243 ordinary shares from the original issue of 1,000 in 1887, bringing the total number of ordinary shares to 1,000.[95] A dividend of £750 was paid on these shares for 1890,[96] giving the Edmondsons a comfortable living from the business. Their income was to improve considerably over the next couple of years.

At an extraordinary general meeting of the Dublin Laundry Co. Ltd, held at 10 Dame Street on 13 April 1892, it was agreed that the share capital of the company should be increased to £5,000 by the issue of 2,000 ordinary shares of £1 each, and 1,000 6 per cent preference shares of £1 each, the shares were to be issued at such times and to such persons as the MD might decide.[97] On 1 July 1892 Ann Edmondson acquired an additional 1,000 ordinary shares; in February 1893 she transferred 500 of these to her husband; on 1 January 1894 Thomas bought 750 shares and Ann 250. On that date husband and wife together owned 2,994 ordinary shares.[98]

The business continued to thrive. At the fifth annual general meeting the salary of the MD was raised to £500, with free house, coal, gas, laundry.[99] By the end of December 1894 the company was in a very healthy state. The liabilities included 3,000 ordinary £1 shares, 2,000 £1 preference shares, debentures (first issue 6 per cent, second issue 6.5 per cent), and loans, bearing 5 per cent interest, of £1,551.17s.3d.[100] For the year ending 31 December 1894 the laundry made a net profit of £3,815.12s.11d. There was a loss of £573.5s.9d on the Dartry Dye Works, which had been launched during that year: £50 was also paid to set up a city office at 5 South Anne Street. A dividend of £120 was paid on the 6 per cent preference shares and £2,400 on the ordinary shares.[101] In that same year there were 140 workers in the Laundry, six vans collected and delivered the washing, and a thirty-horse steam engine had been put in to assist the waterwheel.[102]

CHAPTER THREE

# *Milltown*

MILLTOWN HAD many of the characteristics important to Thomas Edmondson as a site for his new laundry. It was in the country, yet close to the city and not too far from Kingstown, and it was near water. Milltown was a small village three-quarters of a mile from Dundrum, where Thomas had lived and worked for the previous twenty years. It was smaller than Dundrum and was nearer to the city. It may seem surprising that Edmondson decided to start a laundry so close to the Manor Mill. He is reputed to have said that he would put that establishment out of business, but this may have been just a piece of family lore.[1] It was not unusual to have laundries clustered in one district, if water power were nearby and a suitable work force available. At one time fifteen of seventeen laundries in Dublin were located on the south side of the city.[2] As has been seen, commercial laundries did not depend on local business.

The name Milltown reflected the former importance of this village and its surrounding area as an industrial centre. Situated on the banks of the Dodder, whose waters turned the mill wheels, thirty-seven[3] of the approximately 143 mills in County Dublin in the early 1800s were here.[4] As early as the fourteenth century the existence of a mill is mentioned in connection with the lands, then known as 'Milton';[5] the number gradually increased over the succeeding centuries. Among the mills indicated as existing there at different times during the eighteenth and the nineteenth century were corn mills, paper, iron and brass mills, and one for grinding dry woods.[6] These changed hands frequently. The mill acquired by Patrick Gibney, and eventually by Edmondson, had been a cloth mill when it closed in 1850; it had been allowed to become dilapidated when it was taken over by Gibney.[7] The changes in the ownership of mills, closures and changes in use must have caused great upset and hardship to the workers and their families.

All the mills were gradually closed down during the nineteenth century, so the coming of the Dublin Laundry in 1888 and the Dartry

15. Milltown village as it was until the mid-1950s.

Dye Works a few years later were the salvation of Milltown. Not only was the laundry the principal employer in Milltown, it was among the largest employers in the Rathmines township.[8] An article in the *Rathmines News* in January 1896 stated that it employed more people than any other similar industry in the country.[9] Among the requirements when founding a laundry listed by Edmondson was a supply of suitable workers. In this Milltown was eminently qualified to benefit from the boom in the laundry business. Residents of Milltown were used for centuries to the discipline of the mill and the factory. Life was organised around mill hours; the hooter which sounded a warning blast in the morning, ten minutes before the start of work, and a final whistle on the hour, repeated after the dinner break, served as a community timekeeper for the village. In addition, there was a tradition of laundry work in the area. The mill at Dartry, later the dye works, was a laundry, between approximately 1845 and 1860, which was also run by a Quaker, Thomas Bewley.[10] In the 1860s a small laundry was built at Windy Arbour, run off the water from the mill pond, but due to the failure of the water power in the late 1870s it ceased to exist.[11] By far the most important laundry in the area was the Manor Mill, started by Hewetson Edmondson in 1863 (see above).

During the eighteenth century Milltown became the property of the Leeson family, the head of the family acquiring the title of the Earl of Milltown. At that time, Milltown was described as a large and pleasant village, which became a gay and popular resort for Dubliners.[12] Revelling and dancing went on in the dance houses, much to the disapproval of the local priest. It was a favourite halfway house for the citizens on their excursions to the mountains.[13] In the summer months the citizens of Dublin came for a change, the area near the river, known as the Strand, was a special attraction. Until the latter part of the century, when Classon bridge was built by John Classon, the owner of the mill for grinding wood, the only means of crossing the Dodder were by an old bridge, packhorse bridge, which was too narrow for vehicular traffic, or a ford, where the present bridge of Milltown is built. This ford was the cause of loss of life, as people on horseback, reluctant to make the short detour necessary to cross by the old bridge, were sometimes swept away by the rapid waters of the Dodder in flood.[14] The packhorse bridge was a toll bridge, which also may have made people reluctant to use it. The bridge, which is still in existence, has a recess which allowed a pedestrian to stand aside and let horse traffic pass by. There was a hostelry near the bridge, also described as a 'shebeen', where travellers could rest and have a meal, before the final lap of their journey into the city.[15] When, in the 1830s, the ford was replaced by a bridge, Milltown bridge, this greatly facilitated the flow of traffic.

There were many changes to the village in the nineteenth century. A Catholic church was built in 1819 and dedicated to St. Gall and St.

Columbanus, it later became the Church of the Assumption.[16] Before that there had been no chapel nor resident priest. A stable had served as a mass-house. The owner, a Mrs Burke, gave it to Fr Young, from Harold's Cross, who said mass there on Sundays; this became the site for the church. Near the church a school for boys and girls was erected; this was considered necessary to familiarise the children with the fundamentals of Christian belief. The Catholic clergy alleged that the children were being proselytised at the only school in Milltown then in existence. Young was greatly troubled by this. One day he called on the schoolroom, and, seeing some of his flock there, ordered them to leave. The master and his two sons, who ran the school, flung him down the stairs and afterwards brought an action for assault against him. He had no witnesses except the children and feared that a court of law, at that time, would not find in favour of a priest. Fortunately for him, a friendly solicitor took up his case, and placed it in the hands of Daniel O'Connell, who had the real aggressors brought to justice.[17] Milltown has been part of many parishes since Norman times, when it belonged to the parish of St. Sepulchre. At a later period it was part of Donnybrook. Then it belonged to 'St. Nicholas Outside the Walls'. In 1823 it became part of Rathmines. When Rathgar was divided from Rathmines in 1881, it was administered from the new parish of Rathgar. It came under the jurisdiction of Cullenswood (Beechwood) when that parish was founded in 1906.[18]

In 1888, the year the Dublin Laundry opened, the population of Milltown numbered 863 living in 132 houses.[19] The vast majority of these were small; Milltown was a village of cottages which housed a close-knit community and remained virtually unchanged until the middle of the twentieth century.[20] There was much intermarrying among the families, and even in the later days of the Laundry attendances at weddings and funerals caused an appreciable drop in the number at work.[21]

The houses, situated as many of them were on low ground close to the river, were subject to flooding. Of the approximately 140 listed in Griffith's Primary Valuation in mid-century, more than one-third had neither a backyard nor garden.[22] Many were owned by some of the local businessmen. In 1951 fifty-four houses were deemed by the medical officer for health to be unfit for human habitation 'by reason of disrepair and sanitary defects'; they included many on the main street. The medical officer went on to say: 'This constitutes the area in which they are situated an Unhealthy Area for the purpose of the Housing Act, 1931, and in my opinion should be dealt with either as a clearance area or an improvement area.'[23] By the 1950s most of the cottages had been

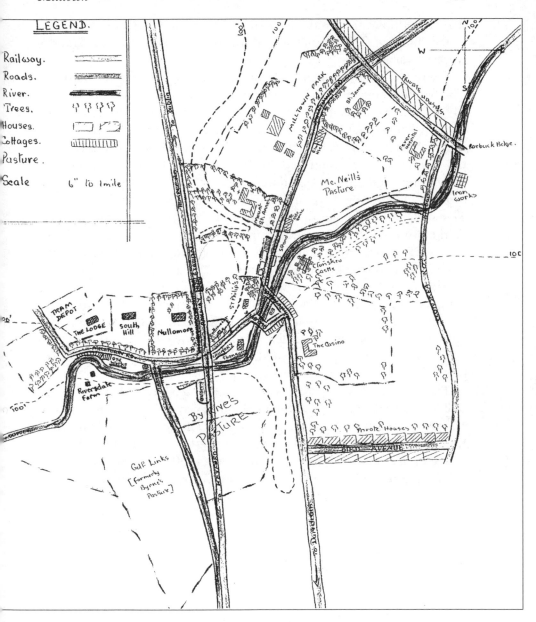

16. Map of Milltown at the beginning of the twentieth century, showing the Dublin Laundry, Shanagarry and the Dye Works; Creevagh was on the corner of Dartry Road and Orwell Park, opposite the tram depot; William Martin Murphy's home (Dartry House) was on the opposite corner (permission of Sr. Margaret Mary Fitzsimons, Caritas, Sandymount, Co. Dublin). See also Figure 11, p. 229.

demolished, and the residents, many reluctant to leave, were removed to new housing. The old village known to Edmondson and his laundry workers was gone for ever.[24]

There were stark contrasts in the village; besides housing the poor, Milltown was home to some of the very wealthy. In the eighteenth century, Mr Jackson, who was the proprietor of ironworks at Clonskeagh bridge, lived in Clonskeagh Castle. Jackson joined the United Irishmen and became involved in the rebellion of 1798, for which he was imprisoned. On his release, he emigrated to America. A later resident, George Thompson, vigorously opposed the coming of the nuns to Milltown (see below).[25] There were several other large houses in the district.[26] Many were built in the first half of the nineteenth century, when large numbers of the professional classes moved from the city to the suburbs. Unlike the cottages, these were built on the rising ground on either side of the river. In spite of the presence of some wealthy residents, Milltown was considered a poor district. It was part of the area chosen for the new Rathmines Township in 1847, but did not become part of it until 1880: the commissioners felt that Milltown, which had so much inferior housing, would be more of a liability than an asset.[27] Edmondson was very conscious of the poverty and bad housing in Milltown, and did his best to help those in need.

The Dublin to Wicklow Railway was built in 1854, calling at Dundrum, Stillorgan, Carrickmines and Shankill, on its way to Bray; Ranelagh and Milltown stations had not yet been built.[28] The spectacular Nine Arch Railway Viaduct was erected to carry the line across the Dodder valley. The station at Milltown opened in the early 1860s, built on the grounds of St. Phillips, which was then owned by Charles Granby Burke, JP. It was built of wood with oil lamps on the platform and in the waiting room.[29] The journey from Harcourt Street to Milltown took five minutes. Not all trains stopped at Milltown, about a quarter of them went straight through to Dundrum.[30] The presence of the wealthy in Milltown and the nearby Temple Road played an important part in the decision to have a station there. St. Philip's Church of Ireland on Temple Road was opened for worship in May 1867, to serve the rapidly-expanding, wealthy, middle class living there.[31] The railway was used mainly by the better off, apart from the cost of travelling by train, the poorer people lived and worked in Milltown or travelled by foot or bicycle to their jobs. The station was a boon to the Laundry, being, as Edmondson constantly told visitors, just two minutes from the laundry; it was also much used for sending and receiving baskets and parcels of laundry.

17. Aerial view of the Laundry and viaduct, early 1950s.

In 1858, Milltown Park, another of the big houses, was acquired by the Jesuits and a noviciate was built there in 1860.[32] In 1879 a second religious order moved to Milltown, when a property on a hill overlooking the village was purchased from Richard Warneford Boyle by the Irish Sisters of Charity and became known as Mount St. Anne's. They moved their novices there from Harold's Cross. They then bought a property, belonging to the Misses Luscombe, which was situated between there and the village. The nuns later added a noviciate, chapel, school and laundry. The work of the order included visiting the sick poor and hospitals, the running of sodalities and teaching.[33] For years at Christmas time, Edmondson, and later Robert Benson, made an annual donation to the sisters for the poor; the nuns sometimes sought work in the Laundry for people they were prepared to recommend. The nuns ran the infants and girls' school, and the boys' school was staffed by lay teachers; Francis Kavanagh was the master in 1888.[34]

Until the coming of the railway, travelling was difficult for those who had not their own horse-drawn transport, although Milltown was a coach stop on the journey between Dublin and Wicklow.[35] Towards the end of the century, people could have used the trams plying between Dartry or Clonskeagh and the city, and walked the remainder of the way. The trams catered more for the middle than for the working class;

the fares were high, higher than in London where the general charge was 1d per mile, and the times of the trams did not suit the working day of the labouring classes.[36] Even carriage-owners considered Milltown a distance from the city, as a letter from Thomas to his mother-in-law Sarah Roberts, who lived on Appian Way, shows: 'If weather keeps as warm as it is—perhaps thou tempted out again soon as far as this?'[37]

Most of the inhabitants were content to live out their lives in Milltown, with perhaps an occasional trip to Harcourt Street on the train, many to shop in Camden Street or Wexford Street.[38] Most of the requirements for day-to-day living were available in the village. In 1888 Milltown had two grocers, four dairies, a public house, a smith and farrier, a horse dealer and a number of carpenters, one also claiming to be a builder. There was a post office and three deliveries of mail daily, the postmaster was Michael Kavanagh, who also ran one of the grocery shops. The second provision shop was run by Thomas Peter Kavanagh, whose family owned a number of cottages in the village.[39] The centre of the village was situated less than half a mile from the Laundry. On the left-hand side, going from Dartry, was the tiny village church and the boys' school. The girls' school, in Mount St. Anne's, was on higher ground overlooking the village. Cottages lined the right-hand side from the bridge, along the banks of the river. They were built of limestone from the nearby quarries, and were whitewashed and thatched. Census returns for 1901 show that a number of dress-makers lived on Milltown Road. As the majority of people at the time had their clothes made for them, it is probable that thirteen years earlier the village was at least as well supplied with this essential service. Those who had gardens probably grew their own vegetables; the Dublin Laundry had a field which was let out in plots to those who had no gardens or wished to till more ground.[40]

The road between Dartry and Clonskeagh, built in 1870, was considered broad except for the part through the village which was very narrow, two people could not walk abreast on the footpath. Like most roads at the time, it was dusty in the summer time and covered with mud when the weather was wet. Roads were surfaced with crushed limestone and clay, sprinkled with water and rolled to give a smooth finish. The *Rathmines News* reported on 20 February 1887 on the deplorable state of the roads; it suggested that granite would be better than limestone. In 1898 Edmondson wrote to Frederick Dixon, at the Town Hall, Rathmines, about the heaps of mud on the road between the Laundry and the village, and also on the road to the railway station; he said that it had not been removed for about a fortnight.[41] Seven years later, he was still complaining that the workmen who repaired the roads were depositing a bank of 'road stuff' along the Laundry wall at Windy Arbour. This would enable trespassers to gain access to his premises. He demanded that it be removed.[42]

Milltown had its share of rowdyism and petty crime, as Edmondson's complaints to the local police show. In August 1891 he wrote to the police in Dundrum and Donnybrook about the men and boys who frequented the banks of the Dodder on Sunday nights. He said that some of these had probably broken into his garden and greenhouse and stolen fruit.[43] A few years later he was drawing the attention of the superintendent at Donnybrook 'to the rowdyism which so often prevails in the streets of Milltown at night'. One of his employees, Mrs Breen, who lived in a corner cottage near the bridge, was frequently annoyed by stones thrown at her front door, this had gone on the previous evening between 11p.m. and 1a.m. He asked for 'stringent measures to repress this kind of thing in our neighbourhood'.[44] In the same year he wrote to Dundrum about a cottage, empty only for a short time, which had been broken into, its windows broken, other damage done and timber stolen.[45] Ryan, the tenant in Clonbeg (see below, p. 81), wrote to Thomas about what he described as 'curious women, idlers and loafers', who were loitering on a piece of land in front of his house, and were 'a perfect nuisance'.[46] Obviously, how to occupy one's leisure, even the restricted free time of those days, posed problems, especially for the young men and boys of the district. The law-abiding inhabitants of the cottages depended on Edmondson and other members of his class to report crime and public nuisances to the police. In 1905 Edmondson wrote to the Royal Irish Constabulary at Dundrum about the rowdyism which so often prevailed, especially on the county side of the river. Stones had been thrown through the windows of two of his employees: Mr Cosgrave, who had a shop on the corner, and Mr Traynor, his foremen, who lived in Bankside cottages. He asked that one or two constables should be constantly on duty in that neighbourhood. He also suggested that the RIC. should co-operate with the Dublin Metropolitan Police for the 'thorough supervision of the whole village of Milltown.'[47] The Milltown bridge separated two policing jurisdictions, the DMP were in charge of Milltown Road, while the RIC were responsible on the County Dublin side. The district inspector in Dundrum replied, saying, that several persons had been fined for disorderly behaviour, and he trusted that this would result in an improvement. He said that it was not possible to have even one constable on constant duty at that point at night.[48] The *Rathmines News* of 18 April 1896 reported that a woman returning on the 11.30p.m. train on Saturday night to Milltown, with a bag of groceries which she had bought at M'Dermott's and Doyle's, of Camden Street, was attacked by three men, who knocked her down, held her by the nose and mouth, used foul language and attempted to indecently assault her. She begged the men to take the basket and not murder her. Later, two constables found tea and sugar in a room in an area near packhorse bridge, known as Concrete, occupied by a James Doyle, a man was charged.[49]

The great majority of the workers in the Dublin Laundry were from the neighbourhood and lived at home with their families. Sometimes several members of the same family worked in the laundry; this was a tradition which lasted down to the final days in the 1980s. When taking on new staff, management tended to favour people from families already employed; this was recognised and accepted policy.[50] Edmondson wanted the staff to stay locally, as he made quite clear to a young woman who thought of commuting by train: 'you would find it very inconvenient not being within walking or biking distance. We start on Mondays at 9a.m. and at 8a.m. on the other days.'[51] For those from a distance he had a hostel; he provided housing for some supervisory staff (see Chapter 4) and helped other workers to get suitable lodgings.

The number of workers living locally can be obtained for 1901 and 1911, the only years for which census returns are available. The exact number can never be ascertained because, as well as errors and omissions, many married women were returned as housewives, not as laundresses. In 1901 thirty-five laundry workers, thirty-three women and two men, lived on the Milltown Road. Henry Waring, the superintending mechanical engineer, lived in Shanagarry, and the manageress, Jemina McCleery and her son, an engineer in the laundry, were in Tinnamullen.[52] In Concrete, sixteen out of twenty-seven dwellings housed laundry workers— thirty-three women and five men. One of these houses, a former tannery, was a tenement, home to fourteen separate families, fifteen of whose members worked in the Laundry.[53]

In 1911, at a time when 260 hands were employed there, at least 220 people living in Milltown and the surrounding areas of Rosemount, Windy Arbour and Farrenboley were returned as laundry workers.[54] Some of these, especially in the Rosemount area, might have worked in the Manor Mill. Concrete was home to fifty-five laundry workers, forty-six women and nine men, twelve of whom lived in the tenement.[55] Seven

18. Dinner hour at the entrance gates to the Laundry; Tinnamullen in the background (Tony Behan Collection).

female laundry workers lived in four of the five houses in Lees Lane.[56] Besides laundresses and van men, some of the foremen, one of whom was Albert Pierce, and a forewoman, lived in Farrenboley. There was also a little colony of Scottish and English dyers, finishers and French cleaners who worked in the Dartry Dye Works.[57] This was one of the areas in which Edmondson took a special interest; in 1904 he arranged to have the Vartry water brought there, and to the eight Bankside cottages; he agreed to pay 1s. in the £ of the valuation for the water.[58]

A number of the returns instance many members of the same family employed in the laundry: in 1901 two of the houses on Milltown Road had three, and one had four workers. The wife and two daughters in one household at Classon Bridge were laundresses. In 1911, in Rosemount Town, two families had four members in the laundry trade and two had three members. A widow and her five daughters who lived in Windy Arbour worked in the laundry. Again the census returns show that the laundry workers were, almost without exception, Catholic. On the other hand, Mrs McCleery and her son were Episcopalians, Mr Waring was a Quaker. The foremen and forewoman living in Farrenboley in 1911 belonged to the Church of Ireland, while the specialists at the Dye Works were Presbyterian, Church of England and Plymouth Brethren.

Milltown was a small, self-sufficient village, home to many families who had lived in the neighbourhood for generations. People knew one another, had gone to school together, worked side-by-side, shopped in the village stores, drank in the local public houses. It was not a pretty village, but it was a friendly place, which, while only $3^1/_4$ miles from the centre of the capital, could have been in the heart of the country. The quietness was disturbed from time to time when the carriages of the gentry, the horses and carts of more humble folk, the coach to Wicklow, the vans of the Laundry, and other delivery vans, trundled by. Traffic from Dublin appeared from under the Nine Arches, negotiating a bend on the road at the base of Richmond Hill, which was considered dangerous even in those days. The silence was completely broken when the train rattled across the viaduct, a reminder that there was an outside world.

At night the blackness was only relieved by pools of dim light cast by the gas lamps and by flickering lamp and candlelight from village shops and cottage windows. When the day's work was done, the Laundry workers streamed through the massive stone gates on to a lonely stretch of the Milltown Road. For those who turned left under the arch, the road between there and Classon bridge was bounded by a strip of land which belonged to the Laundry and was used for grazing. The majority turned right along by the Laundry wall, on the rough and muddy track that passed for a footpath. Ten years after the Laundry was founded, in 1898, Edmondson tried to get the Rathmines Township authorities to put 'a properly constructed footpath' between the end of the wall and the village of Milltown.[59] As the workers went home, the sound of their footsteps, voices, occasional laughter and shouts broke the silence. The noise gradually grew less as they dispersed into their homes along the road and across packhorse bridge to Concrete and the Milltown bridge to Windy Arbour and beyond.

*Note*: the heads of sixteen of the nineteen houses on Milltown Road where laundry workers lived in 1911 had been born in Co. Dublin, one was born in Dublin City.[60] (The enumerator's return for the census only asked people to give the county or city of their birth.) In Windy Arbour in 1911, the heads of twenty-six households out of thirty-seven, 70 per cent, were born in Dublin County or City, the majority in the former.[61] Sixty-three per cent of householders in Concrete were born in Dublin County or City.[62] It is likely that there were even fewer residents from outside twenty years previously.

## CHAPTER FOUR

# Working Conditions in the Laundry Industry

AS WITH ANY OTHER TRADE, or perhaps more than in most trades as legislative control came late, working conditions in laundries varied enormously. While some workers toiled under atrocious conditions, others, as in the Dublin Laundry, enjoyed high standards. There were different types of laundry. Originally, as has been seen, all laundry was carried on privately as a branch of everyday routine. The first commercial laundries grew from this, when enterprising housewives took in the washing of the well-to-do, or at least the better off than themselves. This type of laundry persisted for many years, though with the advent of the power laundries, they gradually decreased in number. These home laundries, sometimes called cottage laundries, were often unhygienic and unhealthy. They were usually carried on in ill-adapted houses, with a few wash tubs, washing boards, scrubbing brushes and a built-in copper or a couple of portable boilers; clothes were dried outside, if possible, or indoors in the work room or living rooms. Clothes were finished using a mangle or flat or box iron, both of which had to be heated on a heating stove or range in the work area. There was almost certainly a scarcity of water, often hard, which required the use of an undue amount of soap or even a strong bleaching agent to try to keep the clothes a good colour. The small, ill-ventilated rooms could not allow for sanitary conditions. The clothes from many households were heaped together on the floor awaiting attention. These laundries were usually run by the proprietress and her family, with perhaps some outside assistance.[1]

Secondly, there were laundries specially built or adapted for the purpose, in which washing machines were used. These might have been worked by hand or by mechanical means. Finally, there were the power laundries, in which most of the machines were driven by mechanical power: gas, water and electricity were all used, but in the majority of cases, steam was used for driving laundry machinery. These concerns were on quite a different level to the previous categories, and with them the trade entered the factory age. There were also laundries which advertised as 'hand laundries, no machinery used', which persisted well into the twentieth century and catered for those who were prejudiced against machinery and could afford the higher prices charged. Some were reputed to send out the major part of customers' work to steam laundries.[2]

There was much criticism of the laundry trade, much of it justified, and directed against the small home laundries as well as the large steam laundries. Until the advent of legislation, everything depended on the proprietor or manager of the individual concern. The nature of the occupation lent itself to abuses and the rapid development of laundry work between the 1860s and the 1920s meant that demand for the service outpaced the ability to provide the proper standard of buildings to house the laundries; many were hastily converted dwelling houses.[3] The failure to include laundries under the Factory and Workshop Act 1867, and the subsequent difficulties in including them in later years exacerbated the situation, and meant that bad conditions in laundries lasted well into the twentieth century.

Many workers had to work in extremely wet conditions; uneven floors and imperfect drainage meant that washers had to stand in pools of water. Tales were told of women standing ankle-deep in water all day.[4] While boards or grids to stand on were advocated by some and were present in many laundries, when these were not firmly fixed to the floor they were dangerous, as workers could slip off them or trip over them; when fixed, they offered a hiding place for foul matter which collected in dirty water. While the 1895 Act required that the floors should be drained, it did not say that the water should be drained *at the spot where it was discharged*. The result was that it was not unusual, to find yellow, foul water from the washing machines at one end of the wash house, flowing all across the floor, over the feet of the workers, until it eventually reached a drain.[5]

Ventilation was often poor and the atmosphere was laden with steam. The principal lady inspector of factories said that often on entering a wash-house the whole place was so pervaded by steam that she could not see the workers.[6] The temperature of ironing rooms was often extremely high, as it was usual to have the stove for heating the irons in the room. In small laundries, where there was no separate drying-room, clothes were often dried overhead in the ironing room, and, since the windows were kept shut to aid drying, this impeded ventilation, and again gave a moisture-laden atmosphere. Miss Abraham, a factory inspector, reported to HM Chief Inspector that she had noticed that the workers' clothes were 'saturated with water'. She suggested that they should have some protection such as that afforded to wet spinners.[7] Where gas irons were used, they often emitted fumes.[8] Sanitary conditions were often inadequate, cases of one lavatory for fifty men and women and two for sixty-two women were recorded.[9] A woman who did holiday work in a laundry when the twentieth century was well advanced, said: 'The lavatories were disgusting. It was an ordeal using them, slipping on the cracked concrete floor swimming in foul water leaking from the broken basins, and barely able to look at the dark, scummy, lavatory bowls.'[10]

Work, even in a well-run laundry such as the Dublin Laundry, was hard. By the nature of the work it meant that the washers were up to their elbows in water, were continually handling wet clothes, were standing on wet floors, working in their bare feet, Wellington boots or wooden clogs, and were exposed to the cloying smell of boiling clothes. As time went on more men were employed in the wash-house, they were better able to cope with the heavy work which mechanisation entailed, such as transferring loads of wet linen from the washing machine to the hydro-extractor. The most unpleasant task in a laundry was the sorting of dirty clothes, this was recognised by both management and workers. Zola, in *L'Assommoir*, has his heroine recoiling 'in a sudden fit of revulsion', '"Madame Gaudron's lot", she said, "I don't want to do her stuff any more . . . I've handled some pretty filthy washing in my time, but I can't stomach this. Enough to make you puke. What can the woman do to get her clothes into such a state?".'[11] Zola located his laundry in a working class area of Paris, just north of the Gare du Nord. However, even laundries with a so-called high-class clientele were liable to receive filthy clothes. A woman who started work in the Dublin Laundry in 1920, when she was sixteen, said that working in the sorting room was 'not nice, some people had no consideration in them in what they sent in, and some of it was disgusting; you had to do it and that was that'.[12] In September 1923 the manager of the Laundry refused to take any further washing from a woman who had sent in verminous clothing two weeks in succession.[13]

Sorters had a very responsible job: every article received had to be checked against the customer's list, if necessary they had to be put aside for marking. 'Shorts' had to be noted so that the office could inform the customer. Any unusual item, or those requiring extra care or time in their laundering, had to be put aside for pricing by the forewoman or manager. Forms had to be filled out for any article requiring special attention, for example, if it was required early; these slips accompanied the article through the laundry. Articles had to be sorted into different categories, for example, shirts, collars and cuffs; ladies' underwear; table linen; bed linen; and coloureds. Tears and stains were 'noted' by tacking coloured thread around them. Pockets were turned out and pins removed.[14] It was understandable that Mrs Edmondson elected to take charge of this department when the Laundry opened. Edmondson said that it required 'correctness, quickness and some ability, to make a good sorter'.[15] In 1895 he advertised for sorters in England, through his cousin Robert Benson. He always took a lot of trouble to fill what might be regarded as an ordinary position.[16] In spite of the unpleasant nature of sorting soiled clothes, sorters and packers considered themselves superior to other workers, probably because they had to be literate,[17] and possibly because they were conscious of the responsibilities involved.

Large ironing rooms were noisy places, with the rush of belting, the irregular sound of reversible rolls and the sharp, quick clamp of metal presses. Some of the machinery needed considerable strength and co-ordination to operate. For sleeve- and body-ironing machines, where two hollow metal rolls were used, the upper one was heated, the lower one not and usually padded. The garment was placed over this lower roll, which was lifted by pressure of a treadle into position against the constantly revolving, upper roll. This was done with the left foot, the pressure had to be steady, for the moment it was lessened the roll fell. To reverse the motion of the top roll, a second treadle was pressed with the right foot; these two motions were repeated until the garment was ironed. In a body ironer, the rolls were 22 to 34in long, with a diameter of $7^1/_2$in for the heated roll, and $5^1/_4$in for the padded roll. The metal was not less than $^3/_4$in in thickness. This operation required continuous muscular exertion. Cuff, neck band and the wing point tipper for collars were operated in a similar way requiring double treadle action. The sheer physical effort needed to press each cuff four times, twice on each side, was said to shake the whole body of the operator.[18]

Power and steam laundries could be particularly dangerous places in which to work. This was reflected in the rates charged by insurance companies; employers paid five times more to insure their manual workers, other than sorters and packers, than their office workers.[19] Washing machines, hydros, calendars, shirt and collar machines, as well as revolving shafting, were all responsible for many accidents, some serious, involving loss of limbs or even death. Particularly horrific were cases where a frail, young girl of fourteen, had both arms caught between hot, heavy, unguarded rollers and could not be released for over an hour; a woman, working on a hydro, had her arm torn off and left in the hydro.[20] Over the years there were a number of accidents in the Dublin Laundry. The engine driver had to go to the Meath Hospital, 'when the upper joint of the middle finger will probably be removed'.[21] Bessie Bell, aged fourteen, who was described as a 'folder', was caught in the gear wheels of an ironing machine when she stooped down to pull out a basket and was pinched in the thigh. 'Had no business to be where she was', was the rather harsh comment of management.[22] A male engine tender fell carrying iron pipes into the basement and bruised his shoulder and arm.[23] Lizzie Short, a mangler, received a compound fracture of her right arm in the mangle.[24] A shirt ironer, while waiting for the machine to heat up, patted the lower roller, her right hand was caught between the rollers and burned.[25] Emily Parr, a machine shirt ironer, in smoothing a crease on a shirt front, had her hand taken under the roller, badly burned and crushed but no bones were broken.[26] In 1899 five girls in the Dartry Dye Works drank tartar emetic, and were, in Edmondson's words, 'half-poisoned'; he wrote to his insurance company The Ocean Accident Association to ask whether he was liable, saying: 'They had no business to touch the drugs.'[27] Workers were held by management to be largely responsible for their own actions. The laundry vans seemed to be involved in quite a number of accidents, from colliding with a van from another laundry,[28] to being accused of causing a man to fall off his bicycle, to damaging a house window in Dalkey[29]. A more serious accident occurred on the corner of Morehampton Road and Belmont Avenue, when a child was knocked down, luckily he was not badly injured.[30]

Laundry work was reputed to be a very unhealthy occupation. A contemporary account talked of the 'seeds of disease' being sown by workers' standing in the wetness caused by defective flooring and drainage, of 'low rooms filled with steam and noisome smell, absolutely without provision for ventilation'.[31] This rendered the workers especially liable to pulmonary complaints. Going home on cold evenings after spending several hours in overheated rooms, with, doubtless, little extra clothing, rendered them liable to chills and colds. Gas fumes from irons and other apparatus made the atmosphere unpleasant and unhealthy.[32] A survey of twenty-eight laundries in Pittsburgh in 1907 stated, that while the effects of operating machinery requiring violent treadle pressure had yet to be closely studied, the testimony of physicians tended to confirm lay observers' opinion that operators were liable to pelvic disorders.[33] Nearly all laundry work was done standing, and the long hours spent in this position could explain the fact that varicose veins, ulcerated legs and uterine displacement were said to be particularly prevalent among laundresses. Miss Deane, an inspectors of factories, investigated the effects of conditions in laundries on the health of the laundry women. She examined the records of patients in the Isleworth, Wandsworth and Clapham Infirmaries, their ages, diseases, and occupations. In 1898 she found one in six laundresses suffering from ulcers of the legs, while, for women in other occupations, the proportion was one in twenty-five; one in ten laundresses suffered from phthisis (any disease that caused wasting of the body, especially pulmonary tuberculosis), while the proportion for other occupations was also one in twenty-five. Results for 1899 were not dissimilar. One in sixteen laundresses suffered from rheumatism, while one in twenty-two women in other occupations had rheumatism; one in five laundresses had bronchitis against one in nine in other jobs.[34]

The Women's Industrial Council, which was founded in 1894, became a pressure group to influence public opinion in the improvement of the social conditions of working women.[35] As part of its inquiries into women's working conditions, it examined the laundry trade. Its report stated that the question of the general healthiness of the trade was usually, and not surprisingly, answered differently by employers and workers. Most employers said that the work was healthy and that the girls got used to the long hours of standing, but some of them acknowledged that it needed a strong constitution. Some of the workers said they were very healthy, but several told a different story. Rheumatism and bronchial complaints were the main illnesses mentioned. The investigator came to the conclusion that the work was healthy, if the laundry were well managed, but stated that there was no doubt that the work was heavy and laborious.[36] Edmondson would have agreed wholeheartedly with the first part of this conclusion, and might well have considered the second part true also. He was always at pains to stress that his work force was very healthy, an indication that this was necessary if one was a laundry proprietor. In a booklet advertising the laundry, issued in 1894, he said that the visitor would probably be struck by the 'order, cleanliness, and healthy appearance of the employees, so different to what may be met with in many other similar establishments'.[37] Again, six years later in a second booklet he stressed the 'healthy appearance of the workers, which is a clear proof that the sanitary conditions of the premises are excellent'.[38]

One of the worst aspects of laundry work was the long hours, and the latitude allowed under the Factory and Workshop Acts of 1895 and 1901 for these to be spread over the twenty-four hours of the day, including Sunday (see below, p. 119). Before the legislation, an eighty-five-hour week was not unusual, and all-night working not uncommon. Factory inspectors reported ironers working continuously from Friday morning until Saturday at midnight.[39] The normal period of twelve hours per day, which the law allowed for a girl of fourteen, could be arranged for any part of the twenty-four, so the girl could actually be kept at work all night. Inspectors spoke of 'the spectacle of young girls from 14 years old and upwards at 10 and 11 o'clock at night tending the machines': they reported seeing legally employed young girls engaged in the mechanical task of 'feeding' the large, steam-heated, power-driven ironing rollers with damp linen, 'a cloud of steam rising as each piece was passed through'. It must have been extremely dangerous to have had overtired, young people engaged in this task. An inspector said, in what can only be described as a gross understatement: 'Working and standing in the steaming hot atmosphere of a calender room from 8 a.m. till 9 or 10 p.m. all the week, with the exception of one day, is an arduous strain on the young constitution.'[40] When the Dublin Laundry first opened laundry staff worked more than seventy hours a week. Edmondson said that when the business settled down he hoped to reduce the hours.[41] When he did so is not clear, but in 1893, when there was a move to include laundries under the Factory and Workshop Act, he stated that laundries must be allowed to work up to sixty-four hours a week, if necessary.

There was no formal training for laundry workers; they were trained 'on the job', and this system lasted until the decline and virtual demise of the business. Former workers said that they were well trained in the Dublin Laundry in the 1920s to 1940s.[42] From the earliest days experienced laundresses could be asked, before being appointed, whether they would help in the training of younger hands.[43] The Laundry did not take pupils, that is people who would then work elsewhere, though they were asked to do so on a number of occasions.[44] Although laundry work was always a part of domestic economy courses which were intended for housewives and those working in the home, there were never any courses offered in Ireland for professional laundry workers or supervisors. There were courses in England; Edmondson's niece Alice Edmondson was a teacher in the Laundrymaids' School at Southport.[45] In 1893 interested women in Ireland were advised that there was a three-month course in the Liverpool Technical School for laundry supervisors.[46] Forewomen might be sent to another laundry to receive training. Edmondson intended sending an applicant for head of the packing department in 1900 to his cousin's laundry in Southport for a month or more of preliminary training.[47] Albert Pierce received his training as foreman for the wash house in 1892 in the Mirror Laundry, Putney. Edmondson sent 10s. for the man in the wash-house for his 'kind attention to our Mr Pierce'.[48] Robert Benson's son Ernest was sent to a number of laundries to get as much varied experience as possible before joining his father in the laundry.[49] Years later, Geoffrey, Robert's grandson, trained for six months in the British Research Association in London; he then had to do about a month's practical work in each department of the Dublin Laundry before he was given any authority.[50] The laundries chosen to provide training for supervisors and future managers all seem to have been in England. Apart from having family and friends in the laundry business in Britain, which made it easy to make these arrangements, Edmondson and Benson would probably have found it unacceptable for 'the largest and best laundry in the country' to seek this type of help from another laundry in Ireland. They, of course, had to be willing to return favours of this kind.

The employees of the Dublin Laundry seem to have been fairly paid. In the week ending the 21 December 1888 there were sixty-three people employed, fifty-six women and seven men and the weekly wages bill was £27.8s.10d. Twelve of the women were piece workers earning sums varying between 8s.3d and £1.5s.7d, depending on how long and how fast they worked. The majority of the workers were on a weekly wage and were called time workers, see Table 4.1.

*Table 4.1*
WEEKLY WAGES OF TIME WORKERS, 1888

| Sex: male [M];<br>female [F] | M | F | F | F | F | F | M | M |
|---|---|---|---|---|---|---|---|---|
| Number | 3 | 5 | 8 | 18 | 8 | 5 | 2 | 2 |
| Wages (shillings) | 4–5 | 4–5 | 6–7.5 | 8 | 8.5–9.5 | 10–13 | 14 | 19–20 |

*Source:* Dub. 56/1, Workmen's Account Book, 8 Dec. 1888–26 July 1889

Those earning between 4s. and 5s. a week were probably young girls and boys. Females earning between 10s. and 13s. were probably in charge of a section or a department. The job done by the individual workers is not specified, but it was policy to pay according to age and experience and to move workers around between different departments, if desired. Edmondson said in November 1888 that they paid their washers 8s. per week, and that ironers, if skilled, could earn 'a deal more', presumably, as piece workers.[51] Wages of the majority of women workers in 1888 were 8s. per week: this was the equivalent of £29.4s.0d (€38.22) in 2003. No woman earned as much as an adult male worker.

In the week ending 6 June 1890 ninety-nine people were paid, ten males and eighty-nine females. Four of the males were evidently boys earning 4s. and 5s. per week. The largest number of the women were still earning from 8s. to 8s.6d a week. Seven of the piece workers paid on 21 December 1888 were still doing piece work at this time.[52] Table 4.2 shows numbers and rates in 1895.

*Table 4.2*
WEEKLY WAGES OF TIME WORKERS, 1895
**Females**

| Wages (shillings) | 4–4.5 | 5–5.5 | 6–6.5 | 7 | 8–8.5 | 9 | 10–11 | 12.5–13.5 | 16 |
|---|---|---|---|---|---|---|---|---|---|
| Number | 9 | 13 | 8 | 21 | 25 | 16 | 7 | 5 | 2 |

**Males**

| Wages (shillings) | 4–7 | 16–18 | 20 | 24–25 | 35 |
|---|---|---|---|---|---|
| Number | 6 | 7 | 2 | 2 | 1 |

*Source:* Dub. 56, Wages Book 1895, 2 Nov. 1895–14 Aug. 1897, week ending 2 Nov. 1895

There were also forty piece workers, many earning between 14 and 17s. weekly, giving a staff of 164. Only two women were earning as much as 16s. a week, the minimum wage for the men. Albert Pierce was in charge of the wash-house on 35s.[53]

*Table 4.3*
WEEKLY WAGES OF TIME WORKERS, 1911
**Females**

| Wages (shillings) | 4–5.5 | 6–6.5 | 7–7.5 | 8–8.5 | 9–9.5 | 10–11.5 | 12–12.5 |
|---|---|---|---|---|---|---|---|
| Number | 43 | 17 | 17 | 30 | 28 | 25 | 5 |

**Males**

| Wages (shillings) | 5–6 | 8 | 12–13 | 15–16 | 18–21.5 | 27–31 | 45 |
|---|---|---|---|---|---|---|---|
| Number | 9 | 1 | 4 | 4 | 10 | 3 | 1 |

*Source:* Dub. 56, Wages Book, 27 Aug. 1910–22 Dec. 1917, week commencing 28 Jan. 1911

Again, a large number of women in 1911 were still paid 8s. to 8s.6d per week. However, the proportion of all women (those paid more than 6s.) earning more than 9s. a week went up from 36 per cent to 48 between 1895 and 1911 (compare Tables 4.2 and 4.3). There were also sixty piece workers. The wage bill for that week came to £117.3s.7d.

It is interesting to note that a Schedule of Minimum Wages, signed by fifteen Dublin laundries in 1916, including the Dublin Laundry, agreed a minimum wage for fourteen- to fifteen-year-old learners of 4s. to 5s. per week, while seventeen- to eighteen-year-olds, with some experience, were to receive 7s. to 8s.6d a week, rates paid by the Dublin Laundry in 1888. However, the 1916 Schedule ensured that workers received a steady increase in wages up to the age of twenty-one, when 12s. a week were paid, something never entertained by Edmondson (see Appendix, Figure 2). Only five of the 165 females recorded above in 1911 were paid 12s. a week. By 1916 the laundry business was responding to trade union pressure.

It will be noticed that the number of young girls rose steadily between 1888 and 1911: in the former year 11 per cent of the females earned less than 6s., by 1911 the proportion was 26 per cent. It is understandable that there would have been few trainees in the first year, as the starting staff, few in number, were obviously experienced hands. When it became necessary within a short time of opening to recruit more staff urgently, again experienced people would have been needed. Once the Laundry became established, the proportion of young to older staff seemed to be about a quarter. Again, in 1888 the piece workers numbered 21 per cent of the total number of women employed; in 1911, it was 27 per cent, a moderate increase.

It is difficult to compare wage rates in different industries since conditions varied, hours of work were different and changed over time; a wide variety of rates were frequently quoted for the same occupation.[54] Women working side by side at the Dublin Laundry were often paid differently, depending on their age, experience and their value to their employers. Of the four men employed there in 1888 two were probably van men, possibly the two earning 14s. and two, the higher paid, were probably in charge of the machinery. In 1893 labourers working for the Dublin Corporation were paid 14s. a week, while skilled men, for example, carpenters, earned 34s., and this did not change until the early 1890s.[55] It is impossible to make a direct comparison except to say that the men were paid at least as much as the unskilled in other trades; they may well, however, have been working longer hours.

Information on women's wage rates is sketchy.[56] From the data that are available, it would appear that the women in the Dublin Laundry were paid a fair wage. Before 1900 beginners at shirt, collar and hand-kerchief manufacturers were paid 2s. a week; an eighteen-year-old girl in cardboard-box making, earned 2s.6d a week in 1912.[57] Girls and boys at the Dublin Laundry were never paid less than 4s. In 1912 sack makers at Keoghs in Dublin, with over twelve years' service, earned 6s. a week for what was heavy manual labour. The majority of women workers got between 2s.6d and 6s. a week for a full week, with a few earning 7s. to 9s.[58] An alternative occupation for laundresses might have been domestic service. In the 1890s a general servant was paid approximately 3s.6d to 5s. a week with full board and lodging. Allowing 5s. a week for her keep, the servant's total remuneration was thus in effect 8s.6d to 10s.[59] Many of these girls were 'on duty' for from fifteen to eighteen hours a day.[60] Louie Bennett has said that when she 'was drawn into the trade union sphere in 1917, the Irish woman worker was a neglected factor in industry, exploited and shamefully underpaid. The working week was generally 54 hours—60 in laundries. There was no annual holiday, no pay for statutory holidays, wages were 5s. to 10s. a week.'[61] It would seem that workers in the Dublin Laundry were paid better and had much better facilities than many other laundry workers. Around 1913, some laundry workers were reputed to be earning as little as 3s. a week, a forewoman earning 3s.6.[62] After the Easter Rising two employers in the laundry business suggested to Bennett that she should organise the workers—they were so concerned about the wretched conditions in the industry.[63]

In 1893 Edmondson said that, in comparing wages in Milltown with London rates, one must bear in mind that things were very different in Ireland, 'wages all round being somewhat less and living much cheaper'.[64] In 1907 the average rate in power laundries in London was 13s.6d; it was 12s.6d for hand laundries. Throughout the Victorian period washers in full-time work earned 2s. to 2s.6d per day.[65] On the other hand, it was pointed out that in the 1890s skilled workers' rates in the building industry were almost identical with those in England and Scotland, and that engine drivers and other skilled railway workers received rates comparable with those in Britain. The unskilled, however—and it is with those that laundry workers would be compared—earned considerably less, approximately one-third less.[66]

Edmondson paid the managerial staff handsomely. In December 1891 he offered Mrs McCleery, who was working in a laundry in Edinburgh and who was evidently known to him, £150 'per diem', to come over to help them when their manageress, Mrs Calcutt (formerly Mrs Walsh) was ill; he also said that he would pay her fare both ways. Mrs Calcutt recovered and he cancelled the arrangement. Two weeks later he wrote again asking her to come for a month or two, as the packing and marking rooms were 'somewhat awry'. If she came, he offered the same salary and said she could stay in his house for a period. He promised that they might make a permanent place for her, 'not, of course, a mere "head packer", but something more responsible'.[67] An assistant to the manageress was offered £100 per annum in 1899.[68] In 1907 a national teacher was paid £100 a year and had none of the 'perks' of the laundry staff; a dispensary doctor earned £120 a year.[69] In 1909 the manager in the Dublin Laundry was paid £208. Ten foremen and forewomen were paid £767, fifty-six sorters and packers received £1,106, an average of about £20 a year. Thirteen clerks received £750, £57.7s. per annum or 22s. a week.[70] Managerial staff also received bonuses. In December 1889, after less than two years' trading, the manageress Mrs Walsh got a bonus of £25; this became £30 the following year.[71] In 1898 Mrs McCleery received a bonus of £18.15s.0d, while the same amount appeared again in the accounts that year as a 'special' for McCleery; £37.10s.0d was set aside for bonuses to 'managing staff'.[72] They also got Christmas presents; in 1907 Robert Benson received £2, Mr Waring, £1.10s.0d, McCleery and Mrs Spencer, £1 each.[73]

There was no salary scale offered to workers in the Laundry. Edmondson said to a woman to whom he was offering a supervisory position in the sorting room in 1889 at 17s.6d per week: 'Altho we never make promises as to raising wages, if we get a good helper, we are always glad "to pay enough to keep her with us".'[74] In 1899 he said, 'we never give any guarantee as to raising wages, but we generally pay people what they make themselves worth to us'.[75] Workers did ask for rises, and there are many records of agents writing in requesting a raise, presumably those working in the laundry itself did so verbally. Sometimes these requests received a favourable response, depending, no doubt, on the efficiency of the worker. Sometimes the request was refused. In January 1898 the woman in charge of the city office wrote to say that she had been doing the job for one year and eight months and was looking for an increase of 3s. a week, which she had expected at the end of twelve months. This was followed by another letter in October, saying that her salary was 'very small at present'. In April 1899 she wrote again to say that she was then three years in the job and had received only one small advance.

She said that the work for both establishments, the Dublin Laundry and the Dartry Dye Works, had greatly increased; for March she had received 291 parcels and sixty-eight calls for the dye works and 365 parcels and 317 small accounts for the laundry, which she expected to increase greatly in the current month. She said that she was not satisfied with the salary she was receiving and asked for £52 a year (it is not known what her salary then was). Edmondson's reply to this was to give her notice. In answer, she said that, as it was not entirely her own wish to ask for so much, that she would be satisfied with '2s. of an advance' and that she had no wish to leave.[76] Edmondson evidently did not reverse his decision, and, later that month, her mother wrote to him protesting at the fact that he would sack her daughter merely for asking for an increase in salary and saying that her daughter would be willing to return at her then salary.[77] Edmondson sent a reply by return of post saying, that his previous letter must still hold good since he did not see any reason to change his mind.[78] The clerk lost her job because she overestimated her value to her employer and made too frequent and too high demands. Edmondson summarised his attitude to staff in the following words: 'our opinion is that only by employing the most efficient workers we can procure, by giving them the most healthy rooms to work in, with good pay and as short hours as possible, can we expect to get good work'.[79]

Edmondson was an exacting employer. In 1899 he asked his solicitors Goodbody and Tisdall to draft a clause restricting the freedom of his employees to seek employment elsewhere within the laundry business. They suggested the following:

> In Consideration of the Employment hereby given the said A.B. shall for the period of years from the time when his (or her) employment hereunder ceases, be subject to the following restriction, that is to say a. He or she shall not accept any employment with any other person carrying on any laundry business in the province of Leinster, Ireland and for the purpose of this clause the word 'Persons' shall be deemed to include any body of persons whether incorporated or not incorporated . . .

To which Edmondson wrote: 'Add all business which it is wished to cover by "laundry business"' in the margin of this document.[80]

Money was deducted from workers' earnings for offences such as, bad timekeeping, talking or singing, careless or bad work, or damage to linen; 244 workers were paid in the week ending 17 November 1906; thirty-six of them were fined.[81] While fines could be as high as 1s. for staying out for a whole day, the usual range was 1d to 4d.[82] Thomas told his cousin D.E. Benson in 1896 that, if time workers were not in within fifteen minutes, they were locked out for two hours and were fined 4d. In the case of piece workers, the fine was 1s.[83] A letter from Hilda Martindale, HM Inspector of Factories, to the Dublin Laundry in 1909 drew the attention of management to a notice in the laundry under the Truck Act, 1896, which covered 'deductions which are not reasonable and are therefore contrary to the Act'. Any worker 'who wilfully or negligently cause injury to the work or other property of the Employers, is liable to be charged a sum which does not exceed the damage or loss occasioned to the Employers by his or her act or omission, and is fair and reasonable having regard to all the circumstances in the case'. This limited the imposition of fines, and, she said, appeared to rule out the fines for 'impertinence'. She thought the fines imposed for absence from work and for coming in ten minutes late were excessive and asked to have the amounts reduced.[84] The Principal Lady Inspector at the Home Office asked to have two fines from the revised list submitted by the Laundry removed. One, she felt, could be dispensed with by any good management; a worker making a disturbing noise could be suspended until she realised that 'such bad manners will not be allowed'.[85] Robert Benson recounted to Martindale the overheard remark of a fifteen-year-old girl: 'we can say anything we like to a Forewoman now, as she cannot fine us, and they cannot afford to do without us'.[86] The realisation of worker power had come to the women and girls of the Laundry.

In addition to basic pay and good working conditions, workers had, in common with workers in most large laundries, certain advantages or perks. They were supplied with uniforms. This was a big saving on their own clothes, especially for van men who had suits and coats supplied. A frieze coat lined with good tweed for a van man was ordered from William James McKnight, tailor, Dundrum, in 1893; it cost £2.10s.0d, and, 'bar accident', was to be kept in repair for two winters. Irish tweed suits for the men were also ordered at a cost of from £2.5s.0d.[87] This was quite expensive, the coat cost about three times the man's weekly wage. In 1924 the same type of overcoat from Pim's cost £3, a rise of 10s., or 20 per cent, in thirty years.[88] It is surprising to learn that some of the men did not wear the uniform; apart from the saving to their own clothes, they must have looked quite smart; however, a note from management in 1897 stated that overcoats were not to be issued to those who would not wear uniform.[89] Other men employed in the laundry wore denim jackets and trousers; women workers wore overalls.[90] In 1921 a hundred 48in and seventy-five 51in overalls for women, with green, blue, pink and plain collars, presumably to denote the different departments, were ordered from Lewis Ltd, Manchester. Six white overalls of a better quality were ordered for heads of departments and khaki overalls for men.[91] Enquiries were made to the Ministry of Munitions Disposal Board, in November 1919, about khaki top coats and women's munition overalls; the Laundry actually bought twenty-five Macintosh capes from the Board for £16.5s.0d, presumably for the van men. Some members of the office staff expressed an interest in these capes and six were ordered for them at a cost, to each individual, of 13s.6d.[92] Footwear, such as clogs and rubber boots, were supplied to certain workers, those working in the wash-house or out-of-doors.[93] Caps were not worn by the women, as they would have been too hot.[94]

Laundry workers could have their own washing done at a considerable discount; staff washing was done at the Laundry for what Edmondson described as a 'nominal sum'. He said that it was 'a great help and privilege for them to get their washing done in this very cheap way'. A woman brought in her washing on Monday, a list was made out and priced and returned to her with the clean clothes, and the cost deducted from her wages.[95] There was no record of workers abusing the system in the early days of the Laundry, though it probably happened. It was quite common to put through personal washing without paying for it at all. It happened in all laundries, certain articles were put through 'on the nod'. A blouse, for instance, was given to the woman who did the washing and she would pass it on to the next person concerned, and eventually it came back to the owner. The amount that could be laundered in this way was obviously small; however, if ignored, it could get out of hand. In the later years of the laundry business, if someone were caught, he or she was severely reprimanded.[96] At the end of the nineteenth century such abusers may have been dealt with more severely.

At a time when workers had no protection in law, Edmondson always took an interest in the health and welfare of his employees. Those who had accidents at work were sent to the Meath Hospital for treatment, with a letter of recommendation from Edmondson. Margaret Flynn had been attending the hospital for treatment for four months in April 1902 when the doctor from there reported that she would not be fit to resume work for another week.[97] The Laundry was informed that Anne McDonald should not do any work which would require the wetting of her cut finger and that she should go every day to the hospital to have it dressed.[98] Workers seem to have been treated free of charge. The Meath Hospital was founded in 1753 by benevolent medical men; it was a voluntary hospital originally intended for the use of 'poor manufacturers' in the Liberties. Later in the century it became the County Infirmary for Dublin and after that it received financial assistance from the state.[99] It could be argued that it was Edmondson's duty to look after those who were involved in accidents, but he did not confine himself to this; those who were unwell were also referred to the hospital. In 1896 he got a report that one of these girls was in the first stages of consumption.[100] In 1900 Edmondson was involved in a controversy with Dr James Craig over a statement made by the latter at a meeting of the Prevention of Consumption Committee to the effect that he got more cases of consumption from the Milltown Laundry than from any other place. Edmondson's initial response was quite restrained; he pointed out that they employed over 300 hands and that they frequently gave hospital recommendations to the relatives and friends of their employees, and 'to others brought under our notice by our District Nurse'.[101] This was followed three weeks later by a stronger letter. He said that he had delayed replying because the District Nurse was on holidays. He said that, having discussed the matter with her, she confirmed his opinion that 'there is not more consumption in this neighbourhood than in other similar districts and also confirmed my impression that the cases which have actually occurred are not in any way attributable to employment in this or any other laundry'. He finished by saying that if Craig had facts which warranted a different opinion, he wanted to know them; if not, he demanded a complete withdrawal of his statement at the next meeting of the Prevention of Consumption Committee.[102] The matter must have been resolved amicably, because Edmondson asked Craig to come to see him to have a friendly conversation and referred to their earlier 'small passage of arms'.[103] Edmondson made an annual contribution of £2 to the Meath and in 1892, took 'this opportunity of expressing our sense of the kindly care received by any patients we have sent to your Hospital'.[104]

In 1893 Edmondson wrote to the lady superintendent of St. Patrick's Home asking whether her committee could arrange, as an experiment, to visit the Dublin Laundry's employees and their families, for a small fee per visit. He said that he was willing to give an annual subscription of £2, and hoped that, in return, they would visit those recommended by him. The subscription was to cover a certain amount of visiting; any extra visits would be paid for additionally at a rate to be arranged.[105] The Secretary of the Convalescent Home at 5 Molesworth Street was asked in 1902 whether a woman could be admitted as a free patient, as he, Edmondson, was a subscriber to the Home. If she could only be taken as a 'pay patient', he would rather pay 5s. a week himself rather than have her refused admission. The following year a similar letter was sent on behalf of a Maggie Murray; again Edmondson offered to pay himself 'for a week or two', if he had to.[106] That year he also wrote to Our Lady's Hospice for the Dying, asking them to admit Peter Kavanagh, a former van man, who was not expected to live many weeks, and offering to contribute a guinea if the man were admitted.[107] In 1902 he also paid for an employee who had to spend ten weeks in the Newcastle Hospital.[108]

In 1899 the Milltown, Clonskeagh and Dundrum Nursing Association was founded, Edmondson was the moving spirit behind it and became chairman and treasurer.[109] In January of that year, the *Rathmines News* announced that the Dublin Laundry had appointed a professional nurse who would look after the wants of the poor people of the district who could not afford to pay a nurse in times of sickness; she would attend, subject to doctor's orders, not only the company's own employees, but anyone else who might require her services. The nurse had to 'practise under the rules of the Jubilee Association which strictly forbad her to interfere with the religious opinions of patients or their families'.[110] In January 1900 Edmondson wrote to Miss Naughton, conveying the committee's appreciation of the valuable service she had rendered during the previous twelve months in an area in which there had never been a district nurse. He said that she had overcome any prejudice that had existed at first 'through ignorance', and that he had heard nothing but expressions of kindly feelings towards her. On the same day he wrote to Kathleen Browne in Limerick, engaging her as the new district nurse at a salary of £35 per annum, with a maximum allowance of 10s. a week board, and 10s. a week lodgings, 2s. per week for light and fire, 2s. for laundry and £2.10s.0d per annum for uniform.[111] The salary was approximately the same as that of a woman in charge of a section in the laundry; the allowances were generous. Edmondson was involved in raising money to pay for the services of the district nurse. A 'drawing room meeting' was held at Dr Usher's in Dundrum in February 1900 for that purpose.[112] In April he wrote to the Queen Victoria Jubilee Institute for Nurses thanking them for the grant of £10 which they had given the Nursing Association.[113]

There is no doubt that Edmondson was concerned about the health and well-being of his employees. If they were injured or ill he considered it his duty to look after them. He also included their families as part of this responsibility. He contributed to hospitals and other institutions which might be required to help in this task, by means of annual subscriptions. He hoped that the workers would be treated free, but, if not, was willing to bear their expenses himself, rather than, as he said about one girl, 'see her miss the benefit of it'.[114] He was also willing to expend time and energy chairing committees and raising money for this cause. This attitude was very much in the Quaker tradition, as, indeed, was his concern that his workers should be properly housed.

A couple of years after starting the laundry, in February 1891, Edmondson offered a young woman from Rathdrum a job in the sorting and packing room at a wage of 9s. a week, 'with lodgings in a comfortable house we have taken for the purpose and furnished'. He stressed that board was not provided, except for tea, which was supplied on five days a week at work. The matron of 'our home' would, he said, be able to cook food for her or she could buy meals in the mess room.[115] There were twenty sorters and packers employed at the time, several of them were lodged in the home.[116] This house was replaced in May 1898 when Edmondson purchased Millmount, on the Dundrum Road.[117] In August he appointed a Mrs Meany as working housekeeper in what was then referred to as the Assistants' Home. In the earlier years it was the sorters and packers who were staying in the home, later, it appeared to be those in charge of departments or sections.[118] It was the policy of the management to recruit local labour; however, there was difficulty in the early years getting sorters and packers, who were, as has been seen, considered to have a very responsible job. Edmondson had to appoint people from outside the district. He had always tended to appoint supervisory and management staff from outside, many from Great Britain. This may have been partly due to the unavailability of this level of staff locally; it also seemed to be associated, to a large extent, with previous knowledge of the individual and her family and religion, preference being given to Quakers and members of the Church of England, and, of course, with her experience and ability to control staff. It would probably have been seen as an advantage, even at the lower supervisory levels, to have strangers in charge of local girls. It was for this type of staff that the hostel was used. Meaney was offered 8s. a week, with an apartment, coals and light, but, as was the case with the young women staying there, board was not included. The Laundry took possession in the last week in August, and Meaney was requested to arrive at 9 a.m. to receive the furniture and take up her duties.[119] She stayed only eleven weeks and

19. Bankside Cottages, built by the Dublin Laundry for their workers.

was succeeded by Miss Whitehall who, as working matron, was there four and a half years, until the hostel ceased to exist. In the reference he wrote for her, Edmondson said she was a good plain cook who kept the house clean and comfortable.[120] The reason for closing the home is not known. The house was done up by Messrs Albert Roberts, all but the large sitting room and room off it; these, in Edmondson's words, being 'sufficiently good'. It was let to Thomas Ryan from August 1903 at a yearly rent of £45 paid to the company;[121] the Ryan family still lived there in the late 1920s. It was a beautiful house, which became known as 'Clonbeg'.[122]

The Laundry also owned cottages which it let to more senior employees such as foremen. The company built cottages near Millmount, known as the Bankside Cottages;[123] they also had a terrace of houses, Coolnahinch, on the Dundrum Road.[124] Sometimes Edmondson had to seek cottages elsewhere, as in 1892, when he wrote to John Sealy of Dundrum, asking what was the lowest rent he would take for his vacant cottage, which he wanted for a foreman, who would be 'a very careful and eligible tenant'. He got the cottage for £20 a year, payable monthly,

20. Coolnahinch, Dundrum Road; houses acquired by the Dublin Laundry for their workers.

'I further agree not to sublet any part of the cottage without your consent, except that I am to be allowed to let Furnished Apartments to one or two responsible persons, not of the artisan or labouring class. I also undertake not to keep any fowl in excess of one dozen . . .'[125] It appears that the foreman was not to get the whole cottage and that Edmondson was making provision for accommodation, probably for some of his office or supervisory staff. The inconvenience of lodging strangers was one readily accepted at the time, many people rented or let rooms even in very small houses. Edmondson, as has been seen, often lodged people in his own home, sometimes temporarily, but sometimes for extended periods; they tended to be Quakers or those with impeccable references from family or close friends. He also expected the manageress to provide temporary lodgings in her house, if required. He always offered to help prospective employees to get accommodation locally.

Edmondson was quite unusual, in the Dublin of his day, in providing housing and lodgings for his workforce. There was little housing provided for the working class either by business or philanthropic interests. This, of course, reflected the lack of large industrial concerns as well as a lack of benevolent individuals or groups able or willing to undertake such a venture. It is interesting to note that one of the first businesses to do so was the Quaker textile firm of Pim, which built cottages for its workers at Harold's Cross in the 1850s. Watkin's brewery, in the Coombe, built eighty-seven dwellings for their workers in the 1860s. The Guinness brewery, the largest in the city, was noted for its interest in the welfare of its workers, but its housing provision was on a relatively modest scale. The railway companies also built houses for their workers. By far the largest scheme, 142 houses, was provided by the Great Southern & Western Railway Co. in the 1870s, at Inchicore. At the end of the century the Dublin United Tramways built over a hundred cottages in small, secluded developments at Terenure, Rathmines, Donnybrook and Dollymount, close to tramway terminals.[126]

Edmondson's interest in housing was not confined to his own employees. In 1894 he spoke to W. Fawcett, secretary of the Rathmines Commissioners, about the urgent need for suitable artisans' dwellings in Milltown.[127] Subsequently he was in touch with Edmond Johnston, Nullamore, asking whether he would be prepared to sell or let a strip of ground between the road and the river which belonged to him, for the building of 'a good class of workmen's dwellings'. He also approached J.F. Lombard, of South Hill with the same request, saying that he was very anxious 'to see something done to improve the style of living of the working people of this neighbourhood—a wish in which I feel you will join'. He added that high prices for land or rent could not be afforded.[128] Two years later he wrote again to Johnson, saying that he had been waiting a very long time to hear from him about the strip of land, and pointing out that 'our poor neighbours around us are miserably housed'. He went on to say: 'Is it not our duty, when we are living in our own comfortable houses, to do what we can for the benefit of these less fortunate ones?'[129]

From time to time the Dublin Laundry management made an effort to provide social and educational opportunities for the staff. Garden parties were given for the hands and their families; in July 1890 about 150 people were present at one, and seats had to be borrowed from the school.[130] In August 1901 Edmondson received a request from C.H. Oldham, Feis Ceoil, 37 Molesworth Street, asking whether a deputation from their committee, who were all professional musicians, could come out to talk to the laundry staff. They were doing a similar exercise for the DBC restaurants; they were bringing a choir 'to give them a sample of what choral singing is like, for many of those girls would be ignorant on the subject, having regard to the class these girls come from'. The Laundry would have to wait until September for this, as the choir was from a school and put at their disposal by Mr Vincent O'Brien.[131] The committee met the employees at an evening meeting in August; September did not suit as Edmondson was going away and he evidently wanted to be present.[132] By January 1902 the Laundry had its own choral society, and Bessie Birelo, as secretary to the local committee, was busy arranging the hire of a piano from Messrs Pigott of Grafton Street at 12s.6d a month or 30s. for three months; she felt it likely that they would keep it for the three months.[133] The choir must have provided much pleasure and excitement, at least for its members. Birelo rather grandly told the secretary of the Feis Ceoil on 7 April 1902: 'I am directed to inform you that our Committee and Musical Director cordially agree to attendance of the performing members of our Choral Society at a massed performance during the Feis week.' Bessie Birelo was sent tickets for the Feis which she was allowed to sell at half price, this gave an opportunity to all employees to partake.[134] In May the 'Prize Choir' was invited to go to Cork. The matter was considered but many difficulties were seen: the members, all working girls, could not be put to any expense, and no day, except a Saturday, could be given up for the purpose.[135] Before his death in 1908 Edmondson had discussed with the Technical Instruction Committee the possibility of putting on cookery classes for the girls in the laundry: when the new School of Domestic Economy opened in Rathmines, Robert Benson, his successor, brought the plan to fruition when he arranged with the principal Miss L.R. Proctor to provide an instructress to give demonstrations and lectures in the laundry, from 7 till 9 p.m. on Monday evenings.[136]

In providing accommodation for workers, hot meals at work, medical services, educational opportunities and social outings, Edmondson was in the Quaker tradition and ahead of the majority of entrepreneurs and managers of his time. Three members of the Society of Friends, all born around the same time as Thomas, Joseph Fry, George Cadbury and Joseph Rowntree, were renowned for their benign treatment of their employees. There were, of course, many enlightened employers outside the ranks of the Quakers, but the Friends set a high standard.[137] George Cadbury, like Thomas, believed that a healthy working environment would benefit both employees and the firm. At Bourneville, playing fields for men and a garden for girls were provided; there were welfare facilities such as a kitchen for heating food and provision for drying wet clothes. Probably his most important measure was the building of estate houses, Bournville Village, which was not restricted to Cadbury workers.[138] Joseph Rowntree, like the other two, had been brought up to believe that the welfare of a firm's work force was the responsibility of the owner.[139] In 1891 he appointed a woman welfare officer to look after the increasing number of young girls who worked in his factory; this was a revolutionary action at the time, and, a year later, an assistant was appointed to help her.[140] He arranged occasional festivities to include the whole firm, such as outings to concerts, providing a substantial meal. The office staff, who were not very numerous then, were often invited to 'social evenings' at Joseph's own home. These developed into organised clubs and societies, such as the cricket, football, cycling, tennis, bowling and camera clubs; singing classes and dressmaking classes were organised. There were plenty of employees to keep these activities going, 1,000, in 1897 and 2,000 in 1902.[141] A concern such as the Dublin Laundry, with 200 to 300 workers, would have found it extremely difficult to sustain clubs and societies.

There is no evidence to suggest that Edmondson was influenced by the emerging theories of management of his day, rather he was inspired by the tenets of his faith and the influence of his family. Quaker entrepreneurs may have used, for that time, enlightened methods in their treatment of employees based on their belief in the equality of all men and women, but they were fully aware of the beneficial effect of this policy to their businesses. In a letter to Edmondson from Benson, in March 1896, Robert mentioned that one of the items coming up for discussion at the next meeting of the Northern Counties Laundry Association (NCLA) in Manchester, was: 'Are treats to hands usual in the trade and beneficial?';[142] obviously they meant beneficial to the industry. Thomas said, having enumerated all that he had done to improve the workers' conditions, 'we expect to get good work, and as good work in our aim throughout, we take every means we can to obtain it'.[143] In this he was no different from those who at a later date set up personnel departments in their factories and firms; they were just slower to realise that the humane treatment of people can lead to greater productivity and lacked the ideological perspective which would have allowed them to find this out sooner. Louie Bennet pointed out that women were as keenly interested in working conditions as in wages; women wanted better ventilation, better sanitary conditions, an acceptable place where they could eat their meals and a clean work area.[144] She also said, in

1917, almost ten years after Edmondson's death, that welfare facilities, health services, canteens and cloakroom accommodation were not considered matters of any importance in this country.[145]

The paternal system, as exemplified by these Quakers, was, at the time, the only bulwark that workers had to cushion them against misfortunes such as the illness of the breadwinner or, indeed, of any member of the family, an accident, funeral expenses or a son getting involved with the police. Employees could count themselves extremely lucky if their master acknowledged any responsibilities other than paying them their wages. Paternalism, however, depended entirely on the character of the employer or manager, and benevolent paternalism could vanish overnight through death or change of leadership for any other reason. Even the most amiable of masters, could, if he considered it necessary, compel an employee to do what he wanted. Edmondson considered himself a kind man, a view doubtless endorsed by family and friends, but he could be ruthless and impervious to the pleas of sacked workers. Until the state, through legislation, intervened and trade unions were formed to protect the majority of workers, employees were literally at the mercy of their employers.

# CHAPTER FIVE

# Continuing Success but 'a Difficult Business'

THE LAUNDRY BUSINESS is difficult 'hard work and worry. Some "novices" think it is an easy thing to "run" but I know of few more difficult businesses.'[1] At least Thomas Edmondson had experience of other trades when he made this statement. A contemporary expert on the laundry business agreed with him, and spoke of the fallacy in the minds of the public that laundering was a very profitable industry at which anyone of ordinary ability could make a comfortable living. He went on to say that this might have been true in the early days of machinery, but that competition had changed that.[2]

The laundry business, even with the advent of machinery, was very labour-intensive; the introduction of machinery having led to a large expansion of the trade. It was a low-status occupation, and for this reason it was sometimes difficult to attract workers. The association of laundry work with domestic service was given as a reason for the low status.[3] Edmondson, who recruited most of his staff from the families around the village of Milltown, did not seem to experience this problem; neither did the occupation, in that location, appear to suffer from any lack of status. However, even in the Dublin Laundry the maintenance of a good staff was a constant preoccupation, and one of the prime requirements for supervisory personnel, as has been seen, was the ability to control and manage a large number of girls. In some laundries in the city centre, where conditions were bad and wages low, the workers were probably rougher and more unmanageable. In England laundresses had a reputation for heavy drinking, encouraged, it was said, by the hot and heavy nature of their work, and the long hours standing, and undoubtedly helped by the tradition of partly paying the workers in beer.[4] Drink was not a problem in the Dublin Laundry, where the use of alcohol was strictly forbidden.

Laundry machinery changed rapidly, and obsolescence, as well as wear and tear, had to be included when reckoning depreciation.

Contemporary advice stressed that depreciation must be taken into consideration if a reliable balance sheet were to be obtained. An annual figure of 10 per cent was suggested, though in large concerns it was advised that the plant should be separated into different groups, with varying rates of depreciation on each, for example, 7.5 per cent on machinery, 15 on vans and 25 on hampers.[5] This is what Edmondson did; in 1889 the depreciation allowed on machinery was 6.8 per cent, on vans 18, on baskets and laundry appliances it was also 18.[6] It was not too dissimilar from the suggested rates, and there could have been different rates of wear and tear in different establishments. It was important that proprietors kept in touch with the latest developments in machinery. This was something Edmondson did through trade journals, machinery suppliers, contact with colleagues in the business, membership of trade associations and visits to other laundries where the latest equipment could be seen in use.

Insurance on laundries tended to be high, and some insurers did not want the business at all.[7] Boiler insurance was compulsory, and it was usual to cover customers' linen under the heading of 'goods in trust', the value being reckoned at twenty times the amount of the week's work, if the goods were lost or destroyed. Another necessary form of insurance was against employer's liability, and proprietors were warned to see that policies provided complete protection.[8] The Employers' Liability Act of 1880 had recognised the responsibility of the employer for insuring his workers against the risks of their calling.[9] Protection for damage caused to others by the collision of vans or other accidents in the street was obtained under 'third party' policies; loss of profits as a result of fire could be guaranteed against by a 'contingent' policy.[10] In 1896 the Dublin Laundry was insured by the General Accident Guarantee and Indemnity Insurance Co. Ltd, 3 Westmoreland Streeet. In January 1898 that company amalgamated with the Ocean Accident Insurance and Guarantee Corporation Ltd of London, though the business in Ireland continued to be carried on from the Westmoreland Street office.[11] In June 1898 the Ocean offered members of the National Laundry Trade Protection Association Ltd, what they ingenuously called a 'Practically Free Policy', covering all employers' liability risks in Common Law, under the Employers' Liability Act 1880, and under the Workmen's Compensation Act 1897. This 'special low rate' was 10s. per cent on the wages bill. By having a large number of members, this could be further reduced to 7s.6d per cent; the cost to an individual employer was 12s.6d. Every member was urged to join by the association so that a saving

21. Hand ironing room, showing gas irons.

amounting to £2.10s.0d on every £1,000 paid in wages could be obtained.[12]

Pricing was a difficult area for the laundry trade. There was the problem of undercutting by other laundries and by small home laundries, which were often run uneconomically—satisfied to make one salary, even though other family members were involved—and, of course, by Edmondson's special *bêtes noires*, the institution laundries. Another pricing difficulty was that the work could not be standardised, either as regards quality or style. Nightdresses were quoted in practically all lists as 'from 3d', depending on the amount of trimming and the type of material; if it was a delicate fabric, a nightdress might cost anything between 4d and 6d. A decision had to be made in the sorting department, if, by an oversight, an elaborate nightdress 'went through' at 3d, it was difficult to get the customer to pay the right price the next time. Laundry proprietors were warned that silk articles, good lace or embroidery, and fancy teacloths, warranted an extra charge as insurance against claims for loss or damage (see Appendix, Figures 6 and 7). The basis of the price charged to a customer for any article was the cost of ironing it by hand, the guiding principle being that the charge must be three times the ironer's wages. This standard was often not obtained. In theory, each article laundered should have borne its proportion of the establishment's charges, but this did not happen. Kitchen cloths, towels, servants' washing and often children's washing did not bear their fair share, and customers would not allow this to be corrected, so other articles had to be priced more highly.[13] Thus proprietors were often guided by what they thought customers would pay. On one occasion, when it was necessary to raise prices, Robert Benson said that the least annoying rise to customers would be for table linen, to a minimum of 3d; the average household sent only one tablecloth per week.[14]

As the number of laundries increased, competition grew. In order to offset the effects of this, an effort was made in 1900 to get all the steam laundries to agree on prices; thirteen did so; one, the Mespil Steam Laundry did not.[15] Laundry associations sought to achieve agreed prices among members. In 1912 a minimum price list was agreed by the members of the Irish Laundries Association, they even agreed to forfeit £20 every time they were proved to have cut prices below those figures, but the laundries tried to keep knowledge of this price fixing from the public.[16] In 1916, due to the war, it was necessary to raise prices; the Association got a unanimous decision for a 10 per cent rise, which some thought insufficient; it was done in two instalments and was announced to customers by circular signed by all the participants, to prevent, as it was said, 'people running from one laundry to another'. When prices went up, laundrymen expected a temporary falling off in business as people did some washing at home, but customers soon tired and things returned to normal. It was difficult to get these agreements to hold and a year later, the Swastika had not 'come into line'.[17] The increase in wages, the rising cost of materials, difficulties in raising prices, requests from contract customers for reductions, all caused the exasperated manager of the Dublin Laundry, Sidney Foster, to say in 1916 that: 'the lot of all laundries is an unenviable one'.[18]

The arrangement of the work had an important bearing on the success of a laundry. If there were a large number of full-time hands, it was important that they should be kept busy over the whole week; if the weekly hours were crammed into four days their labour was not as effective. It was also important not to have machinery standing idle, as could happen with the washing plant at the end of the week and the ironing equipment at the beginning. As has been pointed out, laundry tended to be collected on Monday and Tuesday, and returned on Friday

22. Typical horse-drawn delivery van, in use up to 1949.

and Saturday; customers were resistant to any changes from this, and, indeed, proprietors did not show much inclination to deviate either. Country business was done on a weekly basis, dirty washing was collected and laundered linen returned on the same day each week, so if this was done on Wednesdays and Thursdays, it helped to spread the work. This was the way the Dublin Laundry arranged its business, and it seemed to work well. In 1901 van men were making 400 to 500 calls per day and 75 to 150 long-distance runs. Family clothes collected by Tuesday evening were delivered the same week; long-distance work was delivered on the following Wednesday or Thursday. If the men had any time free, they were sent for stores or to the North Wall to collect goods.[19]

Family work was the mainstay of most laundries, as it was in the Milltown laundry. Many combined contract work with family washing. Contract work had usually to be returned within forty-eight or even twenty-four hours. This work could be undertaken only by laundries that had a large number of calendars and sufficient space to keep the two kinds of work separate. If this could not be managed properly, there was the danger that contract work might take precedence, to the detriment of family business.[20] The punctual return of hotel linen might seem much more important than adhering to the normal routine for individual homes. Edmondson was aware of this danger, and, in his laundry, seemed to combine the two types of business very well, and, of course, had planned for both. Edmondson told Mr Spicer, who was in charge of the Dartry Dye Works, that he knew Spicer had been 'pressed for the Horse Show', but it was important not to get the regular work 'left behind', and added, that they should 'keep our name for punctuality, even if you have to get another hand'.[21] Edmondson could boast to clubs, hotels and institutions of his ability to deal with large amounts of washing, and to return it within a short period: he could also claim that private customers could rely on receiving their clean linen on the same day, and at almost exactly the same hour of that day, each week.[22] Price cutting was particularly common in the contract business as laundries sought to attract important clients. In 1915, when prices for laundry work rose, the manager of the Gresham asked the Dublin Laundry to give a discount on visitors' laundry; he was told that all laundries had agreed to discontinue this practice and he was advised to increase the price to visitors.[23] All hotels made a profit on visitors' washing; Edmondson said that he charged hotels the lowest price on visitors' work, and assumed that they charged their customers about double that amount.[24]

All the commercial laundries in Dublin were located south of the Liffey, due, in part anyway, to the greater availability there of water. This clustering does not appear to have been regarded as a major disadvantage since laundries could not rely on the immediate neighbourhood, but had to draw their custom from a much wider area. This entailed a transport system, which in 1888 meant horses and vans, and men and boys to drive, collect and deliver. Laundry vans were a familiar sight around the city, and the van man, like the bread man, the milkman and the coalman, was a regular caller to many homes. Usually he built up a rapport with the housewife or servant, and was an important link in maintaining customer loyalty. When complaints were received about van men, they were taken very seriously indeed. A customer from Rathmines wrote to complain that the man was insolent to the servant and his wife, and, when the parcel was not ready, went without it. He added that 'plenty of other Family vans come up this way who would be very glad to get the clothes, even if they had to wait a second or two'.[25] Failure to have the dirty laundry ready when the van man called was a fairly common occurrence, which caused much annoyance to the laundry. Again, a resident of Temple Villas complained that the delivery boy broke the lock on the side door and flung the laundry basket into the kitchen.[26] The manager of a branch of the Royal Bank of Ireland wrote

23. Motorised van; 'Dublin Laundry' on other side of name plate.

to say: 'Everything is right in your laundry except the van man who was not very civil, please arrange that "a civil man" could call.' The laundry replied: 'We are sorry to have your complaint as to the van man's incivility and have made arrangements that your linen be collected on Tuesdays by a different man.'[27]

The Dublin Laundry had one two-horse van for steep hills, but considered the single-horse van better value for ordinary purposes. The vans, which were painted a chocolate colour, carried a van boy, some two, as well as a man. They not only collected in Dublin and its neighbouring townships, such as Clontarf, Pembroke, Rathmines and Rathgar, but went as far as Sutton and Howth on the north side, and Kingstown, Bray and Greystones on the south. Edmondson said that the longest distance reached was fourteen miles 'as the crow flies'. The men were expected to groom the horses, wash the van and clean the harness; a yard man and boy were employed to do other stable work.[28] A motor van was ordered for the laundry in July 1901 at a cost of £750.[29] In order to get as much business as possible, five different routes of about twenty-five miles each into the country were planned. Advice on the routes was sought from R.J. McCready, of Dundrum, who was considered the best man in Ireland for the job.[30] Enquiries were made about a 9hp Daimler motor van in January 1902, which had a maximum speed of 12 mph.[31] By 1904 the Dublin Laundry engineer, Mr Waring, was giving advice to other laundries about motor vans, and saying that they should have a long wheel base, solid rubber tyres and a speed of 15 to 20mph.[32] However, the horse maintained its position of importance for many years to come (see Appendix, Figure 10).

As well as vans, the Dublin Laundry had branch offices in several parts of the city where washing could be handed in and collected. These were staffed by a full-time woman, sometimes with an assistant. The first one, which was at 5 South Anne Street, was opened in 1895.[33] It must have been a paying investment since it was followed, early in 1899, by 64 South Richmond Street; the premises were rented for 18s.11d per week, free of taxes, and, in addition to the shop, had two rooms upstairs and a kitchen downstairs.[34] In 1906 South Anne Street was closed and the office moved to 56 Grafton Street.[35] By 1912 there were receiving offices at 33 Madras Place, Phibsborough, 12 Ranelagh, 49 Upper George's Street, Kingstown, and 16 Quinsboro Road, Bray;[36] only one of these was located to the north of the city.

The Dublin Laundry had a countrywide business, and had agencies located in several Irish towns, many in post offices or drapery shops. In October 1901 the postmistress in Kilcullen said she would take on the agency, if she were paid properly, but thought that 1d a parcel would hardly suffice.[37] In November Benson wrote to the postmaster in Enniskerry saying: 'You have probably noticed that our Motor Van passes through your town weekly', a not unreasonable assumption in 1901, and offering the same terms as had been offered to the woman in Kilcullen. The letter was returned by the postmistress, who had written at the end: 'I agree the above terms', and signed her name.[38] Sometimes the initiative came from the laundry and sometimes from a local businessman. Robert Edge, a general draper and outfitter in Westport, wrote to the Laundry suggesting that he become their agent; he said there was no such agency in the district and that he did a good trade.[39] The whole business of establishing an agency was fraught with difficulties. In November 1904 Messrs Henry Lyons, of Sligo, wrote to Milltown seeking an agency. The offer by the laundry was: customers would pay list prices, the agent would receive 15 per cent commission on this, the laundry would pay carriage both ways, but would put 2d in the 1s. on the amount that the customer paid in order to partly cover

24. Delivery van at the Nine Arches, obviously a social occasion.

these costs. It was pointed out that carriage to Sligo was high, 37s.4d per ton of goods. Apart from price lists, further advertising was to be done by the agent. Lyons negotiated a lower freight rate with the railway company and said they did not want their customers charged at all for carriage. The Laundry replied that anything less than £10 a week of business was not likely to pay them for giving the commission, and that Lyons would have to supply strong, locked hampers with a duplicate key for the laundry. The final agreement was that the laundry paid the carriage both ways, and supplied hampers and circulars about the service; Lyons got a 10 per cent commission, which was to be increased if justified by the volume of business. The washing was sent to Dublin on Mondays and returned on Saturdays.[40] The agency does not seem to have done well. In 1910 the Laundry refused to pay for an advertisement in the local press because the profit from Sligo was so small that they could not go to any further expense.[41] It was closed down in 1915 as it was not paying. The laundry said then, that with increased rail charges and the rise in postal rates, they would have 'to drop the idea of agencies until times are normal'.[42] Railway rates were considered reasonable in the beginning and the Great Western Railway carried hampers of linen for half-price in 1896.[43] As time passed, carriage became much more expensive. In 1915 James Nixon, a general draper in Main Street, Ballinasloe, who sought the agency on the death of the former agent, was told that carriage accounted for 5s. of each £1 worth of laundry, and, for that reason, it had been decided to cut out heavy items such as sheets and tablecloths, and to make it a shirt and collar service only. Family work would be taken, if the customer agreed to pay the carriage. Later that year, the Laundry agreed to supply a show case to display a shirt and a few collars or a blouse, pointing out, that unless it is continually renewed, it is not an advertisement.[44] The laundry had an office at 109 The Quay, Waterford, which seems to have been quite successful; the woman in charge was given a rise of 2s.6d. in 1919, bringing her salary to 22s.6d; she also had an assistant.[45] By 1924 she was earning £2 a week and her assistant had £1, though the laundry maintained then, that with the high cost of the office and of carriage, the profit margin for them was low.[46] By 1919 increased labour and material costs were both reducing profit margins in laundries and making agency work, where large discounts were required, freight charges rising and railway schedules becoming more unreliable, extremely difficult.[47] The Laundry certainly did a countrywide business, and, as a 1914 advertisement stated, was receiving work by post from all parts of Ireland.[48] This is substantiated by its railway advertising programme; in 1896 the laundry had show cards displayed in approximately fifty of the Great Northern Railway stations alone, from stations near Dublin, such as Malahide and Rush, to much more distant places, such as Cootehill, Strabane, Ballyshannon and Bessbrook.[49]

Complaints about lost and damaged linen occurred frequently in the laundry business. Many were caused by badly marked linen, missing items from customers' lists, missing lists, and by customer names or addresses being omitted from lists. Damage was often caused by using a tablecloth or sheet to cover soiled linen, and pinning the bundle together. Edmondson used the opportunity presented, when he issued his two booklets, to advise his customers about these matters, and pointed out that the laundry supplied washing books, free of charge, which should be used instead of lists.[50] Instructions about sending the washing, and having it ready when the van man called, were printed on the washing book (see Appendix, Figure 9). When a dispute arose between the customer and the laundry, the matter was often placed in the hands of solicitors. The Dublin Laundry often got solicitors' letters

25. First receiving office at 5 South Anne Street, opened in 1895.

26. Receiving office of the Laundry, 64 South Richmond Street.

demanding payment for lost or damaged articles.[51] One lady demanded, through her solicitor, £2.0s.11d, for two embroidered nightdresses, twenty-three cambric handkerchiefs and one gansey (silken wool), which she said the laundry had lost.[52] In July 1897, Lord Bentick, South Cavalry Barracks, Aldershot, said that he was delaying paying his account until a white waistcoat, valued at £1.11s.6d, was either found or its value refunded.[53] In January 1898, the Hotel Cecil, in London, threatened to sue the Dublin Laundry for damage to 'valuable curtains'; they had refused the laundry's offer.[54] There was often a suspicion that customers' linen increased considerably in value when it was lost or damaged. Where the fault was theirs, the Laundry was always willing to reimburse the customer. In cases where there was doubt, they often employed the services of experts in an effort to arrive at the truth. A number of these cases were sent to the Launderers' Association in London. In one instance the laundry could not think of anything in their process which might have caused a hole in a tablecloth and asked to have it analysed to see whether any chemical might have been responsible: they drew attention to another hole in the cloth which had been darned by the customer.[55] In 1894 the laundry told a customer that the damage to her tablecloths had been done before the Laundry had taken over her business from another laundry, and that it had been pointed out to her at the time. The cloths were obviously mangled or put through the ironer in fold, which the Dublin Laundry never did, cloths were always ironed flat and open. To confirm the matter, they observed that cloths which were new when she came to them, were 'wearing very fairly, indeed'.[56] When the laundry received a claim for a tablecloth which, they alleged, had never been sent, they said that the parcel came without a list, the sorters had to make out one; in addition, no claim nor communication was made for five to six weeks. Both of these were contrary to the rules of the Laundry and no claim could be entertained.[57] Later, from about 1912, damaged goods were sent to The Power Laundry, Farrington Street, London. Once, sheets were sent which the laundry thought might have been torn in the hydro, 'we do not think it vicious, considering all our employees'.[58] There was, of course, a charge for this service, an apron sent for analysis, because several with similar black stains had been received from the same house, cost 2s.6d in 1916. A report on a tablecloth was urgently required, because the manager had an appointment to see the owner, 'a very cantankerous customer'.[59] In 1917 the laundry had a case of a round, white stain on linen, which tore away around the edge. The Power Laundry was not able to solve this problem, so a second opinion was sought in Belfast, for which the Dublin Laundry undertook to defray all the expenses involved. A solution does not appear to have been found, but the manager of the Dublin Laundry noted that some of the American trade journals also reported similar stains and were equally puzzled.[60]

The police were sometimes involved in lost laundry. When a valuable tablecloth, a family heirloom belonging to Dr Ormsley, Merrion Square, was lost, the DMP, was asked to enquire at all the pawn offices.[61] On another occasion, they were told, by Edmondson, that two young women workers could identify a jacket and various articles of linen missing from the laundry; he believed that they were pawned at Potter's, in Bishop Street, as 'the person suspected was in possession of pawn tickets from that establishment'.[62] Just before Christmas 1893 a basket of linen, the property of the hotel, was stolen from the Laundry's van outside Moran's Hotel. Again the police were asked to check the pawnbrokers.[63] A laundry was open to fraudulent claims and had to protect itself; it also had to ensure that processes and machinery were not causing undue wear and tear to customers' linen. Edmondson, coming from a family with a deep interest in technical and scientific matters, gave these the importance they deserved and established a precedent, as he did in so many other aspects of the enterprise, which was closely adhered to by his followers. Robert Benson and his brother played a large part in setting up The British Launderers' Research Association in 1920: it was said to be the second oldest industrial research association to be established.[64]

The Dublin Laundry had a rule, as indeed had all reputable laundries, that no washing could be accepted from a house in which there was a case of infectious disease, and customers were notified to this effect. In fact, customers were asked to sign a form stating that they would appraise the laundry should there be such a case in their house. There was, of course, always the danger that this rule would be ignored, even though the customer was liable for prosecution under the Public Health (Ireland) Act 1878, Section 142. Apart from the danger involved, the least hint that there was an outbreak of infection in an area caused fear and the withholding of clothes, or requests to the laundry to have the rumour verified.[65] In 1903 Mrs Thompson, of Clonskeagh Castle, was assured by Edmondson that the 'supposed case of smallpox in Tracy's Cottages' had been investigated by the Sanitary Officer from Pembroke District Council and was without foundation.[66] The Laundry exercised great caution if there were any danger from infection. In 1895 there was an infectious disease in Concrete Buildings, where many of the workers lived; they were not allowed to come into work, and Dr Usher of Dundrum was asked to say when they could safely do so.[67] Later that year Edmondson told a customer that: 'We do not allow our van to go to any house in which there is infectious illness.' He went on to say that they had received a 'letter of remonstrance' from a lady on her road who had seen the Dublin Laundry van at her door and was aware that there was illness in the house. He concluded: 'We could not think of sending the man until you can furnish us with a doctor's certificate that it is safe to do so.'[68] Medical advice was sought about whether a man who was in charge of machinery should come to work when his child had measles.[69] These were sensible precautions which might have been ignored by less scrupulous employers. The Urban District Council informed a laundry of an outbreak, if they thought washing was sent there. Robert Brown, the Medical Superintendent Officer of Health, wrote to the manager to say that there was a case of scarletina in Belgrave Park, that it was a large family and that great care should be exercised.[70] On another occasion, the UDC wrote to ask whether clothes had been sent to the laundry within the preceding ten days from a house in Ashfield Avenue.[71] A potentially dangerous event happened in 1908, when the UDC wrote to say that the wife of one of their employees had attended the dispensary in Rathmines and was found to have diphtheria. She was told to go straight to hospital and not to go home. She not only went home, but also to see her husband in the laundry, before going to hospital: the manager was asked whether any of his hands were absent due to illness.[72] The local authorities appear to have been vigilant.

A difficulty to which Edmondson would certainly have drawn attention was what he considered the unfair competition from the institution laundries. In this he would have been supported by many other proprietors. These laundries were run by religious and charitable groups—Roman Catholic and Anglican—as a means of supporting and rehabilitating those who were considered 'outcasts' from society (see ch. 6). Since they did not pay wages and remained outside the scope of the Factory Acts for many years, they were in a position to charge less for their services than the commercial laundries. There is no doubt that these laundries were in competition with the commercial laundries where the two types coexisted, as in the cities and large towns. The larger institutional laundries, in addition to providing a service to private customers, did valuable contract work. The Good Shepherd laundry in Limerick, for example, did the washing for the military, Mount St. Alphonsus, Mungret College, St. Munchins College, the Salesian Missionary College, the Convent of Mercy, Tuam and the Mary Immaculate Training College.[73] Many of the convent laundries did a considerable trade of a high-class nature; indeed, much of their work came over from Mayfair or from large English houses.[74] The Revd Mother of the Sisters of Charity, Donnybrook, spoke of 'the miles of frills and flounces which we have to stiffen and puff out, and which are yearly growing more elaborate, more intricate and luxurious—the lingerie of the present day!. The trousseaux we get from Walpole's to make up! They are the delight of the ironing room.'[75] There is no doubt that the convent laundries had some highly skilled and careful laundresses—many had, after all, a lifetime in which to perfect their techniques.

Numerically, the institution laundries posed serious competition to the commercial laundries. Until 1896 there were six of the latter in Dublin; this rose to eight in 1897.[76] Five were situated relatively close to each other, two in Rathfarnham, and one each in Dundrum, Milltown and Donnybrook. Approximately half of these were steam laundries. Growth in the commercial section, up to this time, was comparatively slow. On the other hand, there were at least sixteen institutional laundries in Dublin and its suburbs in 1901, nine Catholic and seven Anglican, and a laundry in Maynooth run by the Presentation Sisters.[77] When it is considered that some of these were large, steam laundries and also that institution laundries were longer established and were deemed worthy of support by the public for benevolent as well as financial reasons, the concern of Edmondson and other laundrymen is understandable.

Other problems were those shared by all businesses, such as the non-payment of debts. The Dublin Laundry used the Mercantile Association of 27 Dame Street to collect their bad debts, and threats to sue were used against recalcitrant customers. Sometimes the Mercantile advised the laundry against taking people to court, that it would not be worthwhile: they said of one whom they could not trace: 'even had we been successful in finding her out, she would hardly be worth suing'.[78] Some of those who did not pay their bills were members of the aristocracy, and their bills tended to be much larger than those of the more lowly defaulters. An earl, in 1901, sent a cheque which was returned by the bank marked 'refer to Drawer', and he did not put the 'matter right', when asked to do so by Edmondson. A titled lady owed £92.11s.11d in 1922.[79]

The Dublin Laundry seemed to have relatively few staff problems. There were strikes in 1897 and 1899 which do not appear to have been too serious; one was described as a 'disturbance of hands', on another occasion some hands left their work. In the latter case, George B. Edmondmon, of the Manor Mill, wrote to ask, whether a particular girl, who had applied to him for work, was involved in the strike; if she had been, they would 'not think of employing her'.[80] Although it was played down at the time, the second incident was more worrying. Thomas confided in his niece Marjorie some time afterwards, that she had 'little idea of the trouble of carrying on this business'. As an illustration, he told her 'privately, as we do not want it talked about', that they had tried to get a better standard of ironing, for which they were willing to pay a little more as it was 'a little more trouble'; the result, however, was that twenty-four ironers walked out of the place and they had 'to some extent, to give in', as they could not replace that number.[81] The laundry business generally does not appear to have suffered unduly from strikes. The manager of the Dublin Laundry said in 1917: 'The few strikes we have had in Dublin Laundries have always been engineered through the van men, they simply hold up the place, refusing to collect or deliver.'[82] As has been seen, there were many cases of insolence involving van men and boys, as these were the ones who met the public. This is not surprising. In 1905 a male employee was told that it was useless for him to apply for work to the Dublin Laundry or the Dartry Dye Works unless he repaid the money he had embezzled; he was told that the Laundry might have to take further action in the matter.[83] A van man was sacked for altering the weekly bills and trying to throw the blame on the clerks in the office; one or two of the junior van men had also been guilty of similar, though much smaller, defalcations.[84] A former laundress was suspected of coming back to steal a coat and hat belonging to one of the workers; the matter was referred to the police at Rathmines, where the suspect lived. A detailed description of the missing articles was given.[85] The dangerous driving of the 'motor man' was the subject of complaint by a number of people; the manager said that he was seeking a suitable replacement, 'when a change will be made'.[86]

Over the years, the Dublin Laundry was accused, by its influential neighbours, of causing environmental damage. Smoke from the laundry was the principal bone of contention. E. Johnson of Nullamore, who wrote to complain in 1898, was told that a new boiler, which was purposely fitted with the best smoke-preventing furnace known, was being installed. This was followed by another letter, two months later, in which Edmondson said that they were often blamed for the dense smoke from the locomotives on the railway. Later that year, he admitted that they were a little disappointed with their new patent furnace and that they were experimenting with several kinds of coal. He feared that they might have to build a much higher chimney and was prepared to do this if necessary.[87] He told Alfred Henshaw, of St. Phillips, in 1899, that he had tried everything with the present chimney, and that he was building a new one 100 feet high, which he hoped would prevent further trouble.[88] It does not appear to have done so since there were still complaints in 1922.[89] The correspondence with these two men was always courteous; however, when there were complaints from William Martin Murphy, who lived at Dartry, Upper Rathmines, about the smoke from the Dartry Dye Works in 1904, the exchange was acrimonious. Edmondson said that they had raised the chimney largely in the hope of meeting Murphy's complaint, and that they were willing to take any other reasonable steps. They brought over an engineer from the Manchester Steam Users' Association to advise on the matter. Edmondson told Murphy that he did not like the tone of his letter, that he had practically accused him of making 'a false statement'; he said they were using smokeless Welsh coal, that he himself had not seen any smoke coming from the chimney that could amount to a nuisance. The feud does not appear to have been resolved and Edmondson said: 'I am sorry that you again reiterate your unfounded opinion that we have no serious intention of doing anything in the matter.'[90] He had had complaints from Murphy some years earlier about clearing the pond and the mill race and about disposing of the mud which Murphy alleged was an 'injury of amenities to my residential property'.[91]

Although Edmondson made it known as early as 1890 that he was seeking help in the management of the laundry and was willing to give an interest in the business to a suitable person (see ch. 2), no one stood out as a possible successor to the first managing director, until Robert Benson joined the firm in 1897. This was a very important happening for the Dublin Laundry, as he founded the dynasty which provided successive managing directors until it closed its doors for the last time in the 1980s. Benson was eminently suited for the role of crown prince. He was the son of Thomas's first cousin Jane, a member of the family that owned the steam laundry in Southport. Robert was born in 1865, twenty-eight years after the birth of Thomas.[92] Robert was a district officer in Nigeria before he entered the family business.[93] He probably had worked in the laundry for only a few years, as he was only thirty-two in the year he came to Ireland. He was evidently interested in laundry work and was active in laundry association circles, and in writing about laundry matters. In 1896 he wrote what his brother referred to as 'Bob's Factory Act pamphlet', entitled 'Laundries and Health', 'which had sold 34,000 copies and was still going well'.[94] There was little in the correspondence during the final months of 1896, which might have explained Robert's decision to move to Ireland. He was obviously playing an active role in the laundry in Southport, and when he did move, D.E.

Benson decided to have the telephone installed in Southport, so that he could speak to Bob at Milltown.[95] The Edmondson and Benson alliance proved successful. The two men, from different generations, worked amicably and productively together in what was probably a kind of father and son relationship. At the tenth Annual General Meeting, held at Milltown on 4 August 1898, Benson was appointed secretary to the Dublin Laundry.

Between 1894 and 1900 the Laundry was further enlarged. The most up-to-date machinery continued to be installed, and money was no object if it was considered that the results justified the purchase. There were now eleven clerks employed in the general office. Nearby were the offices of the MD, the secretary and the chief engineer, all communicating with the office of the typist and shorthand writer. The receiving room had been doubled in size. In spite of the large number of washing machines then in use in the wash house, Edmondson alleged that there was an absence of steam and damp, due to the powerful fan which had been placed at one end of this room. A large plant for filtering and softening water had been laid down, which, it was hoped, would deal with 6,000 gallons of water an hour, and help to obtain 'an even better colour on the linen than at present'. By this time, the linen was all dried indoors, no matter what the weather was like, Edmondson maintaining that: 'By this process the linen is kept purer and sweeter and a better colour than even by open-air drying.' This was a complete volte-face from earlier days, when the drying grounds at Milltown were a selling point for the laundry. No doubt speed and efficiency, in the light of a large increase in trade, not to mention the vagaries of the weather, dictated the decision.

A new collar-ironing room had been built on iron girders over the mill pond. The department was laundering at this time between 40,000 and 50,000 collars and cuffs per week. Special machines were used to iron the edges of stand-up collars and the rounded edge of turndown ones, and also for shaping collars to fit the neck. The flat workroom now held five large ironing machines, and the laundry had earned a reputation for the excellent finish it gave to tablecloths and serviettes. Gas-heated irons were used in the hand-ironing room (see Plates 12 and 21). The room on the top floor, where collars were ironed, was now devoted entirely to the starching and ironing of shirts. The laundering of shirts and collars always played a major part in the work of laundries catering for the household trade, which were, of course, the majority of them. In 1894 the Dublin Laundry did 3,500 shirts weekly; by 1900 they laundered more than double that number.[96]

27. Darty Dye Works, Upper Rathmines, Dublin.

In that same year 300 workers were employed, eleven vans conveyed customers' linen back and forth, a more powerful steam engine had been installed and business had increased enormously. Edmondson felt able to state with confidence, that the Dublin Laundry Co. Ltd possessed the largest laundry in Ireland, and, with few exceptions, in Great Britain or even the world.[97] He had established a hierarchical management team of managing director, manageress, secretary, heads of departments, and assistants. In 1901 the Laundry had eighteen managers, fourteen clerks, 257 workers, eight engine men and twenty-four van drivers.[98] This enabled him to concentrate on tasks, such as policy-making, salesmanship and the appointment of senior staff, and leave the day-to-day running of the laundry to others. He not only believed in delegation, he practised it, as his frequent and sometimes lengthy absences from the business and his involvement in other matters, indicate. Years later, Benson's grandson was to remark wistfully, that his grandfather, who continued the structures established by the founder, had 'a grand old time', and was able to go on two continental holidays in the year, a situation which obviously changed in later days.[99]

A second mill, the next on the river to the Dublin Laundry, was acquired in 1894; it was rented from James W. Drury, The Willows, Bushy Park Road, for £40 a year.[100] It was fitted out as a dyeing and cleaning works. It was felt that there was need for an up-to-date dyeing and dry-cleaning establishment in Ireland, as much of this work was going to England and Scotland.[101] A Mr Spicer, who had worked in the business in England, was appointed to take charge; he was asked to bring price lists and circulars with him which would be useful when they were drawing up their own.[102] The company spent £15,880 on the founding and upkeep of the Dye Works. Unlike the Laundry, it was not immediately successful, losing money for many years.[103]

Eighteen hundred and ninety-six was not a good year for Edmondson. In that year, his wife Nannie met with the accident which was the beginning of her ill health. That year also, he complained of opposition which had started up in the preceding year or two, though he did say that they continued to be extremely busy.[104] There were two new laundries in Dublin, the Donore Laundry Co., Dyeing and French Cleaning, in Dolphin's Barn and the Hygienic Family Laundry in South William Street.[105] These were the first commercial laundries to start up in the city since the Dublin Laundry in 1888. Perhaps the fact that one was doing dyeing and French cleaning, and therefore was a possible threat to the Dartry Dye Works, worried Thomas, or perhaps he did not like to see any new competition. They did not seem to affect the profits of the Laundry. The laundry business was doing extremely well at the time. D.E. Benson reported to Thomas that a syndicate was to visit Dublin with the object of buying up the principal laundries, and that according to the latest reports, Hooley and Rucker, the financial firm that had bought out Dunlop Tyre and many of the cycle companies, were 'casting longing eyes on the Laundry trade as a field for their next financial operations'.[106] It was also the year before Benson joined the company, and as well as worrying about his wife, Thomas might have been feeling overburdened by the task of managing the laundry alone without her support.

In June 1896 Edmondson was approached by the firm Porte and Sykes about having electricity installed in Milltown; they thought that, as it was satisfactory in the Dartry Dye Works, that this might influence his decision.[107] It did not, and he told Egan and Tatlow, 20 Fleet Street at the end of 1898: 'We have indefinitely postponed the placing of the electric light in this concern.'[108] As late as 1916 Benson was threatening the Alliance and Dublin Consumer Gas Co. that he would install electric light if they insisted on charging him for extending some gas piping.[109] The advent of the electric trams was a topic of conversation and contention in Dublin in 1895–96. Edmondson reported in January 1896 that the 'electric tram fight' had reached an acute stage. There were, he said, 'two rival companies each wanting "to completely gridiron the city and suburbs'". The car men opposed the project strongly and trade societies had fallen out with one another in the advocacy of the claims of the different companies. He added: 'Whether the overhead wires will be ultimately ceded, I cannot say. There is a strong feeling on both sides of the question. I think, however, a good many are inclined to waive the ugliness of the thing for the sake of its convenience.'[110] The two companies in question were the Dublin Southern Districts Tramway Company, known as the 'English Company', and the United Tramways Company. The former ran a line from Kingstown to Dalkey by horse traffic for many years without much success, and the Dublin Tramway, which 'worked' all the other city and suburban routes, refused to take it over when it was offered to them. However, when the Southern District Company adopted electricity on the overhead wire system, doubled the speed and attracted customers from all over the city and country visitors to ride on the electric tram to Dalkey, the situation changed. Threats to cross the canal and invade the city with this new contrivance alarmed William Martin Murphy and the United Tramways. A row broke out in which most of the artisans of Dublin agitated through the medium of the Trades Council and allied themselves with the Southern line: the car men's union supported the United Tramways. The trouble ended when W.M. Murphy and United Tramways bought this once despised tram line for over a quarter of a million pounds. The Dublin United Tramways (1896) Company resulted and the electrification of the rest of the system commenced immediately.[111]

A healthy profit of £4,946.4s.7d was realised by the Laundry in 1895, a rise of over £1,100 from 1894. A dividend of £120 was paid on the preference shares, and £2,700 on ordinary shares. The loss on the Dye Works for that year was £822.9s.0d.[112] Profits continued to rise in 1897 to a high of £5,626.19s.6d, they fell after that to £4,463.3s.5d in 1900.[113] Table 5.1 shows Edmondson's and his wife's interests as on 30 June 1897 in the audited accounts.

*Table 5.1*
EDMONDSON SHARE OWNERSHIP IN 1897

|  | Ordinary shares (£) | Preference shares (£) | Debentures (£) | Loans (£, rounded) | Totals (£, rounded) |
|---|---|---|---|---|---|
| Thomas | 1,494 | 1,990 | 50 | 3,386 | 6,920 |
| Anne | 1,500 | 10 | 50 | 3,519 | 5,079 |
| Totals (£) | 2,994 | 2,000 | 100 | 6,905 | 12,000 |

*Source*: Dublin Laundry, Balance Sheets 1888–1936. Audited accounts 30 June 1897

It was decided in 1901 to increase the company's capital by £15,000, and the solicitors to the company, Goodbody and Tisdall, sought counsel's advice on certain matters, including whether increasing the capital in 1892 from £2,000 to £5,000 had been ultra vires, and the position of the Dye Works. Jonathan Pim, counsel, said that the articles of association of the company were 'meagre and insufficient', and the company had no power at all in 1892 to increase the capital without amending their articles, nor had they any power now to increase the capital by £15,000, that is, to quadruple the capital, a major transaction. He said that the Dye Works might be held to be a business 'subservient to or connected with the purpose of a public laundry', but 'until it is so decided, the company can never know their exact position', and he doubted 'if the court would so decide'. In a document dated 11 June 1901, he strongly advised the directors to reconstruct the company under section 161 of the Company's Act 1862. He said that it would cost money, but it would remove uncertainty, and 'so far as past acts are concerned, give a clean slate'.[114]

An Extraordinary General Meeting was held on 12 August 1901, followed by a second EGM on 27 August, at 5 South Anne Street; Edmondson was in the chair, and Anne Edmondson, Calvert Roberts and A.E. Goodbody were present. A new company was formed to take over, as a going concern, without any interruption of business. The nominal share capital of the new company was to be £20,000, £18,000 ordinary shares of £1 each, and £2,000 preference shares of £1 each, the 2,000 shares to be 5 per cent cumulative preference shares. The shareholders of the existing company were entitled, for every preference or ordinary share in that company, a preference or ordinary share in the new company. The remaining 15,000 shares were to be allocated as the director should decide.[115] One of the main reasons for the 'reconstruction of our company' given by Edmondson to Frederick Woods was the desire to put their accumulated profits into shares instead of having them on loan to the company and to 'generally renew our articles of association' This gave Thomas 3,500 and Anne Edmondson 5,500 extra ordinary shares.[116] Thomas was to be director of the new company, which was to take over the assets and liabilities of the existing company at midnight 30 June 1901.

The last years of the old century were extremely profitable for the Edmondsons. The very high dividend on ordinary shares, 90 per cent, which was paid in 1896 continued to be paid until 1901 even though profits had fallen (see above). The last act of Edmondson, as MD of the old company, was, at 11.45 a.m., before the EGM on 27 August, to sign a memorandum declaring a dividend of 6 per cent on preference shares and 90 per cent on ordinary shares up to 30 June 1901.[117] The earnings of the Edmondsons from the laundry for 1897 was approximately £3,665.6, the equivalent of £267,588.8 in 2003 (€347,865.44).[118]

At the First Annual General Meeting of the new company, held at Milltown on 21 March 1902, it was agreed that a dividend of 25 per cent per annum be paid on ordinary shares and 5 per cent on preference shares.[119] The dividend on ordinary shares was reduced to 20 per cent in March 1906.[120] At the Sixth AGM the net profit for 1906 was stated as £6,351.16s.7d, which, when added to £4,884.3s.9d, brought forward from 1905, gave a total of £11,236.0s.4d. The loss on the Dye Works, which had to be deducted from this, was £1,434.6s.9d. A dividend of £100 was paid on preference shares. An interim dividend was paid on ordinary shares for the first half of the year at 20 per cent that cost £1,507.16s.0d, tax on the net balance was £77.7s.7d. When these were deducted, £8,116.9s.11d remained. Out of this the directors proposed paying the second dividend for the year at a rate of 10 per cent, which would absorb £900, and transferring £4,080 to the reserve fund. The balance, £3,136.9s.11d, would be carried forward to the profit and loss account. The appointment of C. Frederic Allen as a director of the company was confirmed at a remuneration of £100; Edmondson's salary of £500 per annum was to remain unchanged, and Benson was to get a salary of £540 as director and secretary. It was also resolved that the allotment of 2,922 ordinary shares to Thomas on the 10 July should be confirmed.[121] The finances of the company were in a healthy state, though there was a loss each year on the Dye Works. At an extraordinary general meeting held at Milltown on 24 April 1907 it was decided to promote a company to be called the Dartry Dye Works Ltd, to take over the Dye Works' branch of the Dublin Laundry. That company's interest in the Dye Works was sold for £15,000, taken in ordinary shares of £1 each.[122] As this new company had no liquid assets, it had to be helped for some years until it got established, and, of course, it was not paying dividends. The extraordinary general meeting was held on the day of Anne Edmondson's death.

# CHAPTER SIX

# The Factory Acts and the Laundry Industry

THE LAUNDRY TRADE was omitted from the scope of the Factory Act 1867 in error. It was the intention to include every kind of employment for profit in which manual labour was engaged. However, the definition clause of the Act referred to the 'preparation of articles for sale', and, as a result, lawyers held that only those laundries that were attached to factories, where shirts, collars, table linen and sheets were manufactured, came under the Act. Only washerwomen employed in such laundries enjoyed the advantages that Parliament had intended: the laundry had to be healthy, safe, properly ventilated, proper sanitary conveniences had to be installed, and hours of work restricted. All other laundry workers, the vast majority, remained at the mercy of employers.[1] Thomas Edmondson opposed the Factory Act, with help from Roger and Cook, one of the largest firms in London and employing about 500 hands, in the obvious belief that laundries would be included.[2]

In the years that followed there was agitation to secure for the washerwomen the advantages which legislation had brought to other trades.[3] The laundry proprietors continued to oppose renewed efforts to bring them within the scope of the Act. In this Edmondson played a prominent part, not only in Ireland, but on the much larger and more influential British front. In August 1893 he told his cousin D.E. Benson, in Southport, that the chief factory inspector for Ireland had visited him, and that he, Edmondson, had explained the 'peculiar difficulties of our business'.[4] In correspondence with Lady Margaret Hamilton, a journalist who was writing an article on laundries towards the end of 1893, Edmondson clearly indicated the fears that the laundry proprietors had about the proposed legislation. He admitted that he thought it likely that the trade would ultimately be put under some modified form of Factory Act, but stressed that there were difficulties attached to the trade that none but those engaged in it completely understood. From the very

110

nature of the business it was impossible to work the same hours in every department. At the beginning of the week the washers had to work long hours—up to 9 or 9.30 p.m. on Monday nights in the busy season— while the ironers worked only very short hours on that day; towards the end of the week the reverse happened, washers worked short hours, while ironers, finishers and packers had sometimes to work till 9.30 p.m. On weeks when general holidays occurred, six days work had to be done in five, therefore, he said, some special provision would have to be made. One of the chief difficulties he foresaw was the granting of a weekly half-holiday commencing as early as 2 p.m.; in the busy season this was impracticable, though 4 p.m. might be managed. Special provision would be required for short-season laundries, such as those in seaside resorts. Edmondson stressed the importance of including what he called small cottage and other laundries under the Act, because, if 'they were allowed to escape', they would compete unfairly with other establishments and, from the sanitary point of view, there was urgent need to have them inspected. Convent laundries doing washing for the public should, he said, be also included. This would prove a difficulty, especially in Ireland, as the convents took the view that placing their laundries 'under the Factory Acts would be "the thin edge of the wedge" for convent inspection', so the Roman Catholic members would strenuously oppose legislation. He made it quite clear that he approved of all laundries being brought under the provisions of the Act which related to the 'fencing of machinery' and 'sanitary matters'.[5] In this he was probably supported by most laundry proprietors. Miss Abraham, the factory inspector, who visited laundries in Dublin, London and Liverpool, reported that no objection was raised to the obligations the 1895 Act would impose regarding the safety of machinery.[6] Finally, Edmondson said that it was not practicable for laundries to work under any Act which did not allow them to work up to sixty-four hours a week if necessary. He suggested that chief inspectors should be allowed more latitude than in other trades, so that they could permit a considerable extension of the hours worked in cases where they were satisfied that the concern was well run with regard to hours of labour, the sanitary condition of the premises and the well-being of the employees. He was at pains to point out to Lady Margaret that his employees were healthy, satisfied with their conditions of employment and well paid. He said 'we endeavour to recognise the claims of labour as well as those of capital'. He did not think, he said, that any 'well-ordered Establishment, such as ours, would have much to fear from a suitably modified Factory Act'.[7]

Early in May 1894 Edmondson wrote to Alfred Webb, MP, noting that the Home Secretary was making another attempt to bring the laundries under the Act, and saying that, from what the Home Secretary had said when introducing the Bill, the steam laundries would be placed at a great disadvantage. He sought Webb's help in preventing that and asked for an advance copy of the Bill.[8] When thanking Webb for it and arranging to meet him in London, he said: 'we steam laundries will have to stir ourselves to try to secure somewhat more favourable terms'.[9] Thomas was not a member of the National Laundry Association at this time, and, indeed, seemed to take a poor view of associations. When D.E. Benson told him about the Northern Counties Laundry Association (NCLA), which he and his brother proposed to found, Thomas was sceptical and said that he did not think that the London Association had done much good, and that there would probably be more personal trade jealousies in the north than in London.[10] Most associations, including the Irish, were founded, principally, to fix prices.[11] They held regular meeting of their members and were seen as ways of communicating with and influencing others in the trade. At meetings, papers relevant to the laundry business were read, for instance, in March 1896 the NCLA planned to discuss the 'Rating of Machinery Bill', while 'Apprenticeship and training of hands' was to be the next topic.[12] Associations also negotiated favourable insurance rates for their members. They requested donations to fund exhibitions and congresses.[13] They also looked for money to help other associations, sometimes in other countries. In 1910 help was given to the Relief Fund for the Blanchisseurs of France.[14] Trade associations tended to thrive in adverse conditions for the business, and, when the Factory Bill became an issue that year, Edmondson, having ascertained that it would be discussed at a meeting of the National Laundry Association (NLA) on 16 May 1894, said that he wished to have a hearing at the meeting and would become a member if necessary. He joined as a country member and paid a subscription of 10s.6d.[15] After that meeting it was hoped to get a general meeting of the steam laundry trade in London for further discussion. There were, Edmondson said, some points in it that 'must be very much modified to enable us to carry on our business at all'. As far as he understood it, the Bill proposed to take away all power of working overtime, not only in laundries but in other places where it had previously been permitted. He commented that the framers of the legislation had completely failed to recognise the 'essential difference between the laundry trade and all others'.[16] A month later Edmondson reported to O'Brien of the Franklin

Laundry, Belfast, that Mr Asquith, the Home Secretary, had not yet consented to receive a deputation from the laundries, saying that, from the state of public business, he did not expect that the measure would become law that session.[17]

In April 1895 a meeting of the laundry trade was held in Dublin to discuss the Factory Act. Thomas obtained beforehand, from Robert Benson, the resolutions passed at the last meeting of the Northern Counties Laundry Association.[18] The Dublin meeting was badly attended, causing Thomas to complain: 'some think they will let others do all the work and reap the benefit, without any trouble to themselves'. He was determined to prepare a memorial, get all the laundrymen he could to sign it and send a copy to every member of the Grand Committee on Trade.[19] A letter was sent to the Home Secretary, specifically emphasising the convent and institution question.[20]

In a letter to Benson, early in April 1895, Thomas said again that he did not expect the Bill to pass that session as the government was not trying very hard to make headway, it was prolonging matters with the objective of staying in office.[21] The Liberal government which took office in 1892 had no effective majority either at Westminster or in the constituencies. It was presided over by Gladstone, who, although still vigorous, was almost 83 years old. His main concern was the Second Home Rule Bill for Ireland, introduced in February 1893, but rejected by the Lords in September 1893. Gladstone resigned in March 1894, and the premiership of this weak government was taken over by Lord Rosebery. The Lords continued to veto most of Rosebery's legislation, and his ministers lived in constant fear of dissolution. The end came on 22 June 1895 when the government resigned.[22]

However, legislation was introduced by the Liberals in 1895, contrary to Edmondson's expectations. The Factory Bill of 1895 met with great opposition in Britain and Ireland, not only from the usual opponents of such legislation, but also from the religious world. The members of the Grand Committee on Trade were besieged by letters and petitions from convents, clergymen and philanthropists, Roman Catholic and Anglican.[23] Mother Devereux, from the Good Shepherd Magdalen Laundry in Cork, was one of the religious superiors who wrote to Asquith pointing out the dangers involved in exposing the penitents to such 'unnecessary intrusions'. She also wrote to all Irish MPs asking them to oppose the Bill.[24] In this she got her wish; the proposed regulations were keenly opposed by the Irish Members, on whose vote Asquith was dependent; the Irish vote, usually with Asquith, turned solidly against him. Because some aspects of the Bill were far too rigid and stringent to be applied to the institutions, the whole of the clause about laundries was rejected. The members of the Grand Committee tried to reconstruct one which would give some help to the oppressed washerwomen, while not offending the institutions. Finally, to compound the muddle, after the new clause had been watered down with the undefined idea of making it universally applicable, a further amendment was carried, exempting institutions altogether. The result was that the section relating to the hours of labour, which became law, was immediately declared by the Home Office experts to be ineffective and was described by others, with perhaps an unconscious contextual association, as a 'mangled clause'.[25]

The hours legally sanctioned in 1895 were those of the worst laundries. As was pointed out at the time, in other trades the practice of Parliament had been to force the bad factories to accept the standards of the good ones; the opposite happened with the laundries. Good employers, who had up to this point limited the day's work by their own sense of justice, were encouraged to extend their hours to those fixed by the Act. Under the law, if two hours were allowed for meals, it was permissible to keep women working continuously from 8 a.m. to midnight (sixteen hours) on two days every week; on two other days, from 8 a.m. to 8 p.m. (twelve hours), on Monday and Saturday, the usual short days in the industry, from 10 a.m. to 8 p.m. (ten hours) and from 8 a.m. till noon (four). This could be done without use of any of the permitted overtime. Up to this point the custom in the trade had been to consider work after 8 p.m. as overtime, and good employers normally paid an extra rate for work done afterwards. Now overtime was reckoned only after the maximum of sixty hours had been worked. The hours of work and of mealtimes could be different in each laundry and could be varied at the will of the employer at the beginning of each day. There was similar scope for the exploitation of 'young persons', girls between the ages of fourteen and eighteen. They could, for instance, be obliged to work overtime, a practice strictly forbidden by the Home Office in all other trades.[26]

While Edmondson was, of course, disappointed that convent and institution laundries were not included under the Act, he was not slow to recognise the latitude it afforded him and other employers. He wrote to Frederick Carr of the Steam Laundry, Wolverhampton, saying, 'I hear the Secretary of State is considering if he will allow the Laundries to be worked in sections. My own opinion, from studying the Act, is that he cannot prevent it as long as no individual works beyond the prescribed hours.' He also reported that the weekly half-holiday was not required under the Act.[27] He saw the possibility of different women working different sets of hours.[28] In fact, that was one of the ambiguities of the Act pointed out by the industrial subcommittee of the National Union of Women Workers,

> it is questionable whether the sixty hours' limit is to be reckoned for each individual woman, or as the total number of hours during which women and young persons are to be at work on the premises. If the former, it is obvious that an employer may extend the working hours of his factory indefinitely, and it becomes absolutely impossible for any Factory Inspector who does not live on the premises of the employer to discover how long any particular woman has been at work.[29]

Benson wrote to Edmondson in January 1896, 'The Factory Act is improving matters for us. We used to stop at 6.30, we now go on to 8.30.'[30]

This, of course, did not mean that Edmondson or those considered to be good employers would exploit their workers, but the ineptitude of the lawmakers in 1895, instead of improving the lot of the washer-women, worsened it, or at least made it possible for employers to worsen their conditions and all 'within the law'. Edmondson also thought that under the Act laundries were not compelled to get certificates of fitness for young persons; he said: 'at any rate we do not have to do it until we see further'.[31] In this he was correct.[32] Compared with others under the Factory Acts, whose day's work began and ended at a definite time, with set meal times, where overtime was prohibited altogether for young persons and only allowed for women under exceptional circumstances, where night work was not allowed for young persons and Sunday work was prohibited altogether, laundry workers were much worse off.[33] The 1895 Act did cover sanitary matters and the fencing of machinery. Stoves for heating irons could not be placed in the ironing rooms, and gas irons emitting noxious fumes were not to be used. Fans were to be installed to regulate the temperature of ironing rooms and to carry away the steam in the wash house. Floors should be kept in good condition and drained.[34]

The Act came into force on 1 January 1896. The effect of the new legislation was reflected in the correspondence of the Dublin Laundry. Edmondson was informed by Gerald Bellhouse, HM inspector of factories, in March 1896, that it was not allowable to substitute another day of the week for St. Patrick's Day, but that he could give an extra day at Easter in lieu.[35] In July Bellhouse was informing him that all accidents must be reported on an official form, Form 43, obtainable from Hodges Figgis.[36] A letter from the Home Office in Whitehall in February 1897 informed Edmondson that, as a result of a recent visit to his factory by the inspector J.W. Neely, it was found that certain safeguards were needed on a flywheel and on a belt drawing wash-house machinery.[37] The report of the inspectors for 1897 stated that the task of improving ventilation, the fencing of machinery, and sanitary accommodation in laundries had progressed very slowly. One pointed out that, on a week in which a statutory holiday occurred, the women had to work the sixty hours in five days, unlike in all other factories and workshops where, even with the full amount of overtime, it could not exceed fifty-five and a half hours. Another reported 'the immensely long hours, the absence of any conditions about meal times, other than there shall be at least half an hour every five-hour spell, and the extraordinary manner in which overtime is at present worked combine to make the inspection of laundries more difficult and more inefficient than in any trade I have under my notice'.[38]

By 1900 the laundry proprietors were mustering their forces again to defend their interests against the next Factory and Workshop Bill. In April it was suggested to Robert Benson that the Laundry Association in Dublin should join a federation of associations to be called the National Laundry Trades Protection Association, as this would be a big advantage in furthering or opposing legislation. A federation fee of 1s. per member per annum should, it was thought, be sufficient as factory legislation was not introduced every year, so funds would build up; it was five years since really expensive legislative work had to be undertaken.[39] In July, L.F. O'Brien of Belfast wrote to Edmondson urging that they should support the Home Secretary in his efforts to bring the charitable laundries under the same provisions as they, the commercial laundries, had to work.[40] The same month, a letter from the National Laundry Trade Protection Association to Edmondson, acknowledged a circular from the Dublin Association about the Factory Bill, and said that it would be put forward in the 'right quarter in the House of Commons' when the Bill reached the report stage. The writer asked Edmondson if he could give any evidence of conventual laundries employing outside labour, or, indeed, provide any other evidence in his possession: 'I know there is some difficulty with you in properly stating the evidence owing to so many of your customers being Catholics . . .' Edmondson was assured: 'from what I can gather in the lobby of the House of Commons,

I think it is very likely that institutional and conventual laundries will be included in the Bill'.[41] O'Brien wrote to Benson in September, saying that they, in Belfast, supported Benson's action by drafting a memorial verbatim with the one Benson had sent, and sending it to those Members of both Houses with whom they had influence*.[42] He said that their association had decided to affiliate with the NLA and/or, if desirable, with the Irish Association, 'so that we may show a united front'.[43]

In the event, opposition to the inclusion of the institutions under the Factory and Workshop Bill 1901 was just as strong as it had been six years earlier and met with the same success.[44] Although in 1895 it was confidently predicted that legislation to amend the hours of labour in laundries would be introduced shortly,[45] the 1901 Act left the subject untouched. In all matters relating to hours of work, laundries were still regulated by the special provisions of the 1895 Act, but were subject to the sanitary and safety requirements of the later Act. Institution laundries were still outside the law.[46]

After the Factory and Workshop Act was passed, the Secretary of State made an effort to get religious and charitable institutions to accept, voluntarily, inspection by factory inspectors. A circular letter was issued by the Home Office in January 1902, to a large number of institutions which took in laundry work from outside as a trade. As the Secretary of State was not able to demand the information he required, the list was compiled from directories of charitable and religious institutions, aided by information from factory inspectors and other sources, and its comprehensiveness could not be guaranteed. In Ireland fifty-six institutions either accepted inspection in response to the Home Office circular or afterwards permitted a visit from lady inspectors. Ten either refused permission or gave no definite answer. Approximately forty institutions in Britain and Ireland which did not reply after a reminder were not named. The tone of the Home Office circular was conciliatory. The help and advice that inspectors could give was stressed. It recognised that modification to the provisions of the Factory Act would be necessary to adapt it to the needs of the institutions. It said that many misconceptions seemed to exist, but that the objectives of Parliament were only to secure in laundries reasonable hours of work, healthy conditions of employment and the prevention of accidents. These requirements, it was pointed out, were only what everyone interested in the welfare of the inmates of these institutions would wish to see achieved. The Secretary of State said that he would be glad if the recipient would let him know, first, whether he would receive visits from factory inspectors and, secondly, if he would wish the visit to be made by a lady inspector. The circular began: 'Gentlemen', although virtually all those addressed must have been women. Interestingly, only two requested a lady inspector, although this was a requirement commonly demanded in the debate about inspection.[47]

The Factory and Workshop Act 1907, which came into force on 1 January 1908, shortly before Edmondson's death, finally brought institution laundries within the ambit of the legislators. It included 'all laundries carried on by way of trade or carried on as ancillary to another business or incidentally to the purposes of any public institution'.[48] The only institutions exempted were those in which the industrial work was inspected by some other government department, by the inspector of reformatories schools, for example, or where the work was done for the use of the institute only.[49] Some convents decided to close their laundries to the public and to use them only for the residents: one of those was the House of Mercy, Baggot Street, which continued to use the laundry solely for the order.[50]

The Acts applied only to the part of the institute's premises in which the work was done. Certain modifications could be permitted:

1. The managers could, with the approval of the Secretary of State, substitute other hours of employment, intervals for meals and holidays, provided, of course, that they were not less favourable to those provided in the Acts.
2. The medical officer of the institution could, if approved, act as the certifying surgeon.
3. The manageress would not be obliged to post up in the premises the abstract of the Acts and other notices, but certain entries would be required to be made in the register.
4. The manageresses of reformatories could give notice to the Chief Inspector of Factories requiring that the inmates should not be examined by an inspector, except in the presence of one of the managers.[51]

A letter from the manager of the Magdalen Asylum, Clare St., Limerick, written on 17 January 1908 to the Secretary of State, requested modifications under the four headings.[52]

The 1907 Act addressed the problem of hours of work in laundries. While allowing some flexibility to employers, women and young persons under eighteen could work only within a fixed period of twelve hours, which could be from 6 a.m. to 6 p.m., 7 a.m. to 7 p.m., or from 8 a.m.

to 8 p.m. Certain exceptions were allowed—a period of thirteen hours could be fixed on three days of the week for women, if the total for the week did not exceed sixty-eight. Also, different periods could be fixed for different days of the week. However, a notice had to be posted up in the laundry and a notice sent to the factory inspector. One day a week had to be a short day. Young people under sixteen years had to be certified by the factory surgeon, if the machinery were power-driven. Certain fixed intervals for meals had to be allowed to women and young persons, and they were not allowed to work on Sundays.[53]

It may seen extraordinary that, almost twenty years after the principle of factory and workshop legislation had been generally accepted, it should have been so difficult to extend the legislation to laundries. It was pointed out that 'the old bogey of foreign competition, which has hitherto loomed large over all projects of factory reform, cannot be raised in this connection'. The housewife was not likely to send her dirty linen across the Channel to be washed.[54] There may have been, of course, some remaining opposition to any legal regulation of the conditions of labour.[55] Objections came from two opposing groups. On the one hand, there were the commercial laundry proprietors, and, on the other, the institution laundries, mainly run by religious.

The principal objections of the former were to set hours of work, holidays and mealtimes, which, they said, were inimical to the laundry trade, where flexibility was essential. Secondly, they were totally opposed to the exclusion of institution laundries and small family-run laundries from the legislation, as this, they said, gave the latter an unfair trading advantage. Miss Abraham, in a report made before the 1895 Act, said that all proprietors in Irish laundries visited by her were opposed to inclusion; if the convent laundries were exempt, this would give them advantages, such as exemption from the cost of fencing machinery and exemptions from regulations affecting child labour.[56] The alleged uniqueness of the laundry trade was, of course, challenged. It was pointed out that, with the advent of machinery and the subdivision of labour, the whole character of the industry had changed and the 'uncertainty' stressed by many as a peculiarity of laundry work, had practically disappeared. The capacity of each machine in the plant was known, and the amount of work that could be dealt with per hour could be accurately calculated, often more so than in many other factories. The trade was compared with that of the dressmaker or the milliner who employed only hand labour, 'dependent on the mere passing whim or fancy of a fleeting season, struggling with "uncertainties" and "rushes" and other difficulties as great as any with which the laundry has to cope and yet successfully complying with regulations which the factory (for such it practically is) could often more easily conform to'.[57] The difference, of course, was that the laundrymen formed a strong pressure group, while dressmakers and milliners were in no position to contest the Factory Acts.

The almost invariable custom of collecting washing on Mondays and returning it on Fridays or Saturdays, thereby hampering the start of the work early in the week and putting undue pressure on the workers towards the end of the week, was questioned. Was there any insuperable objection to work being collected and delivered from about half the customers on Wednesday or Friday instead of Monday, it was asked? It was felt that, if some of the 'better provided' households would agree to this, it would make it possible for the poorer classes to get the 'clean change' for Sunday. While it was said that this arrangement would not entirely remedy the evil of over-pressure, it would prevent the workers from being overwhelmed with work on some days and almost idle on others. It was not expected that employers would change existing arrangements for fear of displeasing their customers, unless forced to do so by the requirements of the law. It was alleged, as an argument against prohibiting Sunday work in laundries, that, if a lady had suddenly to go abroad, it would be very inconvenient not to be able to get her clothes home from the wash on Monday or Tuesday. The personal convenience of private households was used as an excuse for excluding a large class of women and girls from the protection of the law. Members of Parliament, it was suggested, might have feared that regulation of laundry hours might cause personal inconvenience to the mistresses of middle-class households, if accepted routines had to be altered.[58] To what extent MPs might have been influenced in this way it is difficult to say. It would not have been the only time that working-class women's rights were sacrificed to the household convenience and comfort of the better off in society, the social classes to which most MPs belonged. In 1911 a bill to regulate the hours of work, mealtimes and accommodation of domestic servants never became law; in fact, all attempts to bring in legislation in favour of domestic servants failed.[59]

Almost all the objections that are made to limiting the hours of laundry-work would disappear, it was said, if customers would exercise ordinary thoughtfulness and consideration in their demands. Ladies who show sentimental sympathy with the woes of workers have been known to refuse a request from their laundries that they would allow their work to be collected and delivered on days other than the traditional ones. This was an opportunity for displaying a little practical help, which might not be as popular as more conspicuous forms of philanthropy.[60] Finally, proprietors were berated for failing to see the benefits that legislation would bring even from the purely business standpoint. It would increase the trade of the more capable and efficient employers at the expense of the less capable, and surely that was a desirable outcome?[61]

Of course, it was recognised that small home laundries should also be included under the legislation: family-run laundries, employing no more than two persons dwelling outside the home, were exempt.[62] The bad effects of noxious fumes, a steam-laden atmosphere and excessively high temperatures were not confined to power laundries. In fact, some of the worst conditions were probably found in the home or cottage laundry. 'The little dark, narrow entrance passage blocked continually by baskets and heaps of soiled linen, the dark kitchen wash-house crowded with machinery, with proper lighting, ventilation and means of removing steam almost impossible to secure . . .', was how a contemporary described this type of laundry.[63] The report of the Inter-Departmental Committee on the employment of school children said: 'Some of the very worst cases of overworking little girls of which we have heard occurred in the small laundries, which are exempt from the provisions of the Factory Acts.' This exemption had led to the evasion of the law which was unjust, not only to competitors, but to ratepayers. It was common practice to keep only two workers on the premises and to send the others with the dirty linen to a public wash-house, to the exclusion of those for whom the wash house was intended.[64]

In the case of other trades carried on in the home—tailoring and shoemaking—Sir Charles Cameron, Medical Officer of Health of the Corporation of Dublin, in evidence to the commissioners appointed to inquire into the working of the Factory and Workshop Act 1876, said: 'anything more insanitary than the conditions in which they are carried on would be impossible to describe. It must be seen to be understood.' He added that the same could be said for dressmaking and millinery. He was concerned about the health of the people living there and said that it was almost invariably the case that they were sleeping in the room where the work was carried on; they worked in the room all day and sometimes the Saturday work continued until 2 or 3 a.m. on Sunday morning.[65] Another witness, Dr Edward Dillon Mapother, consulting sanitary officer to the Public Health Committee, said about millinery, dressmaking and tailoring: 'to the habit of giving orders immediately before great balls or shows, and to the increasing dressiness of the period, deplorable overwork is often due'.[66] Cameron also said: 'people of the higher ranks will go into a tailor's especially, and want a complete outfit in a couple of days or three days'.[67] The demands of the upper classes for efficient and rapid service from those at the bottom of the social scale influenced conditions in the laundry as well as in the dressmaking and tailoring trades. If the medical officers had been reporting on home laundries they would undoubtedly have been saying something similar.

The principal reason advanced for the exclusion of religious and charitable institutions from legislation was that the objective of their existence was not commercial but educational and reformative. Mother Devereux, in her letter to Asquith, stressed that laundries were established, not for the gain of the nuns, but for the support of the penitents undergoing reform.[68] While the state contributed to the maintenance of children under sixteen years of age in industrial schools and reformatories,[69] there were no grants for those institutions catering for older girls and women.[70] The money earned by the laundries in the magdalen or rescue homes was devoted to the maintenance of the women and the upkeep of the homes; their only other sources of income were charitable donations or chapel collections. Laundry work was also carried on in these institutions as a means of imparting skills which might help the inmates to find work later. The women did not get wages, their maintenance was considered adequate recompense for the work done.[71]

Ann Parrish, Mother Provincial of the Good Shepherd order, described their mission as a 'useful work of charity'.[72] Most contemporaries would have agreed with her. Charitable institutions such as the St. Vincent de Paul and the Sick and Indigent Roomkeepers Societies reserved their help for 'the deserving poor'—those who found themselves in dire straits as a result of sickness, misfortune, accident, lack of work or incompetence. It was said in justification that, if they were to extend their charity to the 'professional sinner', the 'deserving poor' would not apply for help.[73] It is not surprising that, in their differences with the institutions, Edmondson and the commercial laundries did not have the support of the public who not only used the laundry facilities provided by the religious but also regarded their work as a solution to a socially-embarrassing problem. The nuns were considered peculiarly suitable for the task of reforming these unfortunates, 'a considerable majority from the lowest fields of licence; women of weak wills but strong appetites', many of whom were driven by the degradation of their lives to seek solace in drink. Only within a religious atmosphere, it was thought, was there any likelihood of getting the women to abandon their former habits and lead lives, not only of virtue and sobriety, but of restraint: to 'practically look upon the joys of this world as at an end, and to spend their remaining days in works of usefulness and abnegation'. As one nun put it: 'what the fallen woman wants is . . . a spiritual hospital, provided with an experienced staff'.[74] While two Catholic congregations brought into Ireland between 1840 and 1865, the Sisters of Our Lady of Charity of the Refuge and the Good Shepherd Order, had the running of magdalen homes as their primary objective, they did not introduce the concept of the penitents' asylum to Ireland; they merely took over asylums already in existence under lay management. The Irish Sisters of Charity and the Sisters of Mercy also began to run these institutions in this period.[75] The *Freeman's Journal* on 21 October 1916 printed an impassioned appeal for increased aid for the Magdalen Asylum, Gloucester Street, not only from Irish Catholics but from other sects too. The sisters

> not only look after the temporal needs of the poor wanderers who have found a haven of peace in the institution, but—what is of far greater importance—they take care that their spiritual welfare is attended to. The beautiful Gospel incident of the repentance and forgiveness of St. Mary Magdalen may be said to be continually reproduced in the Catholic Magdalen Asylum in which the modern magdalen, having turned away from her career of misery and sin lives in peace and penitence.[76]

The inmates were often referred to as if all were prostitutes and sinners, and, apart from the presumption of this categorisation, these 'wanderers' included, not only prostitutes, but the socially-inadequate, unwanted, single women, often considered a temptation to the community, and those who gave birth outside marriage. They were in the institutions with the knowledge and approval of family, state and church. Without state welfare, the only refuges for these 'outcasts' from society were the workhouses, often regarded as a stepping stone to the lowest life on the streets, and the charitable institutions. The latter fulfilled a need in the morally-righteous, yet grossly hypocritical society of the time. There is no doubt that, in the case of those giving birth outside marriage, many could expect to be turned out of their home and expelled from their community.[77] Family, clergy and the sheer power of public opinion would have forced them to seek refuge in these homes. Much was made of the fact that the women came of their own free will, but most had no other choice. When they left for 'suitable employment', often domestic service, or were returned to their families, they were provided with 'outfits'.[78] Many never left and remained in the homes for the remainder of their lives. This was often regarded by the nuns as a sign of satisfaction with the life, 'our girls are uniformly happy and contented'.[79] The Revd Mother of one of these institutions said: 'to a great many of these poor souls High Park is not a penitentiary but a home, in which all their interests are centred'.[80] It is much more likely that they stayed because they had nowhere to go and because they had become institutionalised, a concept which would not have been understood by many at the time. The nuns had no power to force women to stay, they could use only 'gentle persuasion'. The Revd Mother of the Sisters of Charity in Donnybrook explained that when someone demanded to be released, delaying tactics were employed in getting the keys and in procuring and identifying the girl's clothes, by which time the penitent might have changed her mind and decided to stay another day. The next day was followed by another; weeks stretch into months, and 'at this stage contentment sets in, she becomes assimilated to her surroundings'.[81] While technically the inmates were free to leave at any time, after a few years of community living, every moment of every day planned by others, every effort made to instil obedience, conformity, acceptance and self denial, the penitents would have lost the ability to cope with the outside world, and, what was worse, would have lost the desire; as Revd Mother said, 'contentment would have set in'.

There were differences in policy between institutions regarding the length of stay of inmates. Some stipulated that the women should stay for periods varying from nine months to two years; 'situations' would, if possible, be found for them, usually in domestic service, or they would be fitted in some way 'to earn their bread'. These tended to be Protestant or non-denominational homes run by lay people.[82] The magdalen asylums, where the women tended to stay for years, were the homes run by Catholic religious. In 1897 High Park had four jubilarians celebrating the fiftieth anniversary of their entrance into the penitentiary. Two others had died during the year. Revd Mother explained that the founder of the order envisaged that, when 'penitents had been reclaimed', they would be sent back to their friends or 'respectably settled in the world'. Whereas some left High Park every year to go into service, to emigrate or to marry, the experience of later years make the sisters very loath to grant freedom to those who had once belonged to the class known as 'unfortunate'. She went on to say that in High Park and the asylum of the Sisters of Charity in Donnybrook those in authority had noticed a change in the current penitents. In the middle of the century the 'craving for drink' was a marked feature in the middle-aged and 'sin-hardened'. In the preceding twenty years 'the rare exception is to find a girl between fifteen and five and twenty who is not a victim to this terrible slavery'. She added, that there was 'for women of that class, no safeguard outside the asylum'.[83] Guidelines issued in 1866 for the benefit of Sisters of Mercy running magdalen asylums do not endorse this practice. It is pointed out that establishing an asylum on the condition that the inmates should be confined in it for life or else leave it destitute and unprovided for prevents many from entering. It also encouraged Catholics to enter Protestant asylums in the hope of acquiring a future 'character' and 'situation'. Many who might enter or, having entered, persevered, if they had hope of release, would, 'when grace has achieved the victory, choose to stay for life, in which they ought to be encouraged, but not constrained'. Finally, a reason, which would appear unassailable, for adopting a fixed period, in the case of the mercy order of not less than three years, was put forward, namely: that when penitents left, places were provided for others to enter and receive the 'means of conversion'.[84] Nonetheless, those asylums run by nuns, in orders besides the mercy, developed along lines very different from those originally envisaged, which was as short-term refuges for rehabilitation and training for future employment.[85]

The nuns certainly did not encourage the women to leave, and, as has been seen, sometimes resorted to subterfuges to discourage their doing so. The motivation behind the nuns' actions was said to have been the welfare of the women. Nineteenth-century Dublin, like any other large city, was a dangerous place for women without family support or means, and, of course, the nuns would have been concerned about the next life: 'Our sole object is their welfare, temporal and eternal.'[86] There were other possible considerations. It was not easy to find suitable situations for the magdalen women, against whom there was prejudice in society, and the larger asylums could have had 200 to 300 inmates.[87] A journalist in 1897 exclaimed: 'How few Dublin ladies would be willing to accept as domestic servant, even employ as seamstress or charwoman, a fallen girl who wishes to rise from degradation.'[88] Secondly, an asylum of long-stay inmates was easier to run; the intractable, the difficult and the deeply disturbed would have left or been discharged within a few weeks or months. It was policy to discharge those considered a bad influence and capable of causing disruption.[89] The staffing of the laundry has been advanced as a reason for discouraging the women to leave: it has been suggested that strong, docile women, useful in the laundries, were under most pressure to remain.[90] It is undeniable that a result of this policy meant that there was a stable, experienced body of women available to assist in the efficient running of the laundry. On the other hand, it must be remembered that the asylums supported a number of inmates who were unable to work due to the ravages of drink or disease. High Park was described as 'a hospice for the dying as well as a nursery for the soul struggling from darkness into light'.[91] Also, the asylum had to support those who remained on, in their old age, when they were no longer able to work. The nuns were urged by a superior to treat the aged with kindness, remembering that 'they may have rendered great services in their younger days'.[92]

The guide for magdalen asylums run by the Sisters of Mercy advocated that those admitted as penitents should come freely and should be in good health. It was deemed desirable to cut the hair close to the head before newcomers joined the other penitents; it was claimed that this was the rule in most asylums. The sacrifice of their hair, on which they usually set such value, would bring grace: it was also seen as a test of their motive in entering. As Mary Magdalen, the penitent follower of Jesus, consecrated her hair to her Redeemer as evidence of her conversion, so the inmates were 'encouraged' to imitate her in her penance as they had done in their sins. The final reason given for this practice was wholly practical and of this world, though the ultimate aim was, doubtless, eternal salvation. As penitents wishing to leave were known to defer their departure until their hair would be sufficiently grown, in which time 'grace grew and passion subsided, and they became good penitents', it was advised that they would be encouraged from time to time, 'during their fits of fervour', to make a renewed offering of their hair.[93] The shaving of heads to discourage departure was a practice indulged in by other religious orders and in England and Scotland as well as in Ireland.[94]

On arrival, penitents were 'deprived of all that savours of vanity'. A list of all their belongings was made in their presence and everything was locked away. They were then clothed in 'the modest simple asylum uniform'. Food should be wholesome and sufficient, but plain and simple. It was a mistake 'to suppose that procuring them indulgences . . . will render them contented, it does but awaken their spirit of self-indulgence'. Penitents should never be allowed to be idle. Labour was part of their penance, but they ought not to be overworked nor harassed.

Laundry work was deemed 'well suited to the generality of them'. The more secluded the asylum, the better. All intercourse between penitents and their former companions must be entirely ended. Messages should be transmitted only through the sister-in-charge. Few, if any, secular visitors should be admitted to the parts of the asylum where the penitents were engaged.[95] It has been pointed out that this virtual isolation of penitents from society commenced when the nuns took control of refuges and magdalens.[96]

The Sisters of Mercy, like other religious orders, were themselves committed to religious vows of poverty, chastity and obedience.[97] The renunciation of the flesh was accompanied by abdication of the will, or rather the relegation of it to superiors.[98] Self-denial was part of daily living; anything which encouraged vanity was eschewed. All were dressed alike, from the middle of the nineteenth century, in flowing, sombre robes which hid the shape of the body.[99] Most had their hair cut short and their heads covered by veils or more elaborate headgear. The guidelines for the magdalens were based on principles underlying the religious life suitably adjusted for those considered 'grievous sinners'. The nuns had freely chosen this life,[100] with all its hardships and deprivations. However, the religious life, at this period, held certain attractions for women, even in this world. It conferred a high social status on entrants;[101] it provided useful and perhaps interesting work. For those with ability and ambition, it offered the possibility of yielding power, for which there were then rare opportunities for women. What was described as 'the extremely powerful mystique of the penitents' asylum in this period' attracted many women to the orders which ran the magdalen homes.[102]

The growth of these homes in the nineteenth century was part of a wider growth and development of 'total institutions'. The workhouses were set up in 1838; this was followed by reformatories for juvenile offenders in 1858 and by industrial schools for children exposed to crime in 1868.[103] There was also an increase in the number of orphanages and lunatic asylums, and development of the prison system.[104] The trend at the time was to bring together, under one roof, those with similar needs. This was accepted as the best way of controlling and looking after them, and, of course, it removed them from the wider community. The magdalen asylums provided a refuge for those who were rejected by family, friends, masters and mistresses in their time of need. Life was harsh, as it was in all 'total institutions' of the period. The greatest deprivation was, no doubt, the lack of freedom, and the stark realisation, in many of the magdalen asylums, that there was no release. There seems to have been little attempt made to rehabilitate the women and return them to society. In fact, in three magdalen asylums in Ireland run by the Good Shepherd nuns, only 5 per cent of inmates left for 'situations', and it was as low as 1 per cent for a fourth asylum.[105] While many of the sisters probably treated the women with kindness and understanding, the system was open to abuse. Power was entirely in the hands of the nuns, their work affirmed by church and state, while the inmates, condemned by society, were regarded as 'sinners' and 'outcasts'. Excess of fervour by those deemed the righteous could easily lead to abuse of this power. In the absence of legislation and trade union protection, the poor and the powerless in all walks of life were open to abuse by the influential and powerful, but those in 'total institutions', such as the magdalen women, were especially vulnerable.

To those living in the twenty-first century, the fate of these women incarcerated for life, for perhaps one transgression, is horrifying. When it is remembered that many of these were innocent victims, servants seduced by masters, daughters seduced by fathers, sisters by brothers, it was tragic indeed. In the words of a contemporary, 'a woman fell not to rise again; her past different to the man's, was never past'.[106] The acceptance by society of the confinement of girls, perhaps for life, in magdalen asylums, while their male associates retained their freedom, self-respect and good name, is a sad indictment of the times, which were unfortunately to extend for decades into the future.[107] At the end of a series of articles on the Magdalen Homes in Ireland, Mary Costello appealed in 1897 to her readers to support these 'excellent institutions, which are so silently and perseveringly working for the salvation of their fellow-creatures and for the preservation of society'. She contrasted, in the series, the situation of the man, who while 'sowing his wild oats, retains his place at the home fireplace', and can 'when his blood cools', settle down with wife and children, and 'the companions of these wild days, the majority of whom perish miserably; while others, with almost broken hearts, are forced to continue their pilgrimage of guilt and woe'. She ends, not with a plea for justice, but for generosity in giving yearly contributions to those 'asylums devoted to the restitution of fallen women'.[108]

The institutions maintained that the money they earned was wholly devoted to meeting the expenses of the homes and the inmates, to which cause the nuns also devoted their labour. In 1899 the Good Shepherd in Limerick made £1,832 from the laundry and had £850 in a building fund which seemed to include charitable donations and dowries.[109] In

1901 there were 101 penitents in the Magdalen Asylum,[110] allowing 5s. per week, or £13 per year, living costs for each woman, meant that the sisters had about £500 left from the profits of the laundry towards overheads, such as heating and lighting, maintenance on buildings and machinery, and replacement of machinery, not to mention the living costs of the sisters wholly employed in the magdalen home. This would seem to indicate that it would have been difficult, if not impossible, to pay for any large or unexpected expenditure. However, the Good Shepherd nuns, a congregation of seventy-nine in 1901,[111] also ran an industrial school and a reformatory for which they received grants from the state. At the end of the century the sisters received an annual grant from the government of £1,637, for the 109 girls in these two institutions. The order's other houses which had magdalen asylums in New Ross, Waterford and Cork, also had industrial schools. Indeed, government grants from these were deemed necessary to subsidise the magdalen homes. It was clearly undesirable to have these very different institutions, those for 'fallen women' and young girls, in close proximity, even if in different buildings, and looked after by nuns from the same community.[112] In 1911 the Cork Good Shepherd Magdalen Asylum was in debt and the nuns had to appeal to the public for help; the response was disappointing.[113] This shows that earnings from laundry work and fluctuating contributions from the public could not be counted on to finance the homes satisfactorily and gave rise to undesirable practices and the distortion of priorities. A system which began in the mid-nineteenth century at a time of great poverty in post-famine Ireland, was allowed to continue for over a century, with little change and development, by the neglect of the state and the indifference of the public.

The institutions also contended that the provisions of the Factory Acts were unsuited to the homes and would destroy their usefulness. The visits of a factory inspector would violate the religious feelings and the 'home privacy' of the sisters. They would also deter many penitents and others from coming to or remaining in the homes. The main inducement which took them there was the assurance that their wishes 'to be screened for a time from the eyes of others will be respected, whilst their past errors and attempts at reformation as well as their names and even their sojourn in the house may be unknown to the world at large'. The religious said that the factory holidays would be impossible since the nuns could not receive back into their homes girls or women 'who had for 24 hours been free to go abroad, exposed to the dangers of old associations for many obvious reasons'. The fixed hours of employment and of meals were deemed impracticable. It was pointed out that the total number of hours devoted to laundry work in the homes was much less than those allowed by the Factory Acts, but they were distributed differently and broken by intervals for prayers and instruction and for meals.[114] The daily routine in a penitentiary run by the religious in 1897 was that the women rose at 5 a.m. in summer and at 6 in winter. After morning prayers and mass they had breakfast, followed by half-an-hour's recreation. They worked in the laundry till dinner at 2 p.m. This was followed by an hour's recreation and work in the laundry till supper at 6.30 p.m. Religious instruction, more recreation and night prayers followed, and all were in bed at 9.30 p.m. It was alleged that the women had the same fare as the community; this consisted of 'prime meat, vegetables, potatoes, followed by tea or coffee', for dinner.[115] From this, based on a six-day week, it would seem that the women worked for fifty-four hours in the winter and possibly for sixty hours a week in the summer. If there was a half-day on a Saturday, it was not mentioned by the Revd Mother who supplied the timetable. This shows that the institutions worked fewer hours than those allowed by the Factory Acts, but not 'much less', as claimed by the religious. The homes were conducted, it was claimed, on the principles of a family and the happiness as well as the amusement of the inmates were 'abundantly provided for'. The health of the penitents was good.[116]

The worst fears of Edmondson and his fellow-laundrymen would have been endorsed by the remarks of Mrs Edmondson, matron of the Dublin Female Penitentiary (not a relative but almost certainly a Quaker) to Mary Costello. Having said that she used no force and no urging to get the work done and her wishes obeyed, Mrs Edmondson went on:

> Early and late, when the pressure of laundry work is hard, at hours which no factory statute would sanction, the girls are, of their own free will, at the mangle and washtub, knowing that it is the dream of my life to free the institution of debt, and that with the present high competition of the public laundries, we cannot afford to lose a single customer. I have often to turn off the gas after midnight in order to stop the work.[117]

Miss Martindale, who came to Ireland in 1905 as a factory inspector, was asked, with a colleague, to inspect Irish institution laundries and to report on working conditions. They visited forty-two Roman Catholic and fifteen Anglican and Protestant institutions, and were refused admittance only to five of the former and two of the latter. On the whole they were received with great civility, but were often kept some time in the waiting room, so that in only a few cases were they confident that their visit to the actual laundry was a surprise one. They visited penitentiaries, rescue homes, industrial schools, orphanages and domestic training homes, in each of which a commercial enterprise was carried on and used for the support of the inmates. The conditions varied greatly, in some of the large convents the structural conditions were excellent—large, lofty and well-planned rooms with good floors and drainage; in others the conditions were the reverse. In many of the convents the engines and all the machines and even the steam boilers were attended entirely by women; this seemed to surprise Miss Martindale. One nun confided that her favourite recreation was reading *The Vulcan*, an engineering publication of the time. Martindale found the visits to orphanages often depressing: the sight of little girls of nine years of age employed in a laundry where public washing was done was, she said, disturbing.[118]

The laundries in the rescue or magdalen homes and the training schools for girls were the ones feared by the commercial laundries. Many were large and well-equipped, as is evident from Martindale's report. An article in *The Irish Builder* on 1 June 1878 about the new laundry and magdalen asylum on the Crofton Road, Kingstown, stated that the laundry would be fitted up with 'every modern appliance and requirement for a steam laundry'.[119] It was alleged that these laundries undercut the prices charged by the commercial laundries. It was possible for them to do this, it was said, because they did not have to pay wages. Exemption from the rigours imposed by the Factory Acts would increase this advantage, as they would not have to install expensive fencing equipment for machines, maintain certain structural standards or work prescribed hours.

There is conflicting evidence regarding the prices charged. Two members of the Irish Trades Council, in evidence to the Royal Commission on Labour in 1893, said that 'the prices charged by convents were so low as to force down the wages in ordinary laundries'. This was refuted by another witness, who said that, after comparing the printed lists of prices charged by well-known laundries, that suspicion appeared to be unfounded. 'The prices charged by convents are generally higher, and in no cases we heard of, lower than those of the other laundries.'[120] In view of the widespread belief at the time, and indeed later, that the institutions charged less, it is difficult to believe that this evidence was entirely correct. There was consternation in Limerick in 1913 when the Good Shepherd nuns lost the contract for the Army washing which it had held for fifty years . The Mayor, the local MP, the High Sheriff and the Town Clerk sent a joint letter to the Secretary of State for War in London, recording 'the great public indignation' at the proposal, and saying that they intended taking every step possible to have it replaced as it helped the maintenance of destitute inmates.[121] The War Office explained that the lowest satisfactory tender was always accepted by the Army, and that hitherto the convent had been the lowest, but in 1913 a lower one had been received.[122] Ann Parrish, Mother Provincial, said that the Good Shepherd did laundry work at the 'usual terms of payment'.[123]

The charge of unfair competition levied against the institution laundries is one which continued long after the introduction of the 1907 Act. A spirited attack on the commercial laundries was launched by Fr J. Flanagan, of the Pro-Cathedral, Dublin, in a letter he drafted in 1917, on behalf of the convent laundries to be sent to the Laundry Federation. It was a reply to the assertion that the commercial laundries would willingly pay higher wages to their workers if they could do so without going out of business altogether. They laid the blame for this on the unfair competition from the institution laundries, which undercut the commercial laundries and ran at a loss; this loss was covered by appealing to the charitable public for subscriptions. Flanagan stated that convent laundries were not on an equal footing with commercial laundries. The purpose of the owners of the latter was to provide a livelihood for themselves and their dependants; should the enterprises prove so profitable that they could retire from business, they might sell out or even close altogether, and the fate of their employees would not be regarded as their concern. The convent laundries, on the other hand, were run to provide a refuge for people of whom it might be said that unfitness to earn a decent livelihood for themselves was a common characteristic: this fulfilled a pressing public need. The women could remain until death, if they wished, 'within the sheltering walls of their asylum'. He went on to say: 'If the owners of Commercial Laundries trebled the miserable wages they pay their workers, they would still fall far short of what the Convents do for their inmates.'

Flanagan said that, having examined the price lists of both, the difference was not great. He pointed out that commercial laundries had the distinct advantage of being able to select their workers for their skill and expertise, and they could dismiss unsatisfactory workers. The convents used their laundries as a convenient way of occupying their 'children' and as one way of helping to provide for them.

They are never dismissed for idling, or sulking, as they often do—many of them have to be coaxed to work at all—and the uniform quality of their work can never be expected to rival that done by the workers outside. [Flanagan overlooked the expertise of those to whom the delicate and expensive garments of the upper classes were entrusted.] Consequently, if a standard price were adopted, customers would go where they always got better value for the same money, and the Convents would be driven to depend altogether on the charitable public.

The letter concluded by saying that the convent laundries were the first in the field, and that the setting up of commercial laundries in and around Dublin had been a severe blow to their resources. While it was not for the convent laundries to say, he wondered how many privately-owned concerns failed through want of experience and ability on the part of the management? It was clear that a limit might be reached to the demand for laundries and inability to charge higher prices might be due to the multiplication of competing firms, at least as much as to the existence of the Magdalen Asylums, which were doing such necessary and splendid work.[124]

From the beginning a strong case was made for including institution laundries catering for the public under the Factory Acts, even by those who were sympathetic to the work they did. Speaking on the second reading of the Factory Bill of 1895, Mr Asquith said: 'We cannot concede that they [the institutions] are entitled without inspection to have machinery which is dangerous in its character or operation, or to employ persons for a larger number of hours than the Factory Act allows.' Many of the institution laundries were described as 'practically business establishments competing freely in the open market'. It was pointed out that, though it was stated in Parliament that they did not work for profit, many made large sums of money. The Annual Charities Register for 1901 showed that the Asylum for Penitent Females in Dublin had earnings of £1,046, while income from other sources was £225; Edgar Home, Belfast, made £1,132 from the laundry and £144 from other sources; the Magdalen Asylum, Edinburgh made £5,847 from its laundry and £493 from other sources.[125] These statistics show that the major part of the income of these institutions was obtained from the laundries, and that charitable donations were not sufficient to allow the nuns to run their laundries in an unbusinesslike way by undercharging unduly. Martindale reported that the income derived from the laundry tended to have a far too prominent place in some of the institutes she visited, 'the commercial spirit which arose was apt to swamp the spirit of reform and education which was the *raison d'être* of these homes'.[126]

It was agreed that laundries such as these were in serious competition and that there was justice in the proprietors' demand that charitable and religious institutions should obey the law which commercial laundries had to obey. The reports of the chief inspector of factories for 1898 and 1900 instanced cases of complaint against religious institutions where the inspectors were powerless to act. The necessity not to interfere with the charitable work of rescue or the discipline of the establishment was accepted, but it was felt that this should not be incompatible with occasional visits by women inspectors to check sanitary conditions, the fencing of machinery and hours of work.[127] It was concluded that no laundry should remain exempt from the legislative regulations which experience had shown to be necessary to protect the health and well-being of the laundry workers.[128] The industrial subcommittee of the National Union of Women Workers stated in 1897 that, as the difference between 'religious' and 'commercial' laundries was generally accepted, it would have been quite easy, from the beginning, to have drafted clauses for them; the government did eventually have to make the distinction.[129]

# CHAPTER SEVEN

# The Quaker Influence

FROM THE LAUNCHING of the Dublin Laundry until his death, twenty years later, Thomas Edmondson was the quintessential successful, Quaker, businessman. His life revolved around his family, the Quaker meeting house and his business. He disliked social life, and once said: 'Dinners, balls and suppers are not much in my line', going on to say about the particular dinner in question, 'it rather strikes me that it is a little bit outside the legitimate province of a Laundry Association promoting such affairs'.[1] There is no doubt that Thomas enjoyed quiet evenings entertaining members of his family to dinner, or being entertained by them, summer outings with friends or family, lengthy holidays abroad and at home, and, of course, meetings for worship and business, and the social interaction these entailed. He was described by his fellow Quakers as a 'beloved and effective minister'.[2] He was an indefatigable worker in the community in which he lived, exclaiming at one stage, that he was 'overwhelmed with committees'.[3] In December 1895 he agreed to speak for fifteen minutes at a mothers' meeting, saying that he felt it was time for him to retire from that involvement.[4] For over fifty years he took a prominent part in the preparation of essays and in the debates of the Dublin Friends' Institute, an influential society, which had premises in Molesworth Street and a fine library.[5] In June 1896 he said that he was too busy to read a paper at the Institute, but suggested 'Made in Germany' as a subject to which 'we have given some little consideration on the committee of the Dublin Mercantile Association'.[6] He was willing to give his 'Longfellow lecture' in a school in England in 1893.[7] As has been seen, he was a member of a large, extended family, located on both sides of the Irish Sea, with whom he was in constant communication. He was devoted to his wife Nannie, and probably the greatest tragedy of his life was her accident and subsequent serious illness which left her an invalid.[8] Robert Benson referred to the last few years of Edmondson's life being 'sad and sorrowful ones' due to his wife's illness.[9]

135

With the passage of time and the growth in affluence, some Friends, especially the younger and wealthier members, found the simple life less appealing. This change began as early as the 1860s, when they were 'released from the tyranny of plainness of speech, behaviour and apparel'.[10] The rules of the Society, revised in 1881, for the first time since 1864, still enjoined

> simplicity and moderation in your deportment and attire, in the furniture in your houses and in your style and manner of living. Guard watchfully against the introduction into your households of publications of a hurtful tendency. Avoid such sports and places of diversion as are cruel or demoralising, all kinds of gaming, the needless frequenting of taverns and other public houses, and the unnecessary use of intoxicating drink.[11]

By the turn of the century, Quaker objections to fiction and drama as being untrue, and to musical and theatrical performances as leading to depravity, had eased; they were no longer a cause for reproof and disownment.[12] In 1903 a reviewer of Jane Benson's book, *From the Lune to the Neva*, while pointing out that it was not fiction, but 'founded on fact', said: 'With novels we have not much to do'.[13] There is no evidence that these pursuits held any attraction for Edmondson, though he did encourage his workers to take part in the Feis Ceoil (see pp. 83–4), showing a lack of prejudice against things musical and national. By that time, rigidities of dress and speech had almost disappeared,[14] though Thomas, in common with many Friends, continued to use 'thee' and 'thou', when writing, and presumably when speaking to family members and close friends.

Maurice J. Wigham has advanced the theory that the simple life to which the Quakers aspired was not so much abandoned as transmuted into a belief in quality.[15] Thomas's homes, on which he never spared any expense, exemplified the truth of this observation. In 1898, when he wanted to move to a grander house, he offered Shanagarry to Henry Waring, the chief engineer, and his wife. Waring gratefully accepted, saying that it would be much better for him to be so close to his work, but added that he would have to expend a considerable amount of money on extra furniture as 'our few sticks would make a poor show in your rooms'.[16] Shanagarry was to become the home of the managing director again, when, in the early 1920s, Robert Benson and his family went to live there. Robert added Tinnamullen, formerly the manageress's home, to Shanagarry to make it a much larger house.[17]

28. Thorndale, home of the Edmondsons, 1898–1904.

Edmondson rented a fine house, Thorndale, on Temple Road, at an annual rent of £120, high for the time. Characteristically, he made sure that everything was in order before taking possession. Electric bells were installed at a cost of £12.10s.6d, of which he was willing to pay half. He sought quotations for carpets, buying the best quality Axminster and Brussels carpets, and one of the best Turkey carpets from Messrs Anderson, Stanford and Ridgeway of Grafton Street, at a cost of £58.17s.9d, less 10 per cent discount.[18] The iron work outside was painted a dark bronze-green, as he considered the existing colour 'very ugly'. He complained to the owner, Mrs Henshaw, that the wallpapers she allowed them to select were 'very poor for such a house'. He said that no house of the character of Thorndale would be considered properly furnished unless a frieze were supplied with the paper, and he objected to being charged for the frieze.[19] Later, when he built Creevagh, he lavished money on it to make it as comfortable as possible for his invalid wife. The emphasis on quality was also discernible in his approach to the Laundry, only the very best of materials, machinery and furnishings were purchased: this was a policy which was to continue through the years.[20]

Even during the years when money was scarce, Thomas and Anne Edmondson led the life of an affluent, upper-middle-class couple. As was usual at the time, people of means kept a number of indoor servants. In 1901 the Edmondsons had a staff of five, a housekeeper, housemaid and cook, as well as a companion, Josephine Allen, for Nannie.[21] They kept a carriage and horses and employed a coachman; in 1903 they had a brougham (a four-wheeled, closed carriage) and a Victoria (a light, four-wheeled carriage with a folding hood and two passenger seats). When they took short holidays in Ireland, at, for example, the Grand Hotel in Lucan,[22] or the Grand Hotel in Malahide, they went by carriage, arranging lodgings in the hotels for the coachman and stabling for the horse.[23]

In common with the prominent Quaker business man Joseph Rowntree, who considered money spent on travel never wasted,[24] Edmondson enjoyed lengthy holidays, usually taking two in the year, spring and autumn. Pictures of Italy, included in the booklet 'The Side the Sun's Upon', were from photographs taken by himself when on a 'well earned holiday in the South of Europe'.[25] He and his wife enjoyed other holidays: in England, on the Mediterranean[26] and in Switzerland, sometimes spending as long as six weeks on the continent.[27] In the autumn of 1895 Edmondson took a trip to the United States, where he combined business and pleasure; he also visited Canada. Before the end of that year Nannie and he spent a fortnight in England.[28] In May 1897 they spent six weeks in Norway and Sweden.[29] They visited Mountmellick, Nannie's home town, frequently. In March 1899 Thomas wrote to Mrs Chambers of the Temperance Hotel, to book 'the same bedroom at 4s.6d per night', and asked her to send the brougham to meet the train at Portarlington, where they were due to arrive on Saturday morning.[30] He was interested in the Quaker boarding school in Mountmellick, which had been founded in 1786 for boys and girls from Leinster. The Quakers were very interested in education, which was to them the key to progress and personal development. They considered the education of girls and boys of equal importance. They set up a number of boarding schools to provide education beyond the elementary, especially for rural Quakers. The most famous was at Ballitore in Co. Kildare, founded in 1726.[31]

The Society of Friends supported temperance, and Edmondson was a staunch teetotaller, who poked fun at himself in 'The Side the Sun's Upon' when he said, about the refreshment bar: 'In view of the well-known strong Temperance sentiments of the Managing Director, we need hardly add that this is a Strictly Teetotal Bar!'[32] Sobriety was an important factor when hiring staff, and a point stressed by him when giving a testimonial; satisfactory workers were usually described as 'honest, sober and industrious'.[33] In a testimonial for a man who was 'smart and capable in many ways', Edmondson said: 'He might have been with us still, if he had been a thoroughly sober man.'[34] He noted that a reference for a Miss S. said nothing about sobriety, and asked the former employer if this were simply an omission.[35] An applicant for the position of assistant manageress was asked whether she was a total abstainer.[36] When he was manager of the Manor Mill, he told a woman who applied for a job: 'I have myself been a *teetotaller* for 35 years, and do not allow any such thing as drinking: no one being allowed to bring liquor into the premises. So that unless you could completely satisfy me about *that*, it would be no use going further into the matter.'[37] In 1893 Edmondson wrote to the Revd Father Matthew, Dundrum, bringing to his notice that 'two of his flock, have had to be spoken to about giving way to drink'. They were a married man and a 'mere boy', only about sixteen years old. They had solemnly promised Edmondson that they would take the pledge, and he was asking Fr Matthew to look after them and give them encouragement. He said that he would overlook the offence this time, 'upon the solemn promise of amendment in future'. Edmondson gave the two a leaflet on the teaching of 'your good Cardinal Manning on the question', a copy of which he enclosed for Fr Matthew, hoping that the priest could 'effectively add to his faithful words in speaking to them'.[38] He had strong objections to gambling 'in any shape or form', and would not buy lottery tickets even if they were in aid of a good cause.[39] He also seemed to disapprove of smoking, at least he objected to a 'smoking concert' organised by the laundry association. D.E. Benson said that, while he agreed with Thomas, 'the members seem to like an evening of a social nature and so the concert is arranged'.[40] He was obviously slower to accept change than the younger generation.

Quakers may have become more liberal and tolerant in their approach to dress, speech, personal wealth and the arts, but they continued to uphold an ethical approach to business and a caring attitude to those who were not well off.[41] The revised rules in 1881 reminded Friends that the 'Lord Jesus . . . said "it is more blessed to give than to receive"'. Poor Friends, on the other hand, were sternly told that it was 'their duty, by frugality and industry and strenuous endeavour to maintain themselves and their families . . . and not be dependent on others'.[42] Quakers always sought to instil independence, a valuable characteristic for the successful entrepreneur.

Thomas Edmondson was a charitable man, as his attitude to his employees and their families, and to housing for the poor demonstrates: he gave, not only money, but much of his time to others. He supported projects in which the Society of Friends took a particular interest, such as the lifeboat service and missions. In December 1895 he sent a personal contribution of £5 to the editor of the *Irish Times* for the 'Kingstown Life Boat Disaster Fund';[43] this was for the widows and orphans of fifteen members of the crew, who 'capsized to a watery grave', in the tremendous easterly gales on Christmas Eve. It was a disaster, made more poignant by the time of the year at which it occurred.[44] He replied to a criticism from Sir Charles A. Cameron, the medical officer of health, in the *Irish Times* of 26 December, that there was not a permanent fund for this purpose, by saying, that the Royal National Lifeboat Institution had always given large subscriptions to local funds raised and would, doubtless, continue to do so. There was a standing committee in Dublin of the Irish Auxiliary of the Lifeboat Institution, of which Edmondson was the honorary secretary. He said he was 'always anxious to enrol permanent additional subscribers to the funds of the Institution'.[45] Towards the end of the century Friends were particularly interested in missions in Syria, India, Madagascar, China and Ceylon.[46] He and his wife supported missions in India, and agreed to 'take' one of the orphans and to persuade a few other Friends to take a second. He asked for a portrait of the child; he was, he said, 'interested in seeing a picture of our child in your far-off land'. They also chose a name for the child from a selected list.[47] He contributed, through the Dublin Monthly Meeting, to the Friends' Armenian Relief Fund.[48] In January 1897 Edmondson, as one of the secretaries, invited a speaker from England to visit and address one or more meetings on behalf of the Friends' Armenian Relief Fund. A Miss Mellinger came for a week and was invited to stay in the Edmondsons' home, while Thomas told her that he would probably be able to arrange meetings to occupy her whole time in Ireland.[49]

Thomas continued doing acts of kindness for those he considered deserving, sometimes in secret. He paid £4 to Isaac W. Usher, MD, Dundrum, for his attendance on a Mrs. G, if it arose: 'please only say, that it was paid by two or three of her friends'.[50] On one occasion Edmondson and his wife paid a bill for a needy person which they refused to consider as a loan, saying that they had been so successful, that they could afford to give a little help to others—'we should be very sorry to draw the line of our sympathies at "blood-relationships"'.[51] He wrote to a doctor in Milltown:

> I went as soon as possible to the Town Hall and did not leave until I saw the ambulance despatched. Should there be any other cases on your side of Milltown village, write or send to 'Capt.' Smith (of the Fire Brigade), Town Hall, Rathmines, who has charge of the ambulance and tell him I authorised you to do so, and that I will guarantee his fees. I should be quite willing to do the same for Windy Arbour in case of need.

He went on to say that, 'as I stated, you are quite at liberty to call on me for financial aid in special cases of poverty and illness'.[52] When an employee's husband died, Edmondson wrote to the Controller of the Post Office Savings Bank on her behalf, and lent her the money to pay the funeral expenses. Six months later, when she was unwell, he arranged for the doctor to call, without 'the formality of a red ticket'.[53] At the end of November 1907, just months before his death, there were fourteen donations to charity recorded.[54] However, when asked to subscribe to the presentation to Lord Herbert in 1904, he said: 'The demands on one's purse are so numerous that one really has to select the most deserving cases, and this hardly comes under that category.'[55]

The saga of the Wilkinsons shows the lengths to which Edmondson would go to help those whom he considered worthy of it. In January 1896 the Edmondsons received a letter from a Mrs M.J. Wilkinson who had worked for four years in the office of the Manor Mill when Edmondson was manager, seeking a job for her daughter who was almost fourteen.[56] This was followed by a letter from her daughter. In November 1896 Edmondson wrote to Mrs Wilkinson returning the letter, and saying that 'he would try to bear her in mind', but that she was too young for the office. He enclosed some money 'to get any special little things you may want for the children'.[57] In April 1897 Mrs Wilkinson wrote to say that her husband had been thrown out of a high trap, had fallen on his head and, as a result, had been discharged from the Post Office on pension; with their large family this would mean that they would be much worse off. The secretary of the Post Office arranged to have Eveline, her daughter, taught telegraphy, and she herself was going to apply direct to the Postmaster General, the Duke of Norfolk, for the position of postmistress. She asked Edmondson for a recommendation;[58] a few days later he duly sent her a very good reference.[59]

Mrs Wilkinson does not appear to have been successful and is next heard from in January 1898, when she wrote from Cheshire to where the family had moved. She now wanted to get her two daughters into either the office or the sorting room of the Grosvenor Laundry in New

Brighton, 'none but highly respectable girls are employed there'. She asked Edmondson to write to Mr Bennett, who was in charge or 'some director' of the laundry.[60] As a result of his intervention, her daughters were both employed in the sorting room at 4s. per week for the first four months and would get an increase after that. They signed an agreement under which they would be apprenticed for three years.[61] Margaret Wilkinson reported in July that the girls were getting on well. She asked whether Edmondson would know of a situation that would suit her. She said she had had a lot of trouble lately as her husband was fond of drink. She asked that, 'should he favour her with a reply', he would send it to the Upper Brighton post office.[62] Three months later she wrote again, stating that she was in great trouble and had been obliged to leave her husband on account of his ill-treatment of her, 'in fact it was dangerous for me to live with him any longer, as my life and the dear children were not safe'. He never gave her a penny, he drank everything, he even pawned the children's clothes. The landlord had sold their few belongings as the rent had not been paid. She and the girls were staying in a room for which her sister had paid the rent; she was very poor as she could not yet apply for a separation before the magistrate. She wanted another recommendation since she did not get the other one back from the post office. The girls were getting on well and were earning 6s. a week; Bennett was very good to them.[63]

Mrs Wilkinson came back to Ireland, on account, she said, of her three sons, the eldest had got employment in the GPO and they were in lodgings at 7 Middle Gardiner Street. In August 1899 she wrote again to Edmondson, saying that she had seen an advertisement for sorters and packers in that day's *Irish Times* and she wished to apply on behalf of her daughters. She wanted her girls with her in Dublin, and felt that she could arrange things with Mr Bennett, who had promised, that if she had to leave England, 'he would not bind me to the agreement as regards the girls' apprenticeship'.[64] Edmondson again replied by return saying that they would be quite happy to employ her two girls, but that he would not do anything that Bennett might consider unfair to him.[65] Thomas called at Gardiner Street to see Margaret Wilkinson, got a very poor reception, and probably had to talk to her on the doorstep, because her husband, who was back with the family again, wrote at the end of August to apologise to Thomas. He said that matters had been explained 'honourably' to Mr Bennett, and that the girls had been informed.[66] Bennett was not willing to release the two girls and gave Edmondson information about the family when they lived in England which was not very edifying.[67] As a result, Thomas wrote to Mrs Wilkinson saying that, considering the circumstances of the case, he felt that it would be better if the girls stayed where they were and that he would prefer not to employ them.[68] A letter from Mrs Wilkinson then arrived saying: 'Whether or not Mr. Bennett or his directors are agreeable to my taking the girls away, I shall have them back in Dublin',[69] to which Edmondson replied, that he had told Bennett distinctly, that they would not employ her daughters since they appeared to be 'regularly bound apprentices' to the Grosvenor Laundry.[70] Mrs Wilkinson, who seems to have been a particularly persistent and manipulative woman and who was living once more in England, wrote to Edmondson almost six years later with a further request; however, he had evidently had enough by then of the Wilkinsons and replied briefly that he had no vacancies at present that would suit her daughters.[71]

Mrs Edmondson had what her husband described as a very serious accident in March 1896, which resulted in a compound fracture of the right wrist. In June he said she was getting on better than expected and was able to walk in the garden and go for drives. Her 'poor arm was comparatively useless'. She had two doctors in attendance for weeks and a day and night nurse: a trained nurse was kept on as a companion for her.[72] Towards the end of 1898 she was not well, and he was not sure whether he could leave her to visit Bennett's laundry in New Brighton.[73] On the night of 26 April 1899 Thomas had to return unexpectedly from London on account of his wife's illness.[74] She was laid up for nearly six weeks; although Thomas said in September that she was much better, she had to be carried downstairs every day.[75] In 1903 she was 'so much of an invalid' that they could not entertain guests in their home, Thorndale.[76] Rather than incur the trouble of moving, Edmondson asked the owners whether they would make certain improvements, such as providing a lavatory on the hall floor, as Mrs Edmondson was not allowed to walk upstairs, this, he said, could easily be done. Secondly, they wished to have electric light installed.[77] Agreement was obviously not forthcoming. Edmondson decided to build a house suitable for an invalid on a site in Orwell Park, on the corner adjoining Dartry Road, which was acquired from Wm Martin Murphy.[78] The builder, again, was W.A. Roberts. It was a large house, with two attic bedrooms for servants, four family bedrooms and three sitting rooms.[79] A lift was installed, for the benefit of Nannie; this must have been quite unusual at the time, and cost £82.4s.0d, the quivalent of £6,000.6s.0d in 2003 (€7,800.78).[80] As was to be expected, Edmondson was an exacting taskmaster and complained about many things, including the grates, the lift, that there was a lack of attention to detail, that the handrail of the stairs was not properly polished, and that there was a problem about two of the windows;[81] Roberts was offended and said that he had given the house a lot of personal supervision, had saved Thomas architect's fees and taken £20 off the account, and would have gone to look at the offending sash weights anyway.[82] In September 1903 Edmondson wrote to Murphy, saying that he understood that the Tramway Company had bought the plot of ground adjoining Diamond Terrace for a terminus for the new tramway extension, and hoping that Murphy would make sure that any building erected would not detract from the surrounding property.[83] Two years later he was to complain bitterly to Murphy of the noise of the cars returning to the depot from 9 p.m. until nearly midnight, aggravated by what he deemed 'unnecessary ringing of bells'; this was compounded by repair work carried on during the night which involved hammering. He also wrote to the Dublin United Tramway Co. about the '40 or 50 cars rushing into the Depot at that hour'. Leave was given, he said, for a car shed, not a repair shop, which should be in a non-residential area.[84] Creevagh cost a lot of money, much of it spent on specially adapting it to the needs of an invalid, which, as Edmondson said, would add nothing to its letting value.[85] The Edmondsons moved into Creevagh in the autumn of 1904.[86] Unfortunately, they did not live long enough to enjoy their new house and Creevagh was sold by James Adam and Son in April 1908.[87]

When Nannie became a confirmed invalid, holidays became much more difficult and were confined to Ireland. The spring holiday in 1902 was spent at the Lake Hotel, Killarney, Mrs Edmondson was there with her companion Miss Allen, and Thomas joined them after the Whit weekend.[88] That autumn, the ten-day holiday was spent at the Great Northern Hotel, Bundoran, which was, Edmondson said, the only place where he could get the ground-floor apartments which were essential. Thomas wrote to a cousin, at his wife's insistence, saying that they would be glad if Charlie joined the party. The charge per person was three and a half guineas a week, the hotel had asked for four. He said that, when travelling anywhere with Nannie, they always went first class.[89] Nannie was probably anxious that Thomas should have a companion available who might accompany him on walks and other holiday activities. Early in 1903, when he was building Creevagh, Edmondson also decided to get a holiday home in Greystones. He purchased a nearly completed house, just above one owned by his Quaker friend Mr Jacobs, and near another friend, Mr

29. Creevagh, the house Thomas Edmondson had built and adapted for his invalid wife; the Edmondsons lived there from 1904 until their deaths.

Goodbody. He had a coach house and stable for two carriages and two horses, and a room for the coachman, built at a cost of approximately £200. The lease of the house was to be in the name of his wife.[90] Attanagh became their holiday home for the remaining few years of their lives.

In 1896 Thomas was approached by Benjamin Haughton, a Quaker from Cork, who told him that a group of people from the Cork Timber and Iron Co. Ltd, were thinking of starting a laundry, and asking for his help. Thomas said that, without wishing 'to look a gift horse in the mouth', he was willing to help him 'in any limited way not involving constant or continued sacrifice of time or energy'.[91] In November 1997 Haughton asked Edmondson whether he would be willing to go on the board of the new company. He refused, saying, 'that at 60 years of age a man should be reducing his career'. As the one with technical knowledge, he foresaw that there would be much responsibility on his shoulders.[92] The Cork Steam Laundry Ltd was registered on 29 January 1898. The board was composed almost entirely of the Cork Timber and Iron Company's directors. Recognising that none of the directors was what he called 'practical laundrymen', Haughton and his colleagues were anxious to appoint highly qualified people to fill the responsible posts, such as those of manager and manageress. They were glad to accept Edmondson's offer to purchase the machinery on their behalf, and sought his advice on whether or not they should accept the Cork Electric Tramways and Lighting Co.'s suggestion that they use electricity to drive the machinery: evidently Edmondson advised against, an opinion shared by Haughton. Edmondson was entrusted with the selection of staff, Haughton saying that he would like Thomas to bring some Quaker blood to Cork. Haughton reiterated that they were not experts, neither could they undertake the day-to-day running of the laundry, therefore they wanted thoroughly reliable, trustworthy people, and they were prepared to pay liberally for first-class people. As they wished to keep their venture secret, they advertised in the *Friend*, under an assumed name, for a manager and/or manageress. Miss Dixon, now living in Dover, who had formerly worked for Edmondson (see p. 40), replied. Haughton said that Miss Dixon had one big advantage, she was a Quakeress, repeating: 'I would greatly like to employ a Friend'.[93]

Miss Dixon was offered the position of manageress in June, at a salary of £100 a year with house or apartment, free washing and a commission, to be arranged, when the turnover reached £50 a week. Edmondson considered that she was the right person for Haughton.[94] Haughton told Edmondson that Miss Dixon had accepted the position, and that the building would be finished in time—31 July 1898. He was anxious, he said, to get to work before Musgrave, a rival, started a new laundry at Queenstown, which would have a steam launch to bring the linen to and fro.[95] In May a young man named E.O. Wakefield arrived in Cork, as a 'sort of clerk of works' for the building operation. It is not clear who was responsible for his selection, certainly it does not appear to have been Edmondson, who said that Wakefield struck him as one 'who would never be likely to set the Liffey on fire', but would be dependable in a subordinate role. Haughton wrote to Thomas 'E.O. Wakefield has come on the scene. He is a nice young chap, and I think I can make a good man of him yet for the Laundry.' He saw Wakefield as being a possible assistant to Miss Dixon.[96] Wakefield said of Cork: 'It is the most sleepy and dead and alive place I have ever been in almost.'[97]

Haughton reported to Edmondson before Christmas that receipts were increasing weekly, but not as much as he had expected. They were having great difficulty getting the goods out on Saturday, and were receiving 'enormous complaints' from the public about late deliveries on Saturday nights, and even on Sunday mornings. He assumed that this was almost inevitable in starting a laundry of that size and said 'an expert like your good self should look into this on your next visit'. They were also having problems in getting staff. Miss Dixon had advertised in the Belfast and Dublin papers for 'finery ironers', without success. Edmondson was asked to seek hands and told 'give any pay you like in order to obtain first class Ironers', Haughton adding that he did not wish to raise the rate of pay in the Milltown area, but he would pay even a higher wage than Dublin.[98]

Not only did Wakefield not set the Lee on fire or enliven Cork, he did not stimulate much activity in that part of it owned by the Munster Steam Laundry. By the end of January 1899 Haughton was admitting that Wakefield was not the man for the place and gave him notice. To his surprise, Miss Dixon also decided to leave. There was a hint that she may have left to marry Wakefield,[99] but, although the two were running a laundry in Blackburn, it does not appear to have been true. Edmondson wrote in 1901 to thank Wakefield and Miss Dixon for showing him 'through their laundry'.[100] The next manager was a Mr Tosney, for whom Edmondson had even less respect. 'Mr. T. does not impress me favourably as being thoroughly up to his business.' On Tosney's advice, the company had bought additional machinery in 1899, which he thought unnecessary, and said that it was a pity they had not asked his advice before purchasing. He was also unhappy about other decisions taken, such as changing the position of a fan, and the drying room.[101] In December 1899 Thomas was offered a directorship, which he firmly declined: he did not want the responsibility involved. He offered to go down occasionally for a day or two, and said that 'the place ought to be made to pay if it were decently managed'.[102] The Laundry lost money that year. In April 1900 Edmondson expressed surprised that Haughton had not got rid of Tosney, and said that he hoped Haughton was going to get 'out of the mud and make the concern a paying one'. By the summer, Edmondson was beginning to get exasperated, and, in July, asked Haughton to let him know what benefit he thought would come from a visit to Cork: 'Whilst I might be able to point out some of your defects, unless I took my coat off and stay for weeks, I have doubt whether my help would be of much value.'[103] The news from the Munster Steam Laundry at the end of 1900 was better; they managed to make £83 one week, and the average per week for the preceding eleven months was £51.[104] The Munster Steam Laundry had dispensed with Tosney's services by December 1901.[105]

The founding of the Munster Steam Laundry must have taken up a lot of Edmondson's time and energy, while denying him the satisfaction of helping to launch a success. His friendship with Haughton and the desire to help a fellow Quaker can have been the only reason why he undertook the job in the first instance. There is no evidence that he got a fee for his work; he stipulated that he should get a first-class rail fare to and from Dublin, and on one occasion had to remind them of 'our own little a/c for travelling expenses'.[106] He offered to look for a manageress for the Cork laundry when in London on his own business, he said: 'in which case I suppose you would pay a reasonable proportion of my travelling expenses?' He also expected to be 'put up' when in Cork, and, in fact, often stayed at Haughton's home Arbutus Lodge.[107] He got commission on the machinery he bought for the laundry.[108] From the beginning he did not want to become too involved, and told a friend in August 1898 that he was 'very slightly interested' in a company in Cork.[109] He was aware of the problem of a board of directors from a very different field, trying to run a large steam laundry. Everyone was convinced of the necessity, under those circumstances, of getting a first-rate management team. This they singularly failed to do, and therein, probably, lies the main reason for all the early difficulties. In addition, it was difficult to get good, experienced laundry women in Cork. There was also strong competition from the Metropole Laundry; Haughton reported in 1899, that Musgrave, who was a very energetic man, had practically given up the management of a large wholesale grocery business to devote himself to his laundry on the Lower Road and the Metropole Hotel. That laundry had 1,240 accounts and forty hands at a time when the Munster Steam Laundry had a quarter of the number of customers and about half the staff.[110]

There is no evidence that Edmondson was interested in politics, except in so far that they affected the laundry industry and matters of particular interest to the Society of Friends. He showed keen political awareness and a readiness to adopt the usual tactics of the pressure group when the interests of laundry proprietors and the industry appeared to be threatened by the Factory Acts. In 1896 T.H. Cook of the Beulah Laundry and Cleaning Works in London, a collaborator from resistance to the 1867 Factory Act, urged him to join the United Kingdom Laundry Protection Society: 'Your name should certainly be enrolled and especially as you are such an "old parliamentary hand" . . . we should feel a former brother-in-arms had forsaken us when his strong right hand is much needed.'[111] Edmondson told James Armstrong in 1890, when seeking a new charge-hand, that he did not want 'an Englishman of no discretion, who might make mischief among our hands in any way',[112] thus showing a recognition of the nationalistic sensibilities of some, at least, of his work force. Quakers generally did not take a direct interest in political matters, though from the 1830s this changed slowly, and they took a more prominent part in public affairs. Some went into Parliament, others became interested in municipal matters.[113] They certainly made their views on matters of importance to the Society, such as the sale of intoxicating liquor or the death penalty, known to government, through the Dublin Yearly Meeting. Issues, such as Repeal of the Union and Home Rule, received little sympathy from Friends, who were, on the whole, perfectly happy to be part of the United Kingdom, a world power, capable of providing the stability and infrastructure necessary for economic and commercial success. Quakers were expected to support the state and the law unless their conscience was violated.[114]

Edmondson probably regarded himself as an Englishman living in Ireland. He tended to look eastwards; his knowledge of Ireland seemed to be confined to the Dublin area, holiday resorts, Mountmellick and Cork. He was critical of movements and events which upset the even tenor of life. Of 1880 he said that it was the best yet at the Manor Mill, 'in spite of Parnell and Co.'[115] In 1883 he told a friend 'if matters dont mend in the country soon, we may all have to be off to that more distant "New Holland" in the Antipodes'.[116] The Phoenix Park murders of the Irish chief secretary and under secretary by the Invincibles, an extreme society of Fenian background devoted to political assassination, had occurred a year earlier.[117] The Land War of 1879–82 had resulted in some murders, such as that of Lord Mountmorres, which received a lot of publicity; there was violence and threats of violence, there was torturing and maiming of animals; the confrontation between landlords and tenants and their supporters led to a rapid escalation in the number of evictions.[118] This general unrest in the country evidently had a depressing effect on Thomas and his wife, who said to him on a number of occasions at that time, 'Let us pack up and leave this horrid land and go to Canada' (where they had spent an enjoyable holiday). Thomas was not willing to go to those extremes yet, and mentioned that 'the laundry industry keeps booming', and they could not complain of their prospects in Ireland.[119] When he founded his own laundry, there was no further talk of leaving: he did not even seem to consider it when he was ousted from the Manor Mill. Edmondson's commitment was to the community in which he lived, rather than to his adopted country: this is shown, not only by the way in which he conducted his business, but by his life in

Milltown and his work as a member of the Rathmines and Rathgar Urban District Council.

Edmondson was, like most Quakers, loyal to the Union and the monarch. However, when the Queen visited Ireland in April 1900, his main interest in the event was a commercial one: the Dublin Laundry obtained the contract to do the royal washing. The visit took the whole country by surprise for a number of reasons—the advanced age of the monarch, the length of time which had elapsed since her previous visit, thirty-nine years, and 'the cantankerous state of existing Irish public opinion', said to be due to sympathy for the Boers in their war with Great Britain.[120] In addition, Home Rule and Land Reform were issues of concern in the country at the time.

The Queen, having slept on board the royal yacht in Kingstown harbour on the previous night, landed at Victoria Wharf on 4 April and entered Dublin in state. The streets and principal sites of the city and townships were extensively decorated. The people decorated their own houses. The highlight was the city gate, a magnificent structure, modelled on an old castle, which was erected at the Grand Canal Bridge, Leeson Street, the city boundary. Here the Queen was welcomed by the Lord Mayor. She stayed in Ireland for three weeks in the Viceregal Lodge, Phoenix Park, while Lord and Lady Cadogan and their family moved to Dublin Castle. The Queen was accompanied by her third son and his wife, the Duke and Duchess of Connaught (who stayed at Lord Iveagh's home, Farmleigh), her two daughters, Princess Christian and Princess Beatrice, and a large retinue. The Queen spent the time in Ireland quietly, going for drives in Phoenix Park and through the city, while she and members of the royal party visited hospitals, convents, schools and some of the 'big houses' in the neighbourhood.

The day of the Queen's arrival in Dublin was a general holiday and all banks and businesses were closed.[121] The staff of the Dublin Laundry were free to welcome the monarch, but they did not get an extra holiday on her account, as the day was given in lieu of Whit Monday, 12 May.[122] On her way into the city that day, the Queen passed through the townships of Pembroke and Rathmines,[123] so the workers could have gone to see the procession pass, and even those who may not have approved of the monarch and what she stood for, might have gone along to see what was a rare and wonderful spectacle. The Queen's visit was not universally popular. This was evident on what was called Children's Day, when thousands of children from the city and county were invited to Phoenix Park to see the Queen and be entertained at the expense of

30. Carpets from the Viceregal Lodge, cleaned in Dartry Dye Works before Queen Victoria's visit in 1900.

a Citizens' Committee, led by the Lady Mayoress, the Countess of Fingall and other prominent ladies and gentlemen. The plan was resisted, principally by the Catholic clergy and some of the Catholic press; the children's party was dubbed 'Souperism'. Most of the Catholic children from the national and industrial schools did not attend. A contemporary writer said that it was the 'heritage of Faith' and not political principles that were at stake, basing his argument on the fact that it was the clergy, as managers of the schools, who had kept the children away. Letters to the press, however, show that there were political motives as well. The feast in the Park was said to provide the government with an opportunity 'to parade the exuberant loyalty of the Catholic people', mention was made, by those who opposed the project, to 'the odious and unjust anti-Boer war', and of making 'loyal little Britons of the sons and daughters of Irish Nationalists'. Many firms made donations of food, Messrs Jacob and Co. gave one ton of biscuits, Williams and Woods, one ton of jam and 10,000 bags of sweets, and there were many others.[124] The Dublin Laundry was asked to lend laundry baskets for about three days, in which to pack the sandwiches,[125] Edmondson replied rather curtly, that they could not possibly spare any baskets during this period.[126]

The Laundry did the washing 'to the very great satisfaction' of the lady in charge of the linen.[127] Edmondson was more formally advised by letter from the Royal Yacht, that the laundry had been done 'exceedingly well and given entire satisfaction': this was endorsed by letter from the Viceregal Lodge, saying that: 'The laundry work for the Royal Household has been carried out by the D.L. Co. in the most efficient manner and has given entire satisfaction'.[128] For this, the Lord Steward granted them a Warrant of Appointment as Laundrymen to her Majesty, the persons to represent the company were Thomas Edmondson, the MD and Robert Benson, secretary. They received this honour in time to have it incorporated in the new price list which they issued in June 1900.[129] However, royal contracts were not exempt from the everyday mishaps which beset the laundry trade. Evidently the laundry of some servants, which should not have been included, was charged to the Queen's account. Buckingham Palace told the Laundry that they had been overpaid by £1.11s.7d, and requested a refund. Edmondson duly paid up, and asked, very respectfully, whether the secretary of the Board of Green Cloth would 'favour us with the names and addresses of the persons to whom we should charge the washing'. Respect for royalty did not prevent the tenacious Thomas from bringing to the notice of the Palace, some months later, that they still had some small personal accounts unpaid by some of the servants.[130] In their second pamphlet, 'Success', issued that year, the Laundry sought to achieve as much kudos as possible from the royal honour.[131] In April 1901 the Lord Steward was asked for a renewal from the King of the Warrant of Appointment to the late Queen. In case any evidence of character was needed, it was stated that Edmondson was a member of the Rathmines Urban District Council and was also one of the deputation from the Society of Friends in Great Britain who had the privilege of presenting an address to the King on 12 March. The request was granted.[132] In 1903, on the strength of their success, the Laundry sought the contract for the royal washing for the proposed visit to Ireland of Edward VII, which they obtained.[133]

Edmondson became a commissioner for the Township of Rathmines in the autumn of 1894.[134] In 1898, when a bill completely reorganising local government in Ireland was introduced, existing townships and sanitary authorities became urban or rural districts councils. The Rathmines commissioners became urban district councillors. The first meeting of the Rathmines and Rathgar Urban District Council took place in the Town Hall on 23 January 1899.[135] Thomas was very active on the Council, much of the work of which was carried on by committees. In 1903 he was a member of the public health, lighting, library, school attendance and technical instruction committees.[136] This entailed frequent attendance at meetings, and, as he made clear on a number of occasions, he would not undertake the membership of any organisation unless he could fulfil all the requirements of the position. He was chairman of the Rathmines Technical Instruction Committee when the School of Commrce was established. He negotiated the rental of 24 Rathmines Road as the site of the new school, and thought that the committee should also consider taking number 23; however, the committee did not agree, considering 24 large enough for some time to come.[137] He busied himself with such matters as the preparation of the building, the purchase of typewriters and desks,[138] the design of examination certificates and the issuing of the prospectus in time for the opening session in 1903.[139] Edmondson was elected vice-chairman of the Council in 1902, and re-elected in 1903: he later, in 1905, became chairman.[140] He was chairman in 1907 when his wife died. At a council meeting held on 1 May 1907, with Francis McBride, JP in the chair, the following resolution was passed: 'That we deeply regret the loss our respected Chairman has sustained and we tender him our heartful sympathy in his sad bereavement.'[141]

Edmondson was not slow to bring what he saw as the shortcomings of others to the attention of the proper authorities. When he complained that the sub-postmistress in Milltown had not the postage stamps he required, he received a reply from R.C. Day, for the secretary of the General Post Office, assuring him that it would not happen again.[142] The Dublin, Wicklow and Wexford Railway was the recipient of frequent complaints, about the irregularity of the service, the unavailability of timetables, and the non-labelling of a smoking compartment on the platform side; he often mentioned that others were also complaining about the same things.[143] In June 1903, when he was living for the summer in Greystones, he said that he found the times of the trains very awkward, as the 5.10 from Harcourt Street did not stop at Milltown: he asked whether it could stop there, that he was sure that others going to play golf would find it useful.[144] Messrs Alexander Thom and Co. received a number of scathing letters. In 1903 he wrote, obviously not for the first time, 'Clonskeagh, as we have stated, is not our Post Office, but Milltown. Can you tell us any course to be adopted to ensure accuracy in future?' The 1895 Directory had a number of errors which were noticed after 'casually inspecting it'; one was that the names of three commissioners, including his own, were omitted, he was appointed only the preceding autumn, but the other two were on the board considerably over twelve months.[145] Edmondson would probably have seen this as part of his duty to the community; apart from the fact that he was inconvenienced on each occasion, he would have been conscious that the onus of raising these issues rested with those who had the ability, the self-confidence and the status to do so.

Like many other male heads of family, Edmondson took responsibility for his unmarried female relations living on annuities and inherited wealth. He had two unmarried sisters living in Kendal with whom he was in touch on a regular basis. They both had money invested in the Laundry, and Agnes inherited a loan to the Laundry from Jane Benson of Southport, her first cousin.[146] Thomas acted as sole executor for his sister Anne when she died in 1903,[147] and he asked Agnes, the remaining sister, to visit himself and his wife in Greystones in July.[148] When booking a cabin for them on a cross-Channel steamer in 1896, he described them as 'somewhat of invalids', and asked the Steam Packet Co. to have a cabin reserved for them, 'as comfortable and as near mid-ship as possible'.[149] As he outlived most of his family, this burden increased over the years. When John Edmondson, of Dame Street, died in 1894,[150] Thomas assumed responsibility for his wife Fanny until she died at the end of 1902.[151] When sending in an income tax return on her behalf in 1896, he said that she was 'quite an invalid, unable to understand or sign the document'.[152] On their mother's death, the business in Dame Street was inherited by Fanny's unmarried daughters Margaret and Alice; Thomas was a caring uncle to these nieces. Seven or eight years before her death, Thomas assumed liability for almost the entire expenses of his married sister Fanny Smith, who was in a nursing home in England.[153] It seemed to be assumed at the time that these women, who had never worked outside the home, were quite unable to manage, not only their monetary affairs, but the arrangement of holidays, medical care and change of residence. There also seems to have been an unduly high degree of invalidism among the female members of the family; were they really delicate or was it the result of frustration caused by the life of ease and idleness, which these, no doubt, intelligent women, had to lead? Edmondson said, in 1903, that 'my own family circle, within the last 2 years, has been rapidly diminished by the death of three of my sisters'.[154] In that year also, Thomas's brother Joseph had a paralytic

31. The fraternal delegates from Dublin Yearly Meeting to the Five Years' Meeting of American Friends in Richmond, Indiana, attended by Edmondson (at left), autumn 1907 (*The Friend*, 1907, New Series, 47, p. 790).

seizure, while he was attending the Yorkshire Quarterly Meeting at Leeds.[155] However, he regained his speech and mental faculties and lived for a further five years.[156]

Anne Edmondson, Nannie, died on 24 April 1907.[157] On that day the Extraordinary General Meeting was taking place at Milltown to promote the new company, the Dartry Dye Works Ltd, which was to take over the dye works branch of the company. C. Frederic Allen was in the chair and Messrs Wm. C. Roberts and R. Benson were present (see ch.5). Business went on, but for Edmondson life would never be the same again. He was heartbroken. To help him to recover from the shock and depression after her death, he was induced to undertake a mission for the Friends to the United States in the autumn.[158] He was one of the Irish fraternal delegates to the Five Year Meeting of American Friends in Richmond, Indiana.[159] On his return, he was persuaded to go on a trip to South America with his friend Mr Jacob; Edmondson became ill with pneumonia and was brought to the English Hospital in Rio de Janeiro, where he died on 11 February 1908. His death was registered within the district of the British Consulate General and signed by Arthur Chapman, HM Consul General. He was interred in Rio de Janeiro.[160] Edmondson, who had been re-elected chairman of the UDC, was in the chair for the AGM of the Council on 23 January 1908. A few weeks later Councillor McBride presided, this time at a Special Council Meeting for the sad task of passing a vote of condolence with the relatives of the late Thomas Edmondson. They spoke of his untiring devotion and attention to the affairs of the Council and his unfailing courtesy in discharging his duties, a tribute, no doubt, well merited.[161]

Edmondson had many admirable qualities in which his early upbringing and life as a committed Quaker obviously played a large part. He was a loving husband, brother, uncle and cousin to his large, extended family. He was a good master to his employees. He took an active role in the affairs of the community in which he lived and worked. He had sympathy for the poor and was willing to help those less fortunate than himself. As has been seen, his care for the health and welfare of his employees extended to their families: his interest in housing his employees stretched to trying to improve the housing of the poor of Milltown. Over a period of fourteen years he gave freely of his time—which was probably more precious to him than money—as commissioner, later councillor, for the Urban District Council of Rathmines.

Edmondson, to his family, friends and acquaintances, was kind, compassionate and courteous, but he had another side to his character: he was a tough business man. He summarily dismissed an employee who sought an excessive rise in wages and refused to alter his decision when the girl and then her mother begged him to reinstate her at her then salary. He would have sacked the twenty-four women who thwarted his plan 'to get a better standard of ironing', only he could not find replacements for such a large number. Edmondson gave his employees a fair wage, but, as he said himself, he never promised 'to increase that wage'. He was glad to pay a good worker 'enough to keep her with us': he said that they generally paid people what they 'made themselves worth' to them. It seemed that employees had to ask for a rise or threaten to leave. He operated a fines system, until obliged to discontinue it for trivial offences such as 'singing' or impertinence and reduce it for more serious offences. He had no compunction in dismissing those caught taking drink. Edmondson was not sentimental about workers' woes when they clashed with business interests.

It is worthy of note, that Margaret Forster, in her history of the Carrs of Carlisle biscuit factory, said of J.D. Carr, the founder, also an exemplary

Quaker: 'He was gaining a reputation of an unusual kind, one of compassion and concern running side by side with an aggressive business sense'.[162] She went on to say: 'Sobriety was the watchword and it was rigorously enforced.' He was tough in the cause of righteousness'.[163] Yet Carr, like Thomas, was seen within the family as kind and gentle.[164] He was involved for years in improving conditions for the poor.[165] The success of Quakers in business has been attributed to the fact that they were seen to be honest; also they were happy and fulfilled as business men, the stability and endurance of the business was often achieved because sons and grandsons were content to follow in their father's footsteps. However, the crucial factor was that they were hard-headed business men who adopted a single-minded approach to the furtherance of their industrial and commercial affairs. Edmondson's Quaker friends withdrew the money that they had invested in the Manor Mill Laundry and reinvested it in the Dublin Laundry. This was done in sympathy and friendship, but, in addition, these shrewd men would have considered their money much safer in the capable hands of the man who had run a laundry successfully for twenty years rather than in those of a young man of twenty-three—who was not considered, by Edmondson, ready to be involved in the business at the age of nineteen. They might also have foreseen the damage that a new laundry might do to the Manor Mill by attracting staff and customers.

Joseph Rowntree, like Thomas Edmondson, took great care when choosing men to fill positions of authority—taking into consideration the work, the workers and the personality of the man in charge. Ann Vernon, his biographer, makes the interesting suggestion that the method of worship of the Quakers, depending as it does on the group and the relationship within it, would have alerted Rowntree to what was required within the working group in a factory. In this she thought he anticipated the industrial psychologists.[166] Edmondson also showed this awareness when, for example, he sought a charge-hand who would not make mischief among the 'hands' (see Chapter 7).

Edmondson was devastated when he was ousted from the Manor Mill. This was understandable. He had worked hard to improve the laundry; he had contemplated moving it to a new site and making it into the first-class laundry which the Dublin Laundry was to become. He had a contractual arrangement with his sister-in-law and her family, and looked forward to remaining at the Manor Mill for the rest of his working life. Suddenly, at the age of fifty, this vision was shattered. He was bitter and disillusioned. At times he displayed a vindictiveness which seemed unworthy of a man held in such high esteem by family, friends and colleagues. When telling a friend that things were not going well at the Manor Mill, the addition that the pond overflowed and damaged the new carpet, seemed both gratuitous and somewhat spiteful. His insistence that advertisements for the Dublin Laundry should be placed immediately under those for the Manor Mill was probably done to disconcert his old firm. He was also reputed to have said that he would put the Manor Mill out of business. His anger at his treatment by the Edmondsons of Dundrum was probably deepened by the fact that Quaker families were normally supportive of one another. The greater sufferer in the end was probably the Manor Mill, though it was not put out of business.

Edmondson was very careful about money, as was seen in his business transactions and those relating to his homes; but he spent freely on what was of importance to him: his wife, his homes, his carriages and his frequent holidays at home and abroad. He was willing to pay for a highly efficient management team—indeed, give them a share in the business— if this would relieve him and his wife of some of the burden of running a successful laundry. Business was very important to him, but he maintained a balance between it and his private life. His private life included, as has been seen, attending to the needs of the community and the poor, and helping his friends. He devoted time, over a period of at least four years, to assist his friend Benjamin Haughton when he was setting up the Cork Steam Laundry. Again, he was willing to do all he could to help a former employee of the Manor Mill, Mrs Wilkinson, when she was in trouble. He was involved intermittently with her family between 1896 and the end of 1899. He lost interest in them when he learned that they had behaved in a 'dishonourable' way. Thomas was exacting in his expectations of others, and did not readily make allowances for differences in circumstances. While he would have affirmed his belief in the equality of all, men and women, and always tried to be just in his dealings with others, his attitudes often reflected those of his class. He seemed to regard the lower classes, to which the majority of his workers belonged, with a certain amount of suspicion, which may have been partly due to their being Irish and Catholic. He lacked empathy with those outside his own social class and experience. Whereas he was invariably courteous to employees of his own class, nationality and creed, communications with others could be peremptory and brusque. While his treatment of those considered his inferiors, in the rigidly structured society of the day, was tempered by the Quaker philosophy, he was a product of his time. Remarks made about workers often reflected this, and he obviously felt that a strong hand and extreme vigilance were necessary to ensure that they gave of their best. The word commonly used for workers, 'hands', was symbolic of the attitude of employers, and, indeed, of society generally, to unskilled men and women.

In her will Anne Edmondson left £100 to a cousin, £50 to her housekeeper, Bessie M. Neale and £50 to Josephine Allen, her companion; she also left £50 to Jemina B. Spencer. These were to be paid, free of legacy duty, from dividends received after her death from her shares in the Dublin Laundry. The remainder of her estate was left to her husband for his life. She stipulated that her shares in the Laundry should not be sold by her executors, and that all monies or other shares or stocks lent or left by her in the Laundry, should be retained in the investments in which they held at the time of her death. However, these assets could be changed into other investments at the discretion of her husband.

On the death of Thomas, Anne's estate, shares in the Dublin laundry, shares other than those, debentures, securities for money and monies, was to be divided among her numerous nieces and nephews. Her property, 1 Appian Way and 59 Upper Leeson Street, was left to a nephew Samuel Roberts. Four nieces and five nephews each received a forty-fourth share; six nephews received two such each, and six nieces received four such. One of the legacies was allowed to lapse, that of Herbert Roberts, and the value of it was included in his Schedule of Assets when her husband died. This shows that one forty-fourth share was 193 ordinary shares and twenty-three preference shares and the same fraction of her cash on deposit, £87.7s.1d.[167] The will was signed on 7 January 1902. Anne Edmondson's estate was valued at £19,469.7s.10d; £783.12s.4d was paid in estate duty.[168]

In his will, written on the 15 November 1906, Edmondson appointed Robert Benson and Charles Frederick Allen as his executors. He left his house, Creevagh, and contents, carriages and horses to his 'dear wife, Anne Edmondson' for her use during her life. On her death they were to be sold and the proceeds lodged with the Dublin Laundry. He directed that Benson should have the option of purchasing Creevagh for £1,250, an option obviously not taken up, as Creevagh was sold by Adams in 1908.[169] Bequests of £20 were given to his favourite charities such as the Ragged School and the Association for the Prevention of Intemperance, and to Quaker concerns—the Friends' Institute and the Temple Hill Cemetery Fund. Bessie Neale, his former housekeeper, received £50. He left an annuity of £30 to his niece Marie Smith, for her life, which was to be paid from the dividends and interest on his ordinary shares and any debentures he might hold in the Dublin Laundry. Subject to that, his executors were directed to pay the said dividends and interest to his wife during her life.

On the death of his wife, Edmondson left fifty £1 ordinary shares in the Laundry to Charles F. Allen, 200 ordinary shares to Henry Waring, 100 to Jemina Spencer and 100 to Jemina McCleery. Josephine Allen was to get Attanagh in Greystones, with the furniture and household effects or, if it and the furniture were sold, 400 ordinary shares in the Laundry. This was in recognition of her long and faithful service, and especially in remembrance of her devotion to his wife in her last illness, 'and in accordance with my wife's several times expressed desire that the said Josephine Allen should be provided for'. Benson received half of the remaining ordinary shares, 4,292, and was charged with the payment of the annuity to Marie Smith. Benson was given the option of purchasing an annuity for Marie 'from the Friends' Provident Institution or other leading and solvent Insurance Company and thus freeing the shares'. Edmondson's nieces Margaret and Alice Edmondson received the other half between them. He directed that all monies standing to his credit in the books of the Laundry should be retained by the company, subject to the payment by the company of 5 per cent interest. If the directors and the executors, then the same persons, agreed, the monies could be converted into 5 per cent preference shares. Margaret and Alice Edmondson were named as the residuary legatees. They also received his preference shares and any money credited to him in the Laundry to use the dividends, as they thought fit, to assist his grand-nephews and grand-nieces, or to maintain some portion of his subscriptions to various charities, philanthropic societies or religious objects. The preference shares were to go eventually to his grand-nephews and grand-nieces.

Edmondson added a codicil to his well on 4 June 1907, after his wife's death. He bequeathed articles of furniture, pictures, books and ornaments to specific people. His wife's nephew got two rosewood window seats made for 1 Appian Way; a niece got a mantel clock; cousin Robert Benson, two watercolours, Goerq binoculars and silver fruit knives and forks which were presented to Edmondson by the employees of the Laundry. Cousin Margaret Benson of Southport received two bronze figures given to Thomas on his marriage by her mother and father. Margaret and Alice Edmondson got a photograph of Uncle Thomas and a large framed one of Thomas himself taken in America. Photographs were rare and prized possessions in those days. Other bequests were made with the same meticulous attention to the suitability of the gift to the recipient.[170]

The deaths of the Edmondsons in 1907 and 1908, presented difficulties for the company. Preference shares numbering 1,093 and 9,534 ordinary shares were in the name of Thomas Edmondson, 907 preference and 8,307 ordinary in that of Mrs Edmondson. There was an overdraft in the Royal Bank on Edmondson's personal guarantee of about £4,000, and there were deposits at 5 per cent, amounting to £14,345, which were liable to be called in. The bank wished the overdraft to be paid off at once, and there were no assets available for that purpose. The executors of Mrs Edmondson were anxious to receive payment of the sum she had on deposit, which was £3,941 (part of the £14,345 above). Matters were serious, and if the creditors had brought pressure to bear on the company, it would have resulted in bankruptcy.[171] The accounts of some of Anne Edmondson's nephews were closed only on 30 December 1911.[172] It took years to pay off the indebtedness and proved a handicap from which the company had not fully recovered when the First World War broke out.[173] Edmondson would not have regarded himself as extravagant, and would probably have seen himself as enjoying the simple things of life. However, he had expensive tastes and spent freely on those things which were important to him. He had very heavy expenditures in the few years prior to his death, building the Orwell Park house and acquiring the holiday home in Greystones. His household expenditure was particularly high in the months leading up to his wife's death.[174] The result was that this entrepreneur left the laundry, of which he was so proud, in a very parlous state. Luckily it recovered, but the new managing director, Robert Benson, and the other directors had a difficult task.

# CHAPTER EIGHT

# The Dublin Laundry after Thomas Edmondson

THE YEARS FROM the founder's death until the early 1920s were more difficult than the preceding twenty years. This was due to a number of factors within the company and to outside events over which the directors had no control. These included a series of strikes in Great Britain in 1910–12, the Dublin lockout of 1913, the 1916 rising, the First World War and the Anglo-Irish war from 1919 to 1921. Competition from new commercial laundries also increased over these years.

The balance sheet of the Dublin Laundry for the year ending 31 December 1907 shows the assets of the company as £54,039.17s.0d.[1] Since the founding of the original company it had been customary to place various sums in a general reserve fund each year instead of writing off depreciation on the property and the assets of the company. The managing director told the eighth AGM, held on 23 March 1909, that, while the general reserve was £15,000, 'the buildings and machinery stood in the books at the original sum paid for them'. The directors had decided during 1908, in the interests of the shareholders, to have a valuation made of the property and assets of the company by Messrs. James Adam and Sons. The result of this was that the whole of the general reserve had been absorbed to make the figures for machinery and buildings 'approximate to those certified by the valuers', which suggested that the depreciation was greater than the reserve fund. It was also proposed in future to depreciate the assets instead of placing the money in a reserve fund.[2] At the ninth AGM, held on 23 March 1910, the net profit for the year, after depreciation, was £1,972.12s.2d. A 5 per cent dividend on preference shares and an 8 per cent dividend on ordinary shares was proposed.[3] This is in sharp contrast to the early years of the new company, 1902–06, when a dividend of 20 to 25 per cent was paid on ordinary shares.[4] At the last AGM presided over by Thomas Edmondson, in 1907, the dividend on ordinary shares had dropped to 15 per cent.[5]

162

The uncertain position in which the company was placed by the deaths of Thomas Edmondson and his wife has been mentioned. In addition, Adams drew the attention of the directors to a matter which must have caused great concern. The power of the Dublin Laundry to sublet, sell or assign seemed to be withheld: it was withheld in the original lease, granted by Hogan to Robert Gibney and Son, and did not appear to be granted by the indenture of 11 October 1887 to the Dublin Laundry. The head landlords did not appear to have accepted the Laundry as their tenant, 'but to have simply exercised the right they had, under the lease of 1858, to approve of the assignee or subtenant of their own tenant, Gibney'. Adams concluded that the Laundry appeared to be in the very undesirable position that it could not sell its interest in the premises, 'and consequently, the undertaking connected therewith', without obtaining the permission of the head landlord representatives of Hogan. Such a condition seriously affected the realisable value of the company's property. It was pointed out that any valuation had to proceed on the assumption that the head landlords would not withhold their consent to a sale, if at any time the company wanted to sell.[6] As things happened, the company was not obliged to sell, and does not appear to have considered that option.

The Dartry Dye Works was a continual drain on the profits of the company. From 1911 the directors commenced to write off, as depreciation, £1,000 per year on the 15,000 shares which the company owned in Dartry, and on which no dividend had yet been paid.[7] This continued for the next two years.[8] At the AGM held on the 29 March 1916 Robert Benson said that it was 'found necessary to lend a further sum of £500 @ 5% to Dartry', and 'taking into consideration the poor results of this investment, the Directors propose writing it down by £500'.[9] Two thousand pounds was written off the Dartry investment in 1919 and a further £500 at the following two AGMs.[10] The company made continual loans to the Dye Works: in 1913 the Laundry loan to the Dartry Dye Works was £2,000, by 1923 the loan stood at £6,800.[11]

Building work at the Dublin Laundry continued in the early years of the new century. Plans for extending the office were approved by the Rathmines and Rathgar Urban Sanitary Authority in September 1904; plans were also approved, in January 1905, to build offices and make additions to the Dartry Dye Works.[12] Water closets were erected in Milltown the following year.[13] Between April 1908, which was after the death of Edmondson, and 1912, W. and A. Roberts was in constant communication with Benson about alterations and improvements to the Laundry; these included the enlargement of the board room.[14]

The company had extra expenses in 1912. There was a coal strike at the beginning of the year and the National Health Insurance Act of 1911 had added £78 to expenses for the second half of the year. Turnover for 1912 was only £7 lower than in 1911, but the gross profit was £760 less. The chairman told the meeting that, owing to the number of fires that had taken place in Dublin laundries, the directors thought it advisable to have automatic sprinklers installed throughout the building, involving heavy capital expenditure, but 'a fire in this old building would be disastrous'.[15] Things deteriorated further in 1913. Turnover for the year was slightly lower than in 1912, partly due to labour troubles and partly due to increased competition.[16] Dublin had five more commercial laundries in 1914 than in 1909.[17] As the cost of living had risen in recent years, the directors had 'felt it incumbent on them to increase the pay of many workers and felt it certain that other increases would have to be given'. The National Health Insurance Act added £156 to the wage account for 1913; £1,260 had been spent on the sprinkler system. As gross profit for the year was less than it had been for many years, the directors felt that they could not recommend a higher dividend than 6 per cent on ordinary shares.[18] In 1920 Benson told the secretary of the Meath Hospital: 'When the National Health Insurance Act was thrust upon us, we could do nothing but withdraw all our subs. to such like institutions. However, in view of your great kindness to a few of our employees who attended your Dispensary recently, we intend to break this hard and fast rule.' He sent a cheque for £2.2s.0d.[19]

In 1908 the two directors of the company were Robert Benson, who was also, of course, the managing director, and Charles Frederick Allen. Allen died in 1911, and Benson appointed Frederick C. Sharpe, a solicitor, of 16 College Green, and D. Edmondson Benson, his brother and long-time confidant of Thomas Edmondson, as directors.[20] During 1913 two senior members of staff retired, Mrs McCleery, manageress for many years, and Mrs Spenser, who had been with the company since 1888, and had originally come for a couple of weeks at the end of 1887 to seek contracts for the Dublin Laundry.[21]

The laundry trade in Dublin was not unionised until 1917, when the Irish Women Workers' Union was resuscitated by Louie Bennett.[22] This special union for women had been founded in 1911 after James Larkin expelled women from the Irish Transport and General Workers' Union (they were readmitted in 1918); Larkin was president and his sister Delia,

32. Robert Benson, managing director of the Dublin Laundry, 1908–47.

33. Davis Edmondson Benson, Robert's brother, proprietor of the Southport Laundry, became a director of the Dublin Laundry in 1911.

secretary. It collapsed during the rising of 1916.[23] In a letter to D.E. Benson in August 1917, Sidney Foster, the manager of the Dublin Laundry, said that, as far as he knew, the laundry workers of Dublin were not connected with any trade union. When he added that he had heard only that week, that the van men were either forming one or joining one and that all the Milltown men were involved,[24] he pinpointed accurately the coming of trade unionism to the laundry industry.

The formation of the Irish Trades Union Congress, modelled on the British Congress, in 1894, to which the Irish branches of the amalgamated unions gave their full support, was a big advance for Irish workers, but it left women and the unskilled unrepresented.[25] These were the two categories to which the majority of laundry workers belonged. It was the men, a small minority, who first joined the trade unions. Women were always more difficult to unionise; they were less militant, less politically aware, often unwanted by male trade unionists,[26] many worked part-time, and, if married, had child-care and other family commitments. In addition, women seemed to be more conscious of status and class distinctions, and were reluctant to enrol in unions with those they considered their inferiors. Mr Larkin 'could not for the life of him understand the meaning of the class distinctions existing, particularly among female workers . . . It was time these foolish ideas vanished from their midst because they were all brothers and sisters in one great army.'[27]

Laundry workers did get rid of those 'foolish ideas', and, through union membership, were to win important concessions from employers in the years to come, concessions which eventually benefited workers in other industries, men and women. When Louie Bennett took on the task of reorganising the Irish Women Workers' Union, she decided to start with the women in the printing trade. When they were organised, she turned her attention to the laundry workers. These two groups of workers, in printing and laundry work, became the two strongest sections in the union. (See Appendix, Figure 3.)[28] Louie Bennett could claim in 1919 that the IWWU had 'reduced the hours of the laundry workers by five and doubled their wages'.[29] By March 1918 she had achieved a guaranteed rate of 5s.6d a week for workers over fourteen, for a 50-hour week; 6s.6d for those over fifteen, 8s. over sixteen, and reaching a top rate of 16s. for those over twenty-one. Overtime rates were fixed at 5d per hour, and rates for piecework were also laid down. Later laundry workers won a guaranteed week, which meant that, if they were employed on the Monday, they must be employed and paid for the whole week. Previously they could be kept waiting in the workroom without work or wages.[30] Sidney Foster told James Musgrave of the Metropole Laundry, Cork, in 1918, that he thought it better that laundry workers should be unionised, as the alternative was a Trade Board, and a government-controlled industry. He added: 'I think it would pay you to get them organised, not in the Transport Union, but in the Irish Women Workers' Union which has a Laundry Section'.[31] He probably considered that this might cause fewer problems for employers, that it would be less militant, and that laundry workers were less likely to get involved in strikes by other workers.

In 1926 the Leinster Laundry Association, after a three-year struggle with the union, conceded a one-week holiday for laundresses.[32] However, the finest achievement of the laundry workers was to gain a fortnight's holiday with pay after a strike which lasted for fourteen weeks—from July to the end of September 1945. It was the first strike of laundry workers. The IWWU claimed that it was the pioneer of the tea-break system, when in 1955, an agreement with the laundries included a break of ten minutes in the morning and five in the afternoon for tea, if the working time exceeded four hours.[33]

General labour unrest was, however, widespread in England and Ireland long before laundry workers in Ireland were unionised. Strikes between 1889 and 1891, closely related to the London dock strike of 1889, provided an example to unskilled workers of the possibilities of trade union membership. Strikes in Dublin were unsuccessful, due primarily to the availability of alternative workers. Wages increased in Ireland in the years 1894–98, though, what were described as 'unprecedentedly high' rises occurring in England, did not apply to Dublin. A sixty-hour week was conceded in the 1860s for some groups of workers, and this fell to fifty-six or fifty-eight in the 1870s. In many cases no further reduction was made until the 1890s. By the end of that decade a fifty four-hour week was the norm. This was in stark contrast to the hours worked in the laundry business during these years. Wages remained virtually unchanged between 1900 and 1912. A further wave of labour unrest marked the years after 1905, much of it concerned with trade union membership and working practices; most disputes ended in victory for the employers.[34] The general unrest of these years included a strike by fourteen girls and two van men at the Pembroke Laundry.[35]

Wage stability ended in 1912–13 when the cost of living rose. This was when the Dublin Laundry considered it expedient to give a rise to the workers. Trade union militancy increased greatly, especially among unskilled workers,[36] causing considerable anxiety to employers, even to those not directly involved. Many were affected indirectly by increased costs and delays caused by strikes. The cost of coal for the Dublin Laundry rose by £480 in 1912 as a result of the coal strike in Britain at the beginning of that year, but as the strike had increased prices for all materials, the loss to the laundry was much higher.[37] In November 1911 a representative from the Day Time Registers in London could only hope to be in Dublin next week if 'strikes permitted'.[38] Inconvenience was caused during the 1913 strike when firms, such as the Edinburgh Roperie and Sailcloth Co. Ltd, could not deliver goods as railway companies in Scotland would not accept 'traffic' for Dublin.[39] Again, Pronk Davis of London and Birmingham could not deliver goods due to the strike, and sent '7lb of blue by post to keep you going for a little'.[40]

Disruption reached new heights that year. On May Day what was described as a 'small but representative' group of IWWU members including, among others, factory workers, shop assistants and typists, marched in Dublin for the first time: four months later strikes, demonstrations and riots became widespread in the capital.[41] A number of employers, headed by William Martin Murphy, combined to compel workers to withdraw from the Irish Transport and General Workers' Union or face dismissal. The ITGWU responded by calling out other workers, and by late September some 20,000 were on strike or locked out. The dispute was prolonged and bitter, and ended in defeat for the unions, though the ITGWU, the original target, survived.[42] One of the main reasons for the failure of the strikes was the hiring of alternative labour. A two-week strike of dockers in September 1899 was broken by the importation of 'scabs' from England: in 1900 a strike by dock and coal labourers ended when new workers were sought and English scabs used.[43] Intimidation and violence against scabs and blacklegs meant that, by 1911, employers found it more difficult to find replacements for striking workers; however, alternative labour was still available.[44] In November 1913 The Dublin Employers' Federation Ltd produced literature giving the employers' side of the labour troubles; a dozen copies of the statement were sent to the Dublin Laundry, saying that it would be useful to circulate 'across the water'.[45] The Federation was founded in 1908 to enable employers to engage, and provide housing and maintenance for workmen replacing employees on strike. The wages, travelling and other expenses could be paid from the assets of the Federation. It was also to 'promote the trade interests of the members of the Federation in and about the City of Dublin and its neighbourhood'.[46]

The First World War created great hardship for the Dublin Laundry, and its bad effects were felt almost immediately. From its outbreak in August 1914 there was a drop in turnover of about £30 a week, and the total turnover for the year was £1,255 below that of 1913. The cost of coal and other materials rose.[47] Laundry turnover for 1915 was £1,453 below that in 1913, and about £2,700 less than that in a normal year. On account of this poor performance, a tightening of credit and the high cost of fuel and materials, no dividend was paid on ordinary shares—the first time this ever occurred. Reasons given for the drop in turnover were: the large number of men wearing khaki shirts and collars, the lack of 'gaieties' and the general need for economy.[48] There was a slight rise in turnover in the following year, and a dividend of 1 per cent on ordinary shares was paid,[49] this was maintained in 1917, when another modest rise in turnover was recorded. During the war the Laundry held large stocks of materials in an effort to guard against future scarcities. In 1917 the stocks were valued at £2,635, nearly £2,000 more than those usually held in pre-war days.[50] Turnover for 1918, the last year of the war, was £25,180, £4,982 over that in the previous year. This was due mainly to an increase in charges necessitated by rising wages and the high cost of fuel, materials and fodder. The chairman stated at the AGM held on the 25 March 1919 that: 'Demands for increased wages and shorter hours are constantly being made on us by the unions, and there seems to be no finality about them'.[51]

The war, of course, caused great problems for all laundries in Great Britain and Ireland. At the half-yearly meeting of the Council of the National Federation of Laundry Associations Ltd on 10 November 1914 it was stated that, 'unfortunately all Laundrymen were more or less in difficulties'; washing for troops helped to make up to a certain extent for the loss of ordinary custom, but a workable scheme for 'handling this class of work' had not yet been devised. It deplored what it called 'an epidemic of Price Cutting', and said it was a 'mistaken policy of the gravest kind'.[52] As early as September 1914, Robert Benson was asked by the Dublin Employers' Federation what financial arrangements he had made for the assistance of the dependants of employees 'called to the colours'.[53] In December the editor of *The Laundry Record* asked the management of the Dublin Laundry for its views on the outlook for the industry in Ireland for 1915. Their reply said that most laundries in Ireland had already suffered a considerable loss in turnover, and feared an increasing one as long as the war lasted. The falling off was greatest in the shirts and collars department, which was the backbone of the industry. The shortage of men, heavy taxes and there being no festivities, meant that 'the outlook for 1915 is not a rosy one'.[54]

The complaint about the shortage of men indicates that many employees of Irish laundries enlisted early in the war. In December 1914 a collection was made from staff and employees in the Dublin Laundry so that 'their soldiers, viz. the Royal Dublin Fusiliers, who have done such excellent work at the front, should not go short of their "much loved fag" at Xmas . . . the magnificent sum of £10 was realized.' This allowed the purchase of 22,000 cigarettes. Packages were specially made up with a card enclosed bearing the words: 'Good luck and a safe return, from the Staff and employees of the D.L.C.'. *The Laundry Record* was asked to include this item in its next edition.[55] In September 1915 Benson received a letter from the City and County of Dublin Recruiting Committee: 'We are anxious to get all the principal Employers of Dublin City and County, to undertake to reinstate any of their staff, as far as possible, on their return from the War.' It was felt that, if this were done, 'many men who are now hanging back will come forward'. A stamped, addressed post card was enclosed, and Benson was asked if his name could be added to the list. He agreed.[56] In Britain men were taken from industry for the armed forces and restrictions on the employment of women were abolished.[57] This opened fresh avenues for female labour, many offering higher wages than those paid in the laundry industry and thus posing great difficulties for British laundries. This was not a problem experienced by the Dublin Laundry, nor indeed by Irish laundries. Again, after the war, there were complaints in Britain, that the laundry industry 'lent, something like 150,000 women to the Government for munition work', and when they were discharged they were given an 'unemployment wage of 25s. These women would not return to work as long as this benefit lasts; they have plainly refused to do so.' It was said that they should have got a bonus or gratuity in proportion to the time they had served, instead of a 'positive premium on laziness', 'while their work in laundries and other industries awaits them, they are idling and amusing themselves'.[58]

The war added enormously to the day-to-day difficulties of running a laundry. From October 1914 the reduction in business meant that the management at the Dublin Laundry was struggling 'to keep all our big staff going, so as to prevent any increase of unemployment'.[59] By January 1916 the manager admitted that they had reduced staff in all departments.[60] By March of that year they had to refuse to quote for contract work. Materials were so expensive and so difficult to obtain that they had to conserve stocks for their existing customers.[61] The manageress of the Dolphin Hotel was told that they could not make a reduction in the cost of laundry work. Wages had increased in the last few weeks and 'the enormous and still rising prices for materials "make the lot of all Laundries an unenviable one"'. Benson went on to say that, if he were making the contract with the hotel today, he would be compelled to charge 8s.4d per 100 items, and that these increased prices did not cover the increased expenditure. His shareholders were suffering from lack of dividends. He did not want Mrs Nugent's directors to think 'that we are out for "war profits", but are simply carrying on for the time being'.[62]

There were continual complaints about the difficulty of getting coal and the poor quality of that obtained. The manager said in 1916, of the poor quality of anthracite and slack, we are 'compelled to take anything the merchants send us, or they refuse to deliver at all'.[63] The difficulty in obtaining coal worsened as the war continued. One effect of this was that, in order to conserve their own fuel, the public sent washing to the laundries which they had hitherto done at home.[64] Statistics on the consumption of coal, slack, breeze and anthracite and on the stock of each held had to be sent to the Coal Controller, at 19 Westmoreland Street, regularly; yet another piece of paperwork engendered by the war.[65] In 1918 the boiler in the Dublin Laundry was shut down on Friday nights to save fuel.[66] Foster was part of a delegation to the Coal Controller in July/August, 'we think it necessary to keep the position of the Laundry Industry before him all the time'.[67] That summer the management had to apply for a licence to purchase liquid ammonia.[68] They also wrote to the Ministry of Munitions of War for a 'repairs and maintenance' permit, saying that they had cut their repairs to the lowest possible limit, but now several matters, such as machinery and lift repairs, were absolutely necessary. It even became necessary to apply for a permit to buy matches.[69]

Obtaining a sufficient supply of petrol for the motor vans also became an issue during the war. In May 1917, when applying for a new licence to the Petrol Control Committee of the Board of Trade in London, the manager of the Dublin Laundry complained that they had originally applied for 390 gallons per month, 'an honest estimate of our bare necessities'; they were allowed 258, with the result that two of the four vans were idle and they were compelled to give up a lot of country work, and to reduce staff. He said they understood that a reduction was absolutely necessary, and were willing to accept this, 'but it is extremely annoying to business people doing their best to keep industries going under very difficult circumstances, to see private cars and motor bicycles going about'.[70] The appeal was to no avail, and the ration was reduced by a third. The manager reminded the committee that the laundry had made a case for a higher allowance in 1916, because, when the government took some of their 'best horses' for Army purposes, the laundry was unable to replace them and had to purchased two more vans. He said that other laundries, competing with them, were given an average of sixty to eighty gallons per motor, while they were getting only forty-three. The Dublin Laundry was one of the oldest established laundries in Dublin and employed up to 300 people; the situation was most unfair and he demanded an explanation.[71] He probably did not get one, because a committee for the control of petrol in Ireland was set up the following week. Foster made an immediate application to this committee for a new licence, saying that they were badly treated by the London committee, but they were granted only 172 gallons, instead of the 390 requested. He asked for an interview.[72] The Dublin Laundry was informed by the Petrol Control Committee (Ireland) that they would be issued with a free-of-all duty licence for the purchase of 1,320 gallons of motor spirit, not more than 220 gallons to be purchased in each month. On 20 December 1917 the manager wrote to the London committee complaining that they had not yet received the licence, and that, if they did not receive petrol within the next day or two, there would be a 'stoppage of our works'.[73] By October 1918 he was writing to the Petrol Control Department in Dublin Castle, requesting 400 gallons of motor spirit a month instead of the 220 which they were then getting and which were 'quite inadequate'.[74]

The difficulty in obtaining petrol led in to a certain rationalisation of country work between the Dublin Laundry and the Manor Mill. In October 1916 the manager of the former wrote to Messrs Edmondson and Co. about the Wicklow work, saying: 'we think if the two collections could be merged into one it would pay, with two going and double expenses, there can be nothing for either'.[75] Agreement was reached whereby the Dublin Laundry transferred its customers in Wicklow to the Manor Mill for £35, and the Manor Mill's customers in Kildare were transferred to the Dublin Laundry. Both undertook not to take customers in each other's territory for five years.[76] The feud between the two appears to have ceased, though letters exchanged were very formal. The Pittsburgh Survey of 1909 was critical of the fact that no attempt was made by the laundrymen's association to 'district' that city, which would have led to 'great savings re drivers and agencies'.[77] The same charge could have been made in Dublin, where each laundry sought customers in all parts of the city, and in many of the same suburbs and more distant regions. It took a World War to force two Dublin laundries to introduce even a modest rationalisation.

Again in 1918 there was a problem for laundries when a licence to buy rice starch was required and no other type was available. Foster, as president of the laundry association, wrote to the Royal Commission on Wheat Supplies in London, pointing out that this placed all laundries working the 'boiled starch process', for which only corn and wheat starches could be used, at a disadvantage as compared with those using the 'cold water process', for which rice starch was suitable. The modern plant used for the former was different from that used for the latter, and would necessitate an entirely new plant, which would be 'unobtainable today'. The spectres of a large number of unemployed women and great inconvenience to the general public were again raised. A few days later, Foster was offered sweet potato starch, and ordered ten tons.[78]

As well as all the difficulties posed during the war by the scarcity of fuel and materials, the Laundry had to cope with other problems. Their premises at 2 Upper Sackville Street were damaged during the 1916 Rising.[79] They were affected, as were hundreds of other businesses, by the bad influenza outbreak of 1918. The manager said in October that they were 'full of flu', eighty workers were out one week and only three regular drivers out of twelve were available for work. He had to spend that week on the washing machines.[80] Neither did life return to normal after the armistice. Scarcities continued into the post-war period, the cost of materials remained high and the cost of labour was increasing further.[81] The Anglo-Irish war caused disruption. In 1920, having sought in vain to recruit staff in England, Benson decided to advertise again, saying: 'but I fear we will not get anyone to come to Ireland these days'.[82] The turnover was 'very greatly affected by the Curfew, which ensured that everyone had to be in his own home by nine o'clock in the evening'; this meant that there were no 'entertainments' nor dining out, and consequently few stiff shirts and dress collars.[83]

The antagonism between the commercial laundries and the institutions flared up again when the introduction of a trade board for the laundry industry was mooted. In 1916 pressure was exerted in Parliament by the Irish MPs to have trade boards established in Ireland. A commissioner from the Ministry of Labour, who was making a preliminary investigation, called on the manager of the Dublin Laundry, who was also president of the Leinster Laundry Association. Foster said the association would be compelled to oppose any board being established unless large numbers of charitable institutions were included. If this were not done, it would mean closing down a big industry employing a large number of workers, which Ireland could not afford to allow to happen. The commissioner's reply was that this was 'unthinkable'. He was asked how he proposed including them 'as these people would bamboozle you every time'. The answer was: 'the Labour Party is so strong that the old fear of the Church, even in Ireland, is gone'. His confidence in the power of the Labour Party would appear to have been overrated, as the manager heard nothing further from him.[84]

The first trade boards, also known as joint boards or wages boards, developed in the second half of the nineteenth century. They were committees of conciliation and arbitration for the regulation of hours of work and wages between masters and men. The first statutory trade boards, as opposed to these voluntary ones, developed, not from those already established in the more highly organised industries, but as a consequence of the bad conditions in the 'sweated' industries. It was to deal expressly with wages in the ready-made and wholesale bespoke tailoring business, in paper-box-making, machine-made lace, net finishing and chain-making, that the first Trade Boards Bill of 1909 was passed, establishing trade boards for each of these industries. In addition, the Act empowered the Board of Trade to apply it to other trades where they considered wages to be 'exceptionally low' compared with those in other industries. In 1918 an amendment to the Act of 1909 changed the *raison d'être* of a trade board, from one in which very low wages obtained, to one where 'no adequate machinery for the effective regulation of wages' existed. This widening of the scope of the Act, together with the stimulus of the war, increased the number of trade boards, so that by the end of 1922 there was a total in the United Kingdom of sixty-three, covering thirty-nine trades, governing the wages of about three million workers.[85]

A Trade Board for the laundry business was established in England in November 1919, and this was followed by the Laundry Trade Board (Ireland) in the following year. Irish employers, as Foster said, wished to have the question of the institution laundries settled before a trade board was established. To assist them in this, an effort was made on behalf of the Leinster Laundry Association in 1919 to establish the exact number of institutional laundries catering for the public. A letter was sent to laundry suppliers in England, asking them for the names of the institution laundries with which they did business, and saying that the information was required by the Ministry of Labour. Later it was admitted by the Association that they themselves also wanted a list of these establishments. Not surprisingly, only some, including Armstrong and Co. Ltd, complied with this request.[86] In June 1920 Foster wrote to J.J. Stark of the Federation of Laundry Associations, to whom a report of the first meeting of the Laundry Trade Board (Ireland) had been sent by Robert Benson, remarking 'you will have noted we are fighting the old, old fight against the "Institution Laundries"'. He reported that a special subcommittee had been formed to devise some means of bringing the institutions into line with the commercial laundries, and it was to meet on the following Tuesday, 13 June. Foster said: 'We fear it is only ploughing sand but, as the labour representatives are solid with us on this point, we may make some progress.'

At the first board meeting, it was stated that there were 119 commercial laundries (excluding hotel laundries) in Ireland, and only twenty-three institution laundries—to show, according to Foster, how little effect they had. He said that those statistics were certainly incorrect, that there were definitely not more than eighty of the former and probably as great a number of the institutional laundries, but that it was extremely difficult to get exact figures. He assumed that the numbers quoted were Board of Trade figures, and said that Benson thought that Stark might be able to find out how the figures were arrived at, and also the number of people employed in institutional laundries.[87] In this Stark was not successful. A 'flat wage' rate of 32s. a week was set by the trade board, and this was carried in spite of the opposition of the employers who asked for an adjournment, so that they could place the whole situation before the members of the several laundry associations. The Leinster Association decided to withdraw from the trade board unless the institution question were settled: it was hoped that the Ulster and the Munster Association would support them. The Workers' Union (Eng.) representatives, on behalf of the Belfast workers, had all the information on the English Trade Board's offer of 35s. and 30s, and this influenced the Irish members very much. The question of a lower rate for Ireland, because the cost of living was lower, was held to be no longer true; living in Ireland, especially in cities such as Dublin, was considered to be more expensive than in England and Scotland. Even the employers present agreed to the case made by the union representatives on this point. However, Foster maintained that the laundry workers in Dublin were, on the whole, satisfied with the present rate of 27s.6d for forty-eight hours. It was the executive of the unions who were 'attempting to force the pace'. Foster wrote to Stark: 'You have to bear in mind that the revolutionary spirit over here is well developed among the Labour union Executive. They are openly Bolshevik, and out to do away with the Capitalist class and arguments of any sort are useless'. He added that, if the trade boards failed, the unions would 'naturally put in a very much higher claim and threaten strikes etc.'—'between high prices, and the Institution Laundries grabbing all the work "the lot of the Irish Laundries is not a happy one"'.[88]

At the adjourned meeting of the trade board on 16 June 1920, the rate of 32s. was rejected by the employers, as one they could not pay nor even consider, until the institution question was finally settled. They did not move from this position, and the meeting was adjourned again, this time for a month. The employers assured the labour representatives that they were not just playing for time, and that as soon as matters were sorted out regarding the institutions, they would settle rates and these agreed rates could come into force, and would not be prejudiced by the delay. It was then decided that the special committee elected to deal with the institution question would meet in Belfast in July. The institutions were represented by a Father Lawrence. It was agreed at that meeting that the secretary of the Board of Trade and Fr Lawrence would arrange to hold a conference of representatives of all the religious orders running laundries in competition with the commercial laundries, to be held at High Park Convent, Dublin on 4 August. Foster expected that meeting to provide a settlement. He thought that the institution laundries would agree to charge the current prices charged by the commercial laundries in their districts, with a concession of one penny in the shilling. If there were no agreement, the proprietors intended proposing to the Trade Board (Ireland) that it should recommend that all laundries, including institution laundries, and whether run for purpose of gain or not, should be included in the 48 hour (Government) Bill, and that all such laundries should be subject to inspection in exactly the same way as commercial laundries. Labour would support any such recommendations to government on those lines.[89]

At the 4 August meeting Foster's expectations were not realised, and the institutions refused to have anything to do with the trade board. The chairman proposed to fix rates, an action endorsed by the labour representatives. The employers objected, and were urged by the chairman to withdraw and give the matter further consideration. 'As an act of courtesy' they did. When they returned to the meeting they handed in the following statement:

> The employers' representatives are of the opinion that as no means exist for dealing with the unfair competition of the Institutions, the Laundry Industry is an unsuitable one for administration by a Trade Board and that such a Board should never have been set up. They regret they cannot take any further part in the deliberations of the Board, which is unable to deal with the industry as a whole.

After the withdrawal of the employers, some business was 'ardently transacted', and 32s. was fixed for time workers. The labour representatives were reputed to have spoken very strongly to Fr Lawrence, and said that the institution laundries were 'a menace to Labour', and that they would have to take some action independently. Sidney Foster expected that the commercial laundries would now receive a demand from the union and would 'have to fight it out with them'. He expected the Munster and the Leinster Association to be in agreement about future policy, but that 'Ulster, who never looks at things from "the whole Industry" point of view have already offered settlement to the Workers' Union

(Eng.)'.[90] In a letter to J.J. Stark of the Federation of Laundry Associations, on 3 September 1920, he said that the employers would lodge their objection to the wages fixed by the trade board at the Conference of the Laundry Proprietors of Ireland to be held the following week. The Irish Transport and General Workers Union had lodged the expected claim for laundry workers, an increase of 20s. for men and 10s. for women and proportionate increases for juniors.[91] Benson was to remark in September 1922 that 'perhaps we would have done better for ourselves under the Trade Board'.[92]

Robert Benson had had a ten-year apprenticeship for the position of managing director of the Dublin Laundry when his kinsman, friend and mentor died in 1908. Robert was to spend more than twice as long in that position as Thomas Edmondson. He seems to have run the laundry very much in the tradition established by the founder. The organisation appears to have remained the same, and he delegated responsibility as Edmondson had done before him. When describing the role of H.V. McCleery, he said that McCleery was 'more of an engineer than a manager, though called a "manager"'. His mother, Mrs McCleery, 'had control of the workers and the organisation of different departments, and I dealt with any matters of particular importance'.[93] He was not in the powerful position of the Edmondsons, while he was a major shareholder, he shared that position with Thomas's nieces, Margaret and Alice Edmondson. Also, as has been seen, he had many difficulties to contend with from those caused by the deaths of his predecessor and his wife, to those resulting from a World War and the birth of a new state. He steered the company safely through this turbulent period and, in due course, handed over the reins to his son Ernest.

Like Edmondson, Benson served the community, becoming chairman of the Rathmines Urban Council—as he said himself, 'the highest position in the power of Rathmines to bestow'. In acknowledging the congratulations of W.H. Mellon of the Leinster Laundries Association on his re-election, he said his only regret was that it took so much of his time, and prevented his taking as active a part as he would like in the association.[94] In 1918 the Council elected him to represent them at the annual meeting of the Association of Municipal Authorities of Ireland on 10 and 11 September. He was unable to accept as he was speaking at the Conference of Laundry Proprietors of Ireland in Belfast on those dates.[95] He was, like Edmondson before him, involved in the School of Commerce in Rathmines, now a beautiful new school which was opened in 1913.[96] He also took on, temporarily, the position of honorary

34. Ernest Edmondson Benson, managing director of the Dublin Laundry, 1947–73.

35. David Edmondson Benson, managing director of the Dublin Laundry, 1973–83.

secretary of the Rathmines War Savings Committee, which he had to give up due to lack of time.[97]

Benson continued to play his part in furthering and developing the interests of the laundry trade, and much of his time seemed to be divided between this and his community responsibilities. He wrote a paper, dealing 'largely with the question of research' to be given at the Irish Federation of Laundry Associations' Congress in Cork in September 1919.[98] He could not attend himself, as he had an important Council meeting, so the paper was read by his younger son, and his brother D.E. Edmondson, dealt with 'any remarks thereon'; Foster, as the official representing the Leinster Association, was also present.[99] He was obviously using his experience on the British Launderers' Research Association Council, which he helped to establish and of which he was a member for many years. He went to London several times a year for meetings. His expenses for attending a meeting on 15 November 1921, were £4.11s.7d, for a third-class fare from Dublin to London and expenses, 'necessitating absence for one night, of £1.1s.0d'. In a note attached to the expenses, he wrote, 'really takes 3 days to go to meeting unless one travels on 2 successive nights—too much'.[100] The return journey must have been tiring for a man of his years. Robert was succeeded on the Council by his son Ernest, and, later, by his grandson David, who was vice chairman when the Research Association celebrated its fiftieth anniversary.[101]

Benson felt just as strongly about what he perceived as the unfair trading methods of the institutions as Thomas Edmondson. In October 1916 he complained bitterly that the institutions refused to add a percentage charge to their customers, even though they admitted that extra revenue was necessary; they preferred to appeal to their co-religionists to assist them. At a time when every commercial laundry in Dublin added a 10 per cent increase, the institutions kept their prices at the old rate, hoping, according to Benson, to attract 'work from other places'. Most of the commercial laundries had now added a further charge to meet the increase in wages which the high cost of living had rendered necessary. He accused the institutions of competing unfairly against the wage-paying establishments, of contributing nothing to the state from income tax, insurance or in any other way, and of 'narrowing down the chances of employment for honest girls'. He was not, he said, referring to institutions of any particular denomination.[102]

The immediate post-war years and the early 1920s was not a good time for the laundry trade in Great Britain and Ireland. Laundries were considered to be in a state of crisis. Several in England were closing,[103] as were some Irish laundries; Foster told the proprietor of the Metropole Laundry in Cork, at the end of October 1918, that another unassociated laundry was 'shutting down' that week.[104] 'The present crisis in the Laundry industry' was a topic at the conference of laundries held in Cork in 1920. Benson was asked to open the discussion, and said that he would probably advocate 'the amalgamation of one or two laundries so as to fill one'. He sought advice on how this might be done without 'any money passing', as few laundrymen had any large sums of cash to buy another establishment. He suggested that it might be done by mutual agreement.[105] There is no evidence that this proposal received any support. The Dublin Laundry was asked whether they would purchase the laundry in Portlaw in 1919. They declined, saying that 'labour difficulties were much too annoying to attempt to run a laundry as far away from Head Office and furthermore, there is no encouragement these days to extend one's activities'.[106]

In Ireland, the war of independence, the trade boards, the recalcitrant institution laundries and the emergence of a unionised work force, compounded the problems. The turnover of the Dublin Laundry for 1922 was £30,202.12s.4d, a reduction of £2,898.8s.0d from 1921. This was blamed on disturbances in July, which resulted in the burning down of the Gresham and other hotels, the dislocation of communications and general upset in the country. The departure of the military force had also affected business, especially in the Curragh and Kildare districts.[107] The turnover for 1921 had been slightly lower than that for the previous year due to a lowering of prices from the beginning of November in an obvious attempt to increase business; though wages remained 'at the high level reached in 1920 and there seems no immediate hope of a reduction'.[108] The net profit for 1922 was £2,784.15s.8d, which must be contrasted with a net profit of £4,873.14s.4d, achieved in 1907.[109]

At the beginning of the 1920s there were approximately 150 workers in the Dublin Laundry, half the number employed there in 1900 (see ch.5). Almost one-sixth of the staff was male, a higher proportion than in the earlier days. Albert Pierce was still the highest paid, at 77s.6d per week, six other men earned 65s. or more, and five earned 50s.; boys were paid 12s.6d–14s.6d. The highest paid woman of the waged staff earned 36s. per week; eighty-six women earned 30s. to 35s.; while one girl got 10s. a week; the usual minimum wage paid to females was 12s.6d–14s.6d. There were twenty piece workers earning approximately £1.12s.0d–£2.10s.0d a week.[110]

War, political unrest, worker unrest and increased competition had changed the outlook for commercial laundries dramatically since the heady days in the 1890s and the early 1900s. However, laundries were fighting to recover lost business and attract new customers. With higher overheads and increased wages, efficiency assumed a greater importance. In an effort to price piecework more accurately, the Leinster Laundry Association had the full range of articles sent to a laundry—from plain aprons and pillow cases to tennis skirts and hunting breeches—hand-ironed by workers in different laundries to determine the time taken by an 'ordinary' or 'average' worker.[111] Laundries outside Leinster were also involved. Management also sought to abolish a bonus system which they considered encouraged 'slackers'.[112]

Ways were sought to popularise laundries and to bring them within the reach of more households. Methods known as 'rough dry' and 'semi-finished', where clothes were washed and dried or finished by machine only, were introduced in the early 1920s. The main aim was to encourage the housewife to send the heavier part of the washing, which she now did at home, to the laundry.[113] The Dublin Laundry had introduced a form of 'semi-finished' in the autumn of 1922, when a new department for doing work at 3s.6d for 12lb of clothes and ironing it by machine instead of hand, was started.[114]

Laundries were still an important part of everyday living in the 1920s, and the main factors which brought about their eventual demise, the ubiquitous domestic washing machine and man-made fabrics, were in the future. Although shades of what that future might hold arose at the Dublin Laundry AGM on 22 March 1928. The chairman said: 'Increasing use of artificial silk in the manufacture of ladies' garments affects the Laundry industry—not only because clothes are worn for a longer period, but in many instances, they are washed at home.'[115] While the number of commercial laundries decreased somewhat over the next decades, the situation remained quite stable. There were sixteen in Dublin in 1924 and fifteen in 1951, with very few changes.[116] The Manor Mill closed in 1942.[117] The Dublin Laundry bought the leasehold of the Kenilworth Laundry, subject to a yearly rent of £65, from Roger Webb in 1923. They also bought the movable machinery, fittings, furniture, horses, vans, harness and 'goodwill of the business of a laundry'. They stipulated that 'the vendor was not to carry on, manage or be engaged or interested directly or indirectly in the trade or business of a laundry either alone, in partnership or agent, for a term of ten years from the completion of the purchase, within thirty miles from the City of Dublin'. The vendor and his son were to use 'their best endeavours' to induce the customers, including the Standard Hotel, to continue their custom to the purchaser. Roger Webb was paid £1,600.[118]

From the mid-1920s the fortunes of the Dublin Laundry seemed to improve, although the coal strike in England in 1926, the effects of which were still felt in 1927, adversely affected it.[119] In 1926 the Dartry Dye Works repaid £600 of the loan made to them by the laundry a few years earlier, leaving a sum due by them of £6,000. In 1927 £2,500 was repaid, and the remainder was paid the following year.[120] The business of the Dye Works improved immensely during the Second World War.[121] In 1939, Dartry paid a dividend of £1,453.2s.6d, and £69.18s.11d commission, to the Dublin Laundry.[122] At the AGM held on 25 March 1925, Benson announced a profit of £2,183.14s.7d, and said that the turnover, at £34,493.12s.2d, was the highest figure reached yet. The wages bill, at £16,479, was also a record. A dividend of 5 per cent was paid on ordinary shares, up 1 per cent on 1923 and 2 per cent on 1922.[123]

In 1928 the company's architect advised that it would be necessary to spend a considerable sum in a few years in rebuilding a large portion of the laundry, and possibly reconstructing the whole place. The directors decided that it would be advisable to accumulate a large reserve to meet this expenditure.[124] During 1929 £1,856.7s.0d was placed on reserve towards this fund. A new building for 'flat finish' was erected at a cost of £1,613.11s.11d, additional machinery for this room and elsewhere cost £1,110.11s.3d. The 'head' rent for the premises was purchased from the trustees of William C. Hogan for a sum, including the cost of transfer, of £1,791.15s.1d. This greatly increased the value of the premises and removed the uncertainty to which Adams had drawn attention in 1908 (see above).[125] In 1930 '£850 was paid off the amount standing on deposit in the books of the Company, leaving £2,169 still owing out of the £14,345 on deposit on 31 December 1908', the year of Thomas Edmondson's death.[126] There had been vast improvements in the laundry machinery—enabling a reduction in the number of workers—as well as an improvement in methods over the years. In a letter to J.J. Stark in 1921, Benson asked: 'Do you read London Opinion? They, like so many others, have not yet realised the fact that modern Laundry methods are not unnecessarily destructive to linen. Some day perhaps, the laundry "joke" will be buried in the same plot as the "Mother-in-law joke"'.[127]

The Dublin Laundry lost Sidney Foster, manager for many years, when he left Milltown and Ireland at the end of 1921. The staff and employees of the laundry entertained him 'to tea and an excellent concert' on 23 November. During the evening, Mr Pierce, 'in a neat and appropriate speech' presented him with a silver rose bowl in the form of an ancient Irish potato ring, and wished him well in his future career.[128] Pierce himself, wash house foreman since 1892,[129] retired on pension in 1928.[130]

During 1947 Robert Benson completed fifty years with the Laundry, having been MD since 1908 and chairman since 1912. In a tribute paid to him at the AGM in 1948, it was pointed out that the annual turnover had grown in that period from £23,000 to the then figure of £63,000, and that the business had changed from a predominantly manual one to one 'principally machine operated'. 'The fact, that despite expansion, the business still retains a lot of the family atmosphere is, in no small measure, due to the influence and personality of Mr Benson.'[131] Perhaps the last part of this tribute gave most pleasure to the man, who contributed enormously to the development of the laundry for over half of its long life. He retired in 1947, but continued to act as chairman and 'to give the Board and Company the benefit of his lifelong experience in the Industry'. He died in July 1949.[132]

# *Notes*

## *Abbreviations*

NAI    National Archives of Ireland
NLI    National Library of Ireland
GSIR    Good Shepherd Ireland
T.E.    Thomas Edmondson
R.B.    Robert Benson
D.L.    Dublin Laundry
HC    House of Commons [Papers]
*IT*    *The Irish Times*
*FJ*    *The Freeman's Journal*

## *Primary Sources*

*National Archives of Ireland*
Enumerators' returns for the censuses of 1901 and 1911.
Dub.56: Records of the Dublin Laundry Co. Ltd; all cited materials are located there
    Wills.

*National Library of Ireland*
Commission of Vocational Organisation: typescript copy of the minutes of evidence
    and memoranda submitted to the Commission, including printed items in
    twenty volumes, 1939–40, Mss 922–41.
Griffith's Primary Valuation.

*Valuation Offices, Irish Life Centre*
Cancelled books, townland of Milltown, ED Rathmines, St. Peter's parish.
Cancelled books, townland of Rathmines South, ED Rathmines, St. Peter's parish.
Cancelled books, townland of Churchtown Lower, Taney parish.

*Repository of Quaker Records, Swanbrook House, Donnybrook, Dublin.*
Beale file.
Edmondson family records.
Notice of Interments, 1772–1870.
Mountmellick and Dublin marriage registers.

*Friends' House, Euston Road, London*
*Annual Monitor.*
*Directory of Quaker Biography.*

183

*Dublin City Archives*
Reports and Printed Documents of the City of Dublin.
Reports of the Public Health Committee.
Minutes of the Rathmines and Rathgar Urban District Council.

*Good Shepherd Convent, Clare Street, Limerick*
Archive of the Good Shepherd order.

## Introduction

1 Kelly's *Post Office London Directory*; laundries appeared under other headings in the directories.
2 Patricia P. Malcolmson, 'Laundresses and the Laundry Trade in Victorian England', *Social Studies* 24 (1980–81), pp. 440–1.
3 *Thom's Directory*, 1865, 1888, 1905, 1916. The interesting thing is that the number of laundresses in Dublin city and county dropped in each successive census, from 3,222 in 1881 to 2069 in 1911. This could be explained, to an extent, by a reduction in the number of washerwomen working on their own account in their own homes or in the houses of the better off. Changes in the age profile of the laundresses would appear to substantiate this. In 1881 53.5 per cent were over forty years of age, this had fallen to 41.7 per cent in 1901 and to 23 per cent over forty-five in 1911 (there was a change of age groupings in that census, *Cen. Ire.* 1881 to 1911). Commercial laundries tended to employ young girls and young married women. The growth of commercial laundries also increased the number of men employed in the trade, though it was always a predominately female occupation. The number of women employed in laundry work was almost certainly greater than that recorded in censuses as many working women were simply returned as housewives. Also, laundry work was seasonal, and the end of March, beginning of April, when the census was taken, was a low season when many part-time workers were laid off.
4 Mary E. Daly, *Dublin the Deposed Capital* (Cork: Cork University Press, 1984), p. 118.
5 Malcolmson, 'Laundresses and the Laundry Trade', p. 442.
6 Joanna Bourke, *Husbandry to Housewifery* (New York: Oxford University Press, 1993), p. 218.
7 Ibid., p. 225.
8 Ibid.
9 Ibid., p .243.
10 Mona Hearn, *Below Stairs* (Dublin: Lilliput Press, 1993), p. 31.
11 Dub. 56, Misc. V19, 'The Side the Sun's Upon', p. 4 (a booklet produced by the Dublin Laundry in 1894).
12 John Holohan, 'The History of Donnybrook', lecture to the Rathmines, Ranelagh and Rathgar Historical Society, 21 March 2002.
13 Revd C.J. M'Cready, *Dublin Street Names*, Dated and Explained (Blackrock: Carrig Books, 1998), p. 139.
14 Eamonn Mac Thomais, 'Seven Hills of Dublin', *Dublin Historical Record*, 23, p. 94.
15 Mairin Johnston, *Around the Banks of Pimlico* (Dublin: Attic Press, 1985), p. 27.
16 *Report of the commissioners appointed to inquire into the working of the factory and workshop acts with a view to their consolidation and amendment* [C. 1443–1], HC 1876, XXX, Vol.II. pp. 890, 894.

17 Kevin C. Kearns, *Dublin Tenement Life* (Dublin: Gill and Macmillan, 1994), pp. 6, 9, 20.
18 Pauline Gregg, *A Social and Economic History of Britain 1760–1955* (London: Harrap, 1960), p. 200.
19 Audrey Woods, *Dublin Outsiders* (Dublin: Farmar, 1998), pp. 135–7.
20 Reports and Printed Documents of the City of Dublin [RPDCD], Report of the Public Health Committee [PHC], 1881, No. 190.
21 RPDCD, PHC, 1882, Vol.III, No.267, and Appendix to the Report, pp. 378–80.
22 Ibid., Report of the PHC, 1884, Vol.II, No.66, pp. 2–3.
23 Ibid., Report of the PHC, 1885, Vol.III, No.136, p. 36.
24 Ibid., Report of the PHC, 1888, No.58. Corporation of Dublin By-Laws for the Management, Use and Regulation of the Public Baths and Wash-houses, Tara St., pp. 475–88.
25 Ibid., Report of the State of Public Health during 1890, 1891, Vol.III, p. 68.
26 Ibid., Report of the State of Public Health during 1890, 1891, Vol.III, No.124, Table 1.
27 Ibid., Minutes of the Municipal Council, 1900, p. 284; 1905, p. 414; 1914, p. 170.
28 Samuel Pepys, Diary, 4 April 1666.
29 Cunnington, C. Willet and Phillis, and Charles Beard, *A Dictionary of English Costume 900–1900* (London: A. & C. Black, 1976), p. 56.
30 Samuel and Sarah Adams, *The Complete Servant* (Lewes: Southover Press, 1989), p. 106.
31 Hearn, *Below Stairs*, p. 23.
32 Isabella Beeton, *The Book of Household Management* (London: Ward, n.d.), p. 1044.
33 Ibid., *Mrs. Beeton's Cookery Book* (London/Melbourne: Ward, Lock, 1912), p. 23.
34 Beatrice Bayley-Butler, 'Lady Arabella Denny', *Dublin Historical Record*, 9 (1946–48), pp. 9–10.
35 Association of Charities, *Dublin Charities* (Dublin: Association of Dublin Charities, n.d.), p. 156.
36 Ibid., pp. 152–3.
37 Ibid., p. 152.
38 Ibid., p. 155.
39 Ibid., p. 162.
40 Catriona Clear, *Nuns in Nineteenth Century Ireland* (Dublin: Gill and Macmillan, 1987), p. 106.
41 Mark Girouard, *Life in the English Country House* (Harmondsworth: Penguin Books, 1980), pp. 283–4.
42 Ibid., p. 284.
43 *The Laundry at Castleward* (National Trust).
44 Hearn, *Below Stairs*, p. 70.
45 Malcolmson, 'Laundresses and the Laundry Trade', p .440.
46 G. Cadogan Rothery and H.O. Edmonds, *The Modern Laundry, Its Construction, Equipment and Management* (London: Gresham Publishing, 1909), Vol.1, p. 7.
47 *Rathmines News*, 30 May 1896.
48 Gregg, *Social and Economic History*, pp. 124–6.
49 Ibid., p. 463.
50 *Report of the commissioners appointed to inquire into the working of the factory and workshop acts with a view to their consolidation and amendment* [C 1443–1], HC 1876, XXX, Vol.II, p. 890.
51 Gregg, *Social and Economic History*, p. 464.
52 Ibid., p. 470.

## 1. The Founding of the Dublin Laundry

1  *Dictionary of National Biography.*
2  Jane Benson, *Quaker Pioneers in Russia* (London: Headley Bros., 1902), pp. 23–33, 77–80, 103, 106; Dub.56, Misc. V19, press notices for the book (Headley Bros., 1903, 4 pp.).
3  *Dictionary of Quaker Biography*, Friends House, Euston Rd, London.
4  JB, *From the Lune to the Neva* (London: Saml. Harris, 1879), 'Opinions of the Press', p. 2.
5  *Dictionary of National Biography* [DNB].
6  Press notices for *Quaker Pioneers in Russia.*
7  Dub.56, Misc. V19, Correspondence Out [hereafter: Corr. Out], letters from Headley Bros. to Jane Benson concerning *Quaker Pioneers in Russia*, 6 June 1902, 18 June 1903, 12 Nov. 1903: from Jane Benson's son to Headley, 18 Dec. 1901: acknowledgement on behalf of the Czar.
8  JB, *From the Lune to the Neva*, 'Opinions of the Press', pp. 3–4.
9  *DNB.*
10 Harriet Martineau, 'The English Passport System', *Household Words*, 131, 25 Sept., 1852, pp. 31–4.
11 *DNB.*
12 Corr. Out, 17 June 1880–5 Nov. 1883, T.E. to Cole, 25 May 1882.
13 Martineau, 'English Passport System', p. 34.
14 *Thom's Directory*, 1852.
15 Martineau, 'English Passport System', p. 32.
16 Swanbrook House, Donneybrook, Dublin, Port. 53a, A–F, E II.
17 'Thomas Edmondson', *The Friend*, 1908, New Series, 48, p. 1182.
18 *Thom's Directory*, 1862.
19 Swanbrook House, Port. 53a, A–F, E I.
20 Ibid., MM VIII A 10, Cork 27, 1839–1861.
21 Maurice J. Wigham, *The Irish Quakers* (Dublin: Historical Committee of the Religious Society of Friends in Ireland, 1992), p. 60.
22 Ibid., p .84.
23 Swanbrook House, Mountmellick and Dublin Marriage Register.
24 *Thom's Directory*, 1870.
25 Swanbrook House, Cork Marriage Register to 1859.
26 Ibid., Beale, Fanny, Port 22, No. 62.
27 Ibid., MM VIII A 10, Cork 27, 1839–61.
28 Sr. Katherine Butler, 'Friends in Dublin', *Dublin Historical Record*, 44, p. 34.
29 Wigham, *The Irish Quakers*, p. 15.
30 Butler, 'Friends in Dublin', pp. 34–5.
31 Wigham, *Irish Quakers*, p. 15.
32 Ibid., p. 13.
33 Ibid, p. 15.
34 Butler, 'Friends in Dublin', p .34.
35 Wigham, *Irish Quakers*, p. 40.

36 Ibid., p. 44.
37 Corr. Out, 2 Feb. 1895–26 Apr. 1900, T.E. to Bentley, 2 Oct. 1896.
38 Wigham, *Irish Quakers*, p. 46.
39 Paul H. Wilken, *Entrepreneurialship: A Comparative and Historical Study* (Norwood, NJ: Ablex Publishing, 1979), pp. 12–14.
40 Thos. H. Mason, 'Dublin Opticians and Instrument Makers', *Dublin Historical Record*, 6, 1943–44, p. 148.
41 Wigham, *Irish Quakers*, p. 36.
42 Swanbrook House, Dublin MM Proceedings 1877–94; P.M. Dub. III A3.
43 NLI, *Christian Discipline in the Society of Friends, Ireland 1881*, Rules and Discipline of Dublin Yearly Meeting: Revised Rules of the Society—to come into force First of Ninth Month 1881.
44 Wigham, *Irish Quakers*, pp. 37, 53.
45 *DNB*.
46 *Thom's Directory*, 1871.
47 Swanbrook House, 'The Edmondsons of England' file.
48 Corr. Out, 17 June 1880–5 Nov. 1883, T.E. to Huldah, 20 Apr. 1881.
49 *Thom's Directory*, 1877.
50 Corr. Out, 17 June 1880–5 Nov. 1883, T.E. to Huldah, 20 Apr. 1881.
51 Ibid, T.E. to Huldah, 24 Aug. 1883.
52 Ibid, T.E. to Huldah, 14 June 1882.
53 Ibid., T.E. to Huldah, 24 Aug. 1883.
54 Ibid., T.E. to Huldah, 27 Sept. 1882.
55 Ibid., T.E. to Mrs Moran, 29 Dec. 1882.
56 Ibid., T.E. to Huldah, 24 Nov. 1882.
57 Ibid., T.E. to Roberts, 17 July 1880.
58 Ibid., T.E. to tradesman, July 1882.
59 Ibid., T.E. to Blandford, 18 Aug. 1881.
60 Ibid., T.E. to Huldah, 24 Aug. 1883.
61 Ibid., T.E. to Moore, 27, 30 Jan. 1882.
62 Ibid., T.E. to Drury, 16 Jan. 1882.
63 Ibid., T.E. to Moore, 13 Sept. 1881.
64 Ibid., T.E. to Moore, 30 Nov. 1881.
65 Ibid., T.E. to Moore, 27 Jan. 1882.
66 Wigham, *Irish Quakers*, p. 60.
67 Corr. Out, 17 June 1880–5 Nov. 1883, T.E. to solicitor, 7 Feb. 1882.
68 Ibid., T.E. to Messrs Gilltrap and Roberts, 18 Feb. 1882.
69 Ibid., T.E. to Moore, 20 March 1882.
70 Ibid., T.E. to Moore, 27 July 1882.
71 Ibid., T.E. to cousin, 14 Aug. 1882.
72 Ibid., T.E. to Moore, 12, 16 Feb. 1883.
73 Ibid., T.E. to Drury, 16 Jan. 1882; T.E. to O'Toole, 1 June 1883.
74 Ibid., T.E to Millar and Richard, 20 Feb. 1882.
75 Corr. Out, 15 Feb. 1887–13 Dec. 1887, T.E. to Sinden, 29 July 1887.
76 Ibid., 21 Nov. 1887–14 May 1890, T.E. to Machinery Supplier, 13 Apr. 1889.
77 Ibid., 15 Feb. 1887–13 Dec. 1887, T.E. to Hogan, 29 July 1887.
78 Ibid., T.E. to Sinden, 27 July 1887.
79 Ibid., T.E. to McAdam, 16 March 1887.
80 Ibid., T.E. to Manager *Irish Times*, 15 Aug. 1887.
81 Ibid., T.E. to McAdam, 1 Sept. 1887.

82 Ibid., T.E. to Bradford, 22 March 1887.
83 Ibid., T.E. to Gibney, 17 March 1887, and letter a few days later, n.d.
84 Ibid., T.E. to Harvey, 3, 14 May 1887; T.E. to Cole, 5 May, 17 June 1887.
85 Ibid., T.E. to Gibney, 26 Apr. 1887.
86 Dub.56, First Annual Report of the Dublin Laundry Co. Ltd, for 1888, Corr. Out, 15 Feb. 1887–13 Dec. 1887, T.E. to West, Cardiff, 16 Sept. 1887.
87 Corr. Out, 15 Feb. 1887–13 Dec. 1887, T.E. to Charlotte Edmondson, 15 June 1887: T.E. to Roberts, 15 June 1887.
88 First Annual Report.
89 Dub.56, Dublin Laundry Co. Ltd, Inventory and Valuation 1908, James Adam and Sons, 17 Merrion Row, Dublin, p. 1.
90 Corr. Out, 15 Feb. 1887–13 Dec. 1887, T.E. to Woods, 21 Oct. 1887.
91 First Annual Report.
92 Corr. Out, 15 Feb. 1887–13 Dec. 1887, T.E. to C. Edmondson, 15 June 1887.
93 Ibid., 17 June 1880–5 Dec. 1883, T.E. to Roberts, 24 July 1880.
94 Ibid., 2 Nov. 1887–14 May 1890, T.E. to Spenser, 10 Dec. 1887.
95 Ibid., 15 Feb. 1887–13 Dec. 1887, T.E to Hogan, 29 July 1887.
96 G. Cadogan Rothery and H.O. Edmonds, *The Modern Laundry, Its Construction, Equipment and Management* (London: Gresham Publishing, 1909), vol.2, p. 173.
97 Central Statistics Office, Central Bank of Ireland Forecast (Databank, Code CPAQ001).
98 Corr. Out, 15 Feb. 1887–13 Dec. 1887, T.E. to Bradford, 22 March 1887.
99 Ibid., T.E. to Chandler, 4 Aug. 1887; T.E. to Nottingham firm, 4 Aug. 1887.
100 Wigham, *Irish Quakers*, p. 143.
101 Corr. Out, 15 Feb. 1887–13 Dec. 1887, T.E. to West, 16 Sept. 1887.
102 Ibid., T.E. to Bradford, 16 Sept. 1887.
103 Ibid., T.E. to Wright, 24 Oct. 1887.
104 Ibid., T.E. to Broadbent, 16 Sept. 1887.
105 Ibid., T.E. to Birmingham firm, 22 Sept. 1887.
106 *Rathmines News*, 30 May 1896, advertisement for Manor Mill Laundry.
107 Dublin Laundry Co. Ltd, Issue of £750 in 6 per cent Debentures, Lynton, Dundrum, 6th of Sixth month 1887, Dub. 56, Corr. Out, 15 Feb. 1887–13 Dec. 1887, T.E. to Goodbody,17 Aug. 1887; T.E to Frank (Roberts), 13 Oct. 1887.
108 Swanbrook House, MM II F4, pp. 197–9.
109 Ibid., Notice of Interments 1772–1870.
110 Corr. Out, 15 Feb. 1887–13 Dec. 1887, T.E. to Fred, 15 June 1887.
111 Dub.56, Articles of Association of the Dublin Laundry Co. Ltd, p. 4.
112 Corr. Out, 15 Feb. 1887–13 Dec. 1887, T.E. to Goodbody, 1 Oct. 1887; T.E. to Frank, 13 Oct. 1887.
113 Ibid., T.E. to Wood, 21 Oct. 1887.
114 Ibid., 31 Oct. 1887.
115 Ibid., T.E. to McAdam, 16 Mar. 1887.
116 Ibid., T.E. to McAdam, 1 Sept. 1887.
117 Ibid., 2 Nov. 1887–14 May 1890, T.E to Roberts, 13 Dec. 1887.
118 Ibid., 15 Feb. 1887–13 Dec. 1887, T.E. to McAdam, 16 Mar. 1887.
119 Ibid., T.E. to Armstrong, 6 Oct. 1887.
120 First Annual Report.
121 Corr. Out, 15 Feb. 1887–13 Dec. 1887, T.E. to Alliance Gas, 3 Aug. 1887.

122 Ibid., T.E. to Alliance Gas, 18 Oct. 1887.
123 Ibid., T.E. to Heiton, 4 Nov. 1887.
124 Ibid., T.E. to Greenbank, 5 Aug. 1887.
125 Ibid., T.E. to company engineer, 19 Nov. 1887.
126 Ibid., T.E. to Enamel Co., Wolverhampton, 17, 30 Sept. 1887.
127 Ibid., T.E. to contractors, 22 Sept., 7 Dec. 1887.
128 Ibid., T.E. to Wood, 2 Nov. 1887.
129 Ibid., T.E. to Central Hotel, 18 Nov. 1887.
130 Ibid, 2 Nov. 1887–14 May 1890, T.E. to Bottomly, 28 Nov. 1887.
131 Ibid., T.E. to telephone company, 13 Dec. 1887.
132 Ibid., 15 Mar. 1890.
133 Ibid., 15 Feb. 1887–13 Dec. 1887, T.E. to *Thom's*, 14 Oct. 1887.
134 Ibid., T.E. to Nevins, 30 Sept. 1887.
135 Interview with David Benson, 19 June 1995.
136 Corr. Out, 15 Feb. 1887–13 Dec. 1887, T.E. to contractor, 8 Nov. 1887.
137 Ibid., 21 Nov. 1887–11 May 1890, T.E. to Spencer, 10 Dec. 1887.
138 Ibid., 15 Feb. 1887–13 Dec. 1887., T.E. to Smyth, 22 Nov. 1887.
139 Ibid., reference for Lizzie Sproule, 31 May 1887.
140 Ibid., 21 Nov. 1887–11 May 1890, T.E.'s 'note for bearer', for Mrs Walsh, when she was seeking orders for Dublin Laundry, Dec. 1887 (p. 46).
141 Ibid., T.E. to Butler, 14 Jan. 1888.
142 Ibid., T.E. to Lady Cloncurry, 24 Sept. 1888.
143 Ibid., 15 Feb. 188713 Dec. 1887, T.E. to West, 16 Sept. 1887.
144 Ibid., T.E. to Armstrong, 21 Sept. 1887.
145 Ibid., T.E. to Wood, 21 Oct. 1887.
146 Ibid., T.E. to Central Hotel, 18 Nov. 1887.
147 Ibid., T.E. to McAdam, 27 Apr. 1887.
148 Ibid., 21 Nov. 1887–14 May 1890, T.E. to Roberts, 22, 24 Nov. 1887.
149 Ibid., T.E. to Alliance Gas, 22 Nov. 1887.
150 Ibid., T.E. to Pim, 8 Dec. 1887.
151 Ibid., T.E. to Wood, 24 Dec. 1887.
152 Ibid., T.E. to Mayhew, 2 Feb. 1888.
153 Ibid., T.E to *Freeman's Journal* and *Daily Express*, 24 Dec. 1887.
154 Ibid., T.E. to Spencer, 10 Dec. 1887.
155 Ibid., T.E. to Roberts, 10 Jan. 1888.
156 Dub.56, Minute Book, General Meeting of Shareholders, 12 Jan. 1888.
157 Corr. Out, 21 Nov. 1887–13 Dec. 1890, T.E. to Goodbody, 6 Mar. 1888.
158 Ibid., T.E . to Mamma (Roberts), 7 Mar. 1888; T.E. to Cousin Bessie, 8 Mar. 1888.
159 Ibid., T.E. to Wood, 20 Mar. 1888; T.E. to Williams, 27 Apr. 1888.
160 Articles of Association of the Dublin Laundry, p.4.

## 2. *The Early Days at the Dublin Laundry*

1 First Annual Report of Dublin Laundry, for 1888.
2 Dub. 56, Misc. V19, Dublin Laundry, 'Success: A Story of Twelve Years' (1900), p. 2.
3 Dub. 56, Corr. Out, 21 Nov. 1887–14 May 1890, T.E. to Cousin Bessie, 8 Mar. 1888.

4  Dublin Laundry, 'Success', p. 2.
5  Corr. Out, 21 Nov. 1887–14 May 1890, T.E. to Goodbody, 6 Mar. 1888.
6  Ibid., T.E. to Armstrong, 22 Feb. 1889.
7  Dub. 56, Minute Book, Weekly Receipts from 23 Jan. 1888.
8  Corr. Out, 21 Nov. 1887–14 May 1890, T.E. to Mamma, 7 Mar. 1888.
9  Ibid., T.E. to Cousin Bessie, 8 Mar. 1888.
10 Ibid., T.E. to Davis, 6 Apr. 1888.
11 Ibid., T.E. to McGeough Home, 7 Apr. 1888.
12 Ibid., T.E. to Wood, 21 Apr. 1888.
13 Maurice J. Wigham, *The Irish Quakers* (Dublin: Historical Committee of the Religious Society of Friends in Ireland, 1992), p. 13.
14 Corr. Out, 21 Nov. 1887–14 May 1890, T.E. to the editor of *Laundry Journal*, 27 June 1888.
15 Ibid., T.E. to Wood, 17 Aug. 1888.
16 Ibid., T.E. to unknown, 16 Feb. 1889, p. 571.
17 Ibid., T.E. to *IT*, 14 Feb. 1888.
18 Ibid., T.E. to *IT*, 7 Apr. 1888.
19 Ibid., p. 275.
20 Ibid., T.E. to the editors of *Laundry Journal* and *Laundry News*, 27 June 1888.
21 Ibid., T.E. to Butler and to Lamb, 23 Mar. 1888.
22 Ibid., T.E. to Wood, 6, 21 Apr. 1888.
23 Ibid., T.E. to Ward & Co., 7 Apr. 1888.
24 Ibid., T.E. to advertising company., 4 Feb. 1890.
25 Dublin Laundry, 'The Side the Sun's Upon' (Dublin, 1894), pp. 13, 15.
26 Corr. Out, Book 3, 18 Jan. 1895–11 Feb. 1898, T.E. to Registrar Horse Show, 10 July 1896.
27 Corr. Out, 21 Nov. 1887–14 May 1890, T.E. to Spencer, 10 Dec. 1887, 11 Jan. 1888.
28 Ibid., 'The bearer, Mrs Walsh', p. 46.
29 Ibid., T.E. to Todd Burns, 28 Apr. 1888.
30 Ibid., T.E. to Arnotts, 11 July 1888.
31 Ibid., T.E. to Shelbourne Hotel, 26 May 1888.
32 Ibid., T.E. to Philpon, 26 May 1888.
33 Ibid., T.E. to Tomlinson, 28 Apr. 1888.
34 Ibid., T.E. to Bewley, 4 May 1888.
35 Ibid., T.E. to Davis, 28 July 1888.
36 Ibid., T.E. to United Service Club, 29 Sept. 1888.
37 Ibid., T.E. to Lady Cloncurry, 24 Sept. 1888.
38 Ibid., T.E. to Campbell, 15 Nov. 1888, 13 Dec. 1888.
39 Ibid., T.E. to President Officers' Mess, 10 Dec. 1889.
40 Ibid., T.E. to Somerville, 21 Dec. 1889.
41 Ibid., T.E. to President Officers' Mess, 7 Jan. 1890.
42 Ibid., T.E. to Commander–in–Chief, 20 Feb. 1890.
43 Ibid., T.E. to Willmott, 10 Mar. 1890.
44 Ibid., T.E. to secretary, Dublin Mercantile Association, 29 Mar. 1890.
45 Ibid., T.E. to anon., 10 Apr. 1888, p. 250; T.E. to Royal Bank, 13 Apr. 1888.
46 Ibid., T.E. to Armstrong, 21 Feb. 1889.
47 Ibid., T.E. to Central Hotel, 19 Jan. 1889.
48 Ibid., T.E. to business associate, 20 June 1889.
49 Ibid., T.E. to Ball, 17 Apr. 1890.

50  Ibid., T.E. to Austin, 23 Mar. 1888.
51  Ibid., T.E. to Goodbody, 5 Apr. 1888: letters to three girls in May, pp. 300–1.
52  Ibid., T.E. to Lilley, 22 May 1888.
53  Ibid., T.E. to Waring, 17 Mar. 1888.
54  Ibid., T.E. to Robinson, 13 June 1889.
55  Ibid., T.E. to Armstrong, 16 Aug. 1889.
56  Ibid., T.E. to Jacob, 4 Mar. 1889.
57  Ibid., T.E. to Waring, 17 Nov. 1888.
58  Corr. Out, Book 1, 14 May 1890–20 Aug. 1892, T.E. to Williams, 17 Jan. 1891.
59  Corr. Out, 17 June 1880–5 Nov. 1883, T.E. to Dietrich, 2 Dec. 1882.
60  Ibid., 21 Nov. 1887–14 May 1900, T.E. to Waring, 9 Apr. 1889.
61  Ibid., T.E. to Mrs A., 24 Nov. 1888.
62  Ibid., T.E. to Armstrong, 15 Apr., 6 May 1889.
63  Ibid., T.E. to Haughton, 12 Apr. 1889.
64  Corr. Out, Book 3, 18 Jan. 1895–4 Feb. 1898, T.E. to Benson, 1 May 1895.
65  Corr. In, Box 4, Goode to T.E., 7 Mar. 1896.
66  Corr. Out, 21 Nov. 1887–14 May 1890, T.E. to Williams, 26 Apr. 1888.
67  Ibid., T.E. to West, 5 May 1888.
68  Ibid., T.E. to Wood, 17 Aug. 1888.
69  Ibid., T.E. to Walpole, 3, 10 Jan. 1889.
70  Ibid., T.E. to Mooney, 28 Mar. 1889.
71  Ibid., Draft advertisement, ? mid-May 1889, p. 702.
72  Ibid., T.E. to Robinson, 13 June 1889.
73  Ibid., T.E. to Ruscoe, 19 June 1889.
74  Ibid., T.E. to Baker, 20 June 1889.
75  Ibid., T.E. to Dixon, 22 June 1889.
76  Ibid., T.E. to Dixon, 2 July 1889.
77  Ibid., T.E. to Armstrong, 1 Jan. 1890; draft advertisement, p. 894.
78  Ibid., T.E. to Ruscoe, 19 June 1889.
79  Ibid., T.E. to Armstrong, 19 Apr. 1890: draft advertisement, p. 996.
80  'The Side the Sun's Upon', pp. 16–17.
81  Ibid., p. 18.
82  G. Cadogan Rothery and H.O. Edmonds, *The Modern Laundry, Its Construction, Equipment and Management* (London: Gresham Publishing, 1909), vol.1, p. 254.
83  Dublin Laundry, 'The Side the Sun's Upon', p. 21.
84  Elizabeth Butler, *Women and the Trades: The Pittsburgh Survey* (New York: Charities Publication Committee, 1909), p. 165.
85  Ibid., pp. 176, 362.
86  Dublin Laundry, 'The Side the Sun's Upon', p. 21.
87  Ibid., pp. 22, 24, 26.
88  Ibid., pp. 18, 27.
89  Ibid., p. 18.
90  Rothery and Edmonds, *The Modern Laundry*, vol.1, p. 8.
91  Corr. Out, 21 Nov. 1887–14 May 1890, T.E. to Knight, 27 Dec. 1888.
92  Ibid., T.E. to Holmes, 27 June 1889.
93  Ibid., T.E. to Sparrow, 8 June 1888.
94  Minute Book, Second Annual Report of the Dublin Laundry Co. Ltd for 1889.
95  Dub.56, 256 Share Ledger: Dublin Laundry Co., 1888–1900, p. 1.
96  Minute Book, Third AGM, 10 Mar. 1891.
97  Minute Book, EGM of the Dublin Laundry Co. Ltd.

98 Dub.56, 256, Share Ledger, pp. 1–2.
99 Minute Book, Fifth AGM of the Dublin Laundry Co. Ltd., 28 Feb. 1893.
100 Dub.56, Dublin Laundry Co. Ltd, Balance Sheets, 1888–1936: Profit and Loss Account for year ending 31 Dec. 1894.
101 Minute Book, Seventh AGM of the Dublin Laundry, held at 5 South Anne Street, 20 Apr. 1895.
102 Dublin Laundry, 'Success', p. 2.

## 3. Milltown

1 Interview with David Benson, 19 June 1995.
2 Jim Nolan, *The Changing Face of Dundrum* (Dublin: Dundrum Books, 1993), p. 59.
3 John Taylor, *Map of the Environs of Dublin . . . by Actual Survey* (Dublin, 1816).
4 Joseph Archer, *Statistical Survey of the County Dublin* (Dublin, 1801), pp. 203–9.
5 Francis Elrington Ball, *History of the County Dublin* (Dublin: Alex. Thom, 1903), vol.2, p. 110.
6 Ibid., p. 112.
7 Cancelled books, townland of Milltown, ED Rathmines, St. Peter's Parish (Valuation Office, Irish Life Centre).
8 Dub.56, Corr. Out, Book 3, 18 Jan. 1895–11 Feb. 1898, T.E. to Taylor, *Rathmines News*, 31 Dec. 1895.
9 'South Dublin Industries', *Rathmines News and Dublin Lantern*, 25 Jan. 1896, p. 2.
10 Cancelled books, townland of Rathmines South, ED Rathmines, St. Peter's Parish.
11 Cancelled books, townland of Churchtown Lower, Taney Parish.
12 Ball, *History of the County Dublin*, vol.2, pp. 112–13.
13 Revd Myles V. Ronan, *An Apostle of Catholic Dublin* (Dublin: Richview Press, 1944), p. 98.
14 Ball, *History of the County Dublin*, p. 112.
15 Peter Costello, *Dublin Churches* (Dublin: Gill and Macmillan, 1989), p. 146.
16 Ibid., p. 146.
17 Ronan, *An Apostle*, pp. 98–9.
18 Revd Michael G. Murphy, 'The Story of Milltown', 'A Section of Many Parishes' in *Blessing and Dedication of the Church of the Immaculate Virgin Mary of the Miraculous Medal, Clonskeagh, 8 September 1957*.
19 *Thom's Directory* 1888.
20 'Pre–Danish Dublin Village Will Vanish Soon', *IT*, 1 Sept. 1955.
21 Interview with D. Benson, 19 June 1995.
22 Griffith's Primary Valuation for Co. Dublin : Barony of Uppercross, pp. 54–5.
23 Reports and Printed Documents of the City of Dublin [RPDCD], Report of the Housing Committee to Dublin City Council, 1951, No.141, pp. 344–6.
24 'Pre–Danish Dublin Village'.
25 Peter Pearson, *Between the Mountains and the Sea* (Dublin: O'Brien Press, 1998), p. 348.
26 *Thom's Directory* 1888.
27 Séamus Ó Maitiú, *Rathmines Township, 1847–1930* (Dublin: Rathmines Senior College, Rathmines, 1997), pp. 9, 25.
28 Michael H. Coote (ed.), *A Short History of Taney Parish* (Dublin: Select Vestry, Taney Parish, 1968), p. 41.
29 Nolan, *Changing Face of Dundrum*, p. 40.

30 *Gratis, Dublin, Wicklow and Wexford Railway, Arrangements of Trains*, 1 August 1870.
31 Douglas Bennett, *Encyclopaedia of Dublin* (Dublin: Gill and Macmillan, 1991), p. 138.
32 *Centenary Year. Short History of Milltown Park. The Irish Province. First Dublin Residence, 1814–1914* (Dublin: O'Brien and Ards, 1914), p. 12.
33 Murphy, 'The Story of Milltown'.
34 *Thom's Directory* 1888.
35 'Pre-Danish Dublin Village'.
36 Mary E. Daly, *Dublin the Deposed Capital* (Cork: Cork University Press, 1984), pp. 172–4.
37 Corr. Out, 21 Nov. 1887–14 May 1890, T.E. to Mamma, 7 Mar. 1888.
38 Nolan, *Changing Face of Dundrum*, p. 83.
39 *Thom's Directory*, 1888.
40 Corr. Out, Box 8–9, 12 Oct. 1923–31 Dec. 1924, secretary of Dublin Laundry to Quinn, 3 Nov. 1923.
41 Ibid., Book 4, 12 Feb. 1898–16 March 1900, T.E. to Dixon, 20 Oct. 1898.
42 Ibid., Book 6, 9 Oct. 1905–15 Nov. 1907, T.E. to Collen, Co. Surveyor, 15 May 1905, 29 Dec. 1905.
43 Ibid., Book 1, 14 May 1890–20 Aug. 1892, T.E. to Head Constable, Dundrum, 18 Aug. 1891.
44 Ibid., Book 5, 11 Nov. 1902–7 Oct. 1905, T.E. to Superintendent of Police, 26 Aug. 1903.
45 Ibid., T.E. to Inspector of Police, RIC., 29 Apr. 1903.
46 Corr. In, Box 28, Ryan to T.E., 29 May 1904.
47 Corr. Out, Book 6, 9 Oct. 1905–15 Nov. 1907, T.E. to Winder, 13 Nov. 1905.
48 Corr. In, Box 28, District Inspector, RIC. to T.E., 14 Nov. 1905.
49 *Rathmines News* (18 Apr. 1896), p. 3.
50 Interview with D. Benson, 19 June 1995.
51 Corr. Out, 28 May 1903–21 Dec. 1905, T.E. to Perry, 4 Sept. 1903.
52 NAI, Census 1901, Dublin 62/62.
53 Ibid., Dublin 90/20.
54 Census 1911, Dublin 60/101, 89/8, 89/9.
55 Ibid., 1911, Dublin 89/7.
56 Ibid., 1911, Dublin 60/101.
57 Ibid., 1911, Dublin 89/3.
58 Corr. In, Box 28, Rathmines Urban District Council to Manager Dublin Laundry, 18 Jan. 1913.
59 Corr. Out, 2 Sept. 1898–19 Nov. 1898, T.E. to Dixon, 20 Oct. 1898.
60 Census, 1911, Dublin 60/101.
61 Ibid., Dublin 89/9.
62 Ibid., Dublin 89/7.

## 4. *Working Conditions in the Laundry Industry*

1 G. Cadogan Rothery and H.O. Edmonds, *The Modern Laundry, Its Construction, Equipment and Management* (London: Gresham Publishing, 1909), vol.1, pp. 4–5.
2 Ibid., p. 6.
3 Fabian Society, 'Life in the Laundry', Tract No.112 (London: 1902), p. 11.

4 Margaret MacDonald, 'Report on Enquiries into Conditions of Work in Laundries', Ellen Mappen, *Helping Women at Work. The Women's Industrial Council, 1889–1914* (London: Hutchinson/The Explorations in Feminism Collective, 1985), p. 80.

5 Fabian Society, 'Life in the Laundry', p. 12.

6 Ibid., p 4.

7 *Reports of Inspectors of factories as to hours of work and dangerous machinery in laundries and to their sanitary condition* [C 7418], HC 1894, XXI, 709 p. 714.

8 Ibid., p. 712.

9 Ibid.

10 Margaret Forster, *Hidden Lives: a Family Memoir* (London: Viking, 1995), p. 228.

11 É. Zola, *L'Assommoir* (Penguin Books), p. 151.

12 Interview with Aggie McGattachy (aged 92), 20 June 1996.

13 Dub.56, Corr. Out, Book 7, 7 Nov. 1922–11 Oct. 1923, manager to Donnelly, 24 Sept. 1923.

14 Rothery and. Edmonds, *The Modern Laundry*, vol.1, pp. 253–7.

15 Corr. Out, Book 1, 14 May 1890–20 Aug. 1892, T.E. to Manning, 14 Feb. 1891.

16 Ibid., Book 3, 18 Jan. 1895–4 Feb. 1898, T.E. to Benson, 23 Mar., 1 May 1895.

17 Interview with John McKinney, former manager of Kelso, 8 May 1996.

18 Butler, Elizabeth, *Women and the Trades: The Pittsburgh Survey* (New York: Charities Publication Committee, 1909), pp. 178–80, 82.

19 Corr. In, Box 30, Gibson, Lloyd and Co. Ltd, to D.L., 4 June 1915.

20 Hilda Martindale, *From One Generation to Another* (London: Allen and Unwin, 1944), p. 93.

21 Corr. Out, Book 3, 18 Jan. 1895–4 Feb. 1898, D.L. to Bellhouse, 9 Dec. 1897.

22 Ibid., R.B. to Bellhouse, 17 Dec., 1897.

23 Ibid., 11 Feb. 1898.

24 Ibid., Book 4, 12 Feb. 1898–16 March 1900, D.L. to Moore, 5 Mar. 1898.

25 Ibid., Book 5, 21 March 1900–11 Nov. 1902, D.L. to secretary, Patriotic Assurance, Accident Form, 26 Dec. 1901.

26 Ibid., D.L. to Ocean Accident Guarantee Corporation, Accident Form, 14 Jan. 1901.

27 Ibid., Book 4, 12 Feb. 1898–16 Mar. 1900, T.E. to Ocean Accident, 8 June 1899.

28 Ibid., Book 5, 21 Mar. 1900–11 Nov. 1902, T.E. to Metropolitan Laundry, 28 Feb. 1901.

29 Ibid., D.L. to Ocean Accident, 31 Jan. 1901, 10 Apr. 1901.

30 Ibid., D.L. to Ocean Accident, 28 May 1902.

31 'Law and the Laundry', *Nineteenth Century* (Feb. 1897), p. 224.

32 Butler, *Women and the Trades*, pp. 180, 360–1.

33 Ibid., p. 361.

34 Fabian Society, 'Life in the Laundry', pp. 7–8.

35 MacDonald, 'Report on Enquiries into Conditions of Work', p. 12.

36 Ibid., pp. 79–80.

37 Dublin Laundry, 'The Side the Sun's Upon' (Dublin, 1894), p. 26.

38 Ibid., 'Success: A Story of Twelve Years' (Dublin, 1900), pp. 11–12.

39 *Reports of Inspectors of factories* [C 7418], HC 1894, XXI, 709, pp. 711–12.

40 Fabian Society, 'Life in the Laundry', p. 6.

41 Corr. Out, 21 Nov. 1887–14 May 1890, T.E. to Haughton, 12 Apr. 1889.

42 Interviews with former workers: Mrs Moran (10 May 1996); Essie Nolan and Aggie McGattachy (20 June 1996).

43 Corr. Out, Book 4, 12 Feb. 1898–16 Mar. 1900, T.E. to B. Haughton, 30 Dec. 1898.
44 Ibid., Book 5, 11 Nov. 1902–7 Oct. 1905, T.E. to Smith, 26 June 1905; Corr. In, Box 4, Hampson to T.E., 29 Jan. 1897.
45 Corr. Out, 21 Nov. 1887–14 May 1890, T.E. to Robinson, 13 June 1889.
46 *Lady of the House* (13 Feb. 1893), p. 8.
47 Corr. Out, 21 July 1900–26 May 1903, T.E. to Williams, 21 Sept. 1900.
48 Ibid., Book 2, 21 Aug. 1892–17 Jan. 1895, T.E. to Jones, 20, 23, 27 Sept. 1892.
49 Ibid., Private Book, 23 Oct. 1919–17 Aug. 1920, R.B. to Jackson, 3 Apr. 1920.
50 Interview with G. Benson, 8 May 1996.
51 Corr. Out, 21 Nov. 1887–14 May 1890, T.E. to Waring, 17 Nov. 1888.
52 Dub.56/2, No. 4, Workmen's Account Book, 18 Jan. 1890–6 June 1890.
53 Corr. Out, Book 5, 21 Mar. 1900–11 Nov. 1902; testimonial for A. Pierce, p. 502.
54 Daly, Mary E., *Dublin the Deposed Capital* (Cork: Cork University Press, 1984), p. 67.
55 Ibid., p. 70.
56 Ibid., p. 67.
57 Mary Jones, *The Obstreperous Lassies* (Dublin: Gill and Macmillan, 1988), pp. 2, 7–8.
58 Ibid., p. 8.
59 Hearn, M., *Below Stairs* (Dublin: Lilliput Press, 1993), pp. 48, 51.
60 Ibid., p. 55.
61 Fox, R.M., *Louie Bennett* (Dublin: Talbot Press, 1957), p. 68.
62 Ibid., p. 43.
63 Ibid., p. 66.
64 Corr. Out, Book 2, 21 Aug. 1892–17 Jan. 1895, T.E. to Lady M. Hamilton, 15 Nov. 1893.
65 Malcolmson, Patricia P., 'Laundresses and the Laundry Trade in Victorian England', *Social Studies*, 24 (1980–81), p. 447.
66 Daly, *Dublin, the Deposed Capital*, p. 68.
67 Corr. Out, Book 1, 14 May 1890–20 Aug. 1892, T.E. to Mrs McCleery, 2, 9, 22 Dec. 1891.
68 Ibid., 2 Feb. 1895– 26 Apr. 1900, T.E. to Sullivan, 10 May 1899.
69 Tony Farmar, *Ordinary Lives* (Dublin: A. & A. Farmar, 1995), p. 22.
70 Corr. Out, Inside Letter Book, 3 Sept. 1909–3 July 1912, D.L. to Launders Mutual Insurance Co. Ltd, 11 Nov. 1909.
71 Second Annual Report of the Dublin Laundry for 1889: Third AGM, 10 Mar. 1891.
72 Dub.56, 258 Ledger 1898–1903, Wages and Salaries, pp. 149–53.
73 Dub.56, 96 Cash Book 1907, entry for 21 Dec.
74 Corr. Out, 2 Nov. 1887–11 May 1890, T.E. to Rinfell, 2 Dec. 1889.
75 Ibid., 2 Feb. 1895–26 Apr. 1900, T.E. to Porter, 2 May 1899.
76 Corr. In, Box 3, PAA–PAM, E. Parker to T.E., 8 Jan. 1898, 17 Oct. 1898, 14 Apr., 15 Apr. 1899.
77 Ibid., Mrs Parker to T.E., 18 Apr. 1899.
78 Corr. Out, Book 4, 2 Dec. 1898–16 Mar. 1900, T.E. to Parker, 18 Apr. 1899.
79 Dublin Laundry, 'Success', p. 12.
80 Dub.56, Deeds and Leases, Goodbody and Tisdall to T.E., 1 Aug. 1899.
81 Dub.56, Wages Book, 24 Dec. 1904–17 Nov. 1906.
82 Ibid., 2 Nov. 1895–14 Aug. 1897, wages for 1895.
83 Corr. Out, Book 3, 18 Jan. 1895–11 Feb. 1898, T.E. to D.E. Benson, 8 July 1896.
84 Corr. In, Box 30, FAA–GY, Martindale to D.L., 19 Aug. 1909.
85 Ibid., Martindale to D.L., 21 Sept. 1909.

86 Corr. Out, Inside Letter Book, 3 Sept. 1909–3 July 1912, R.B. to Martindale, 23 Sept. 1909.
87 Corr. In, Box 9, McH–McK, McKnight to D.L., 21 Feb. 1893.
88 Ibid., Box 39, PIE–PIZ, Pim Bros. to D.L., 1 Sept. 1924.
89 Dub.56, Queries Book, 12 Feb. 1897–13 Mar. 1902, 4 Nov. 1897.
90 Corr. In, Box 39, PES–PEN, Peck and Co. Ltd, Liverpool to D.L., 11 Jan. 1921.
91 Corr. Out, Private Book 1921, No. 5, 12 May 1921–6 Dec. 1921, D.L. to Lewis, 13 Jan., 25 Oct. 1921.
92 Ibid., Private Book, 23 Oct. 1919– 17 Aug. 1920, D.L. to Disposal Board, 11,21 Nov. 1919, 12 Dec. 1919, 19 Jan. 1920.
93 Ibid., D.L. to Gamages, London, 31 Oct. 1919.
94 Ibid., Private Book 1921, No. 5, 12 May 1921– 6 Dec. 1921, R.B. to Corrigan, 25 Oct. 1921.
95 Ibid., 21 July 1900–26 May 1903, T.E. to Squire, 28 July 1900.
96 Interview with J. McKinney.
97 Corr. In, Box 9, McN–McZ, house surgeon to D.L., 19 July 1901, 19 Apr. 1902.
98 Ibid., MEA–MEL, Falkner to D.L., 8 Mar. 1899.
99 Helen Burke, *The People and the Poor Law* (Women's Education Bureau, 1987), p. 7.
100 Corr. In, Box 4, GOM–GOO, Goodbody to T.E., 10 Dec. 1896.
101 Corr. Out, 21 July 1900–25 May 1903, T.E. to Craig, 2 July 1900.
102 Ibid., Book 5, 21 March 1900–11 Nov. 1902, T.E. to Craig, 24 July 1900.
103 Ibid., Book 5, 11 Nov. 1902–7 Oct. 1905, T.E. to Craig, 16 Feb. 1903.
104 Ibid., Book 1, 14 May 1890–20 Aug. 1892, T.E. to Penrose, 24 Mar. 1892.
105 Ibid., Book 2, 21 Aug. 1892–17 Jan. 1895, T.E. to Howell, 2 Nov. 1893.
106 Ibid., Book 5, 21 March 1900–11 Nov. 1902, T.E. to secretary, convalescent home, 26 July 1901 and 20 Feb. 1902.
107 Ibid., T.E. to Superioress, Our Lady's Hospice, 8 Sept. 1902.
108 Ibid., T.E. to registrar, Newcastle, 1 July 1902.
109 Ibid., 2 Feb. 1895–26 April 1900, T.E. to Naughton, 10 Jan. 1900.
110 *Rathmines News* (7 Jan. 1899).
111 Corr. Out, 2 Feb. 1895–26 Apr. 1900, T.E. to Naughton and T.E. to Browne, 10 Jan. 1900.
112 Ibid., T.E. to Martin, 27 Feb. 1900.
113 Ibid., T.E. to Queen Victoria Jubilee Institute for Nurses, 26 Apr. 1900.
114 Ibid., Book 5, 21 Mar. 1900–11 Nov. 1902, T.E. to secretary, convalescent home, 20 Feb. 1902.
115 Ibid., Book 1, 14 May 1890–20 Aug. 1892, T.E. to Manning, 14 Feb. 1891.
116 Ibid., T.E. to Rowan, 10 Dec. 1891.
117 Corr. In, Box 4, GOM–GOO, Goodbody and Tisdall to T.E., 31 May 1898.
118 Interview with D. Benson, 19 June 1995.
119 Corr. Out, Book 4, 2 Dec. 1898–16 Mar. 1900, T.E. to Meany, 22 Aug. 1898.
120 Ibid., Book 5, 11 Nov. 1902–7 Oct. 1905, testimony for Mrs Whitehall, 11 Apr. 1903, p. 165.
121 Ibid., T.E. to Mrs Ryan, 7 July 1903; T.E. to Mr Ryan, 18 July 1903.
122 Interview with G. Benson, 8 May 1996.
123 Corr. In, Box 12, Dublin Corporation to D.L., 15 June 1898.
124 Interview with D. Benson, 19 June 1995.
125 Corr. Out Book 2, 21 Aug. 1892–17 Jan. 1895, T.E. to Sealy, 30 Nov., 16 Dec. 1892.
126 F.H.A. Arlen, 'The Working Class Housing Movement', in Michael J. Bannon (ed.), *The Emergence of Irish Planning* (Dublin: Turoe Press, 1975), pp. 142–5.

127 Corr. Out, Book 2, 21 Aug. 1892–17 Jan. 1895, T.E. to Fawcett, 13 Mar. 1894.
128 Ibid., T.E. to Johnson, 28 Aug. 1894; T.E. to Lombard, 28 Aug. 1894.
129 Ibid., Book 3, 18 Jan. 1895–11 Feb. 1898, T.E. to Johnson, 24 Aug. 1896.
130 Ibid., Book 1, 14 May 1890–20 Aug. 1892, T.E. to Revd Moffat, 5 July 1890.
131 Corr. In, Box 3, C.H. Oldham to T.E., 16 Aug. 1901.
132 Corr. Out, Book 5, 21 Mar. 1900–11 Nov. 1902, T.E. to Oldham, 15, 17 Aug. 1901.
133 Ibid., Birelo to Pigott, 1 Jan. 1902.
134 Ibid., Birelo to Oldham, 7 Apr., 12 May 1902.
135 Ibid., T.E. to Coffee, 29 May 1902.
136 Corr. In, Box 28, RAP–RAU, Fawcett to R.B., 17 Aug. 1908 and Proctor to R.B., 12 Apr., 9 Sept. 1910.
137 David J. Jeremy (ed.), *Dictionary of Business Biography* ( London: Butterworth, 1984), vol.2, p. 438; Anne Vernon, *A Quaker Business Man: The Life of Joseph Rowntree, 1836–1925* (London: Allen and Unwin, 1958), p. 93.
138 Jeremy, *Dictionary of Business Biography*, vol.1, pp. 549–51.
139 Vernon, *A Quaker Business Man*, p. 93.
140 Ibid., pp. 97–8.
141 Ibid., pp. 99, 124.
142 Corr. In, Box 8, BEN–BEQ, Bob (R.B.) to T.E., 11 Mar. 1896.
143 Dublin Laundry, 'Success', p. 12.
144 Fox, *Louie Bennet*, pp. 67–8.
145 Ibid., p. 68.

## 5.  *Continuing Success, but 'a Difficult Business'*

1 Dub.56, Corr. Out, 21 Nov. 1887–11 May 1890, T.E. to Bough, 20 Aug. 1889.
2 Rothery, G. Cadogan and Edmonds, H.O., *The Modern Laundry, Its Construction, Equipment and Management* (London: Gresham Publishing, 1909), vol.2, p. 210.
3 Butler, Elizabeth, *Women and the Trades: The Pittsburgh Survey* (New York: Charities Publication Committee, 1909), p. 175.
4 Malcolmson, Patricia P., 'Laundresses and the Laundry Trade in Victorian England', *Social Studies*, 24 (1980–81), p. 460.
5 Rothery and Edmonds, *The Modern Laundry*, vol.2, pp. 208–9.
6 Dub.56, D.L., Balance Sheets 1888–1936, Balance Sheet, 31 Dec. 1889.
7 Rothery and Edmonds, *The Modern Laundry*, vol.2, p. 209.
8 Ibid.
9 Gregg, Pauline, *A Social and Economic History of Britain 1760–1955* (London: Harrap, 1960), p. 470.
10 Rothery and Edmonds, *The Modern Laundry*, vol.2, p. 209.
11 Corr. In, Box 4, General Accident to D.L., 18 Apr. 1896, 22 Jan. 1898.
12 Ibid., Box 3, National Laundry Trade Protection Association, circular concerning insurance for members, 9 June 1898.
13 Rothery and Edmonds, *The Modern Laundry*, vol.2, pp. 210–11, 214, 216.
14 Corr. Out, 12 Mar. 1913–18 Oct. 1913, R.B. to Webb, Kenilworth Laundry, 8 Oct. 1913.
15 Ibid., Book 5, 21 Mar. 1900–11 Nov. 1902, R.B. to Thompson, 15 May 1900.
16 Ibid., Inside Letter Book, 3 Sept. 1909–3 July 1912, R.B. to Coats, 13 May 1912.

17 Ibid., Private Letter Book (2), 1916–17, 1918, D.L. to Musgrave, 19 Dec. 1917.
18 Ibid., Transferred from Private Letter Book, Dub. 57/2, 13 Jan 1916–24 Nov. 1916, Foster to Nugent, 24 Aug. 1916.
19 Corr. In, Box 4, FOZ–FRA, O'Brien, Franklin Laundry, to T.E., 10 July 1901.
20 Rothery and Edmonds, *The Modern Laundry*, vol.2, pp. 216–7.
21 Corr. Out, Book 3, 18 Jan. 1895–11 Feb. 1898, T.E. to Spicer, 21 Aug. 1896.
22 Dublin Laundry, 'Success: A Story of Twelve Years' (Dublin, 1900), p. 14.
23 Corr. Out, Private Letters Book (2), 1913–15, Book 1, Foster, to Doyle, 20 Apr. 1915.
24 Ibid., Book 2, 21 Aug. 1892–17 Jan. 1895, T.E. to West, 13 Dec. 1892.
25 Corr. In, Box 4, Galashan to D.L., 11 May 1897.
26 Ibid., Gifford to R.B., 15 June 1897.
27 Corr. Out, Inside Letter Book, 3 Sept. 1909–3 July 1912, D.L. to Fawcett, 1 June 1911.
28 Corr. In, Box 4, FOZ–FRA, O'Brien to T.E., 10 July 1901.
29 Corr. Out, 21 July 1900–26 Mar. 1903, D.L. to Hutton, 15 July 1901.
30 Ibid., D.L. to McCready, 21 Aug. 1901.
31 Corr. In, Box 5, Daimler Motor Co. Ltd to Hutton, 25 Jan. 1902.
32 Corr. In, Box 28, Queenstown Steam Laundry to R.B., 7 Dec. 1904.
33 Corr. Out, 2 Feb. 1895–26 Apr. 1900, T.E. to Wood, 1 Apr. 1895.
34 Corr. In, Box 12, Carpenter to T.E., 24 Sept., 1898.
35 Corr. Out, Book 6, 9 Oct. 1905–15 Nov. 1907, T.E. to Midlands Great Western Railway, Broadstone, 5 Sept. 1906.
36 *Thom's Directory*, 1912.
37 Corr. In, Box 5, Egan to R.B., 11 Oct. 1901.
38 Ibid., EJ–EL, R.B. to postmaster, 7 Nov. 1901.
39 Corr. In, Box 29, Edge to D.L., 11 Oct. 1909.
40 Corr. Out, Book 5, 11 Nov. 1902–7 Oct. 1905. Correspondence between D.L. and Lyons, 28 Nov. 1904; 20, 24 Jan., 21, 23 Feb. 1905. Other letters, pp. 658, 691, 702, 711, 717.
41 Ibid., Inside Letter Book, 3 Sept. 1909–3 July 1912, R.B. to Lyons, 18 Mar. 1910.
42 Ibid., Private Letter Book, 1913–15, D.L. to Lyons, 29 Oct. 1915.
43 Corr. In, Box 9, Midlands Great Western Railway to D.L., 5 Mar. 1896.
44 Corr. Out, Private Letter Book, 1913–15, D.L. to Nixon, 29 June, 25, 28 July 1915.
45 Ibid., Private Letter Book, 8 Jan. 1919–21 Oct. 1919, manager to Whalley, 20 June, 23 Oct. 1919; secretary to Whalley, 30 Mar. 1920.
46 Corr. Out, Private Letter Book, 12 Oct. 1923–31 Dec. 1924, D.L. to Whalley, 6 Nov. 1924.
47 Ibid., Dub. 56/4, V19, Private Letter Book, 8 Jan. 1919–21 Oct. 1919, D.L. to Armitage, 28 Aug. 1919.
48 Corr. In, Box 35, Draft advertisement in R.B.'s handwriting for the Constabulary Gazette, Ltd, Fleet St.
49 Corr. In, Box 3, Otley and Co. Ltd to D.L., 7, 10 July 1896.
50 Dublin Laundry, 'The Side the Sun's Upon' (Dublin, 1894), p. 19; 'Success', pp. 8, 9.
51 Corr. In, Box 9, MacDermott to D.L., 31 Aug. 1896.
52 Ibid., McMullan to D.L., 18 July 1903.
53 Corr. In, Box 5, DUA–DUM, Bentick to D.L., 20 July 1897.
54 Ibid., Duggan to D.L, 17 Jan. 1898.
55 Corr. Out, Book 6, 9 Oct. 1905–15 Nov. 1907, p. 725, D.L. to Coates, 6 Mar. 1908.
56 Ibid., Book 2, 21 Aug. 1892–17 Jan. 1895, T.E. to Ryan, 30 Nov. 1894.

57 Ibid., 12 Mar. 1913–18 Oct. 1913, Foster to Barron, 30 July 1913.
58 Ibid., Private Letter Book, 1913–15, D.L. to Power Laundry, 22 Jan. 1914.
59 Ibid., Transferred from Private Letter Book, Dub.57/2, 13 Jan. 1916–24 Nov. 1916, D.L. to Power Laundry, 9, 19, 21 Feb. 1916.
60 Ibid., Dub.56, V19, Private Letter Book(2), 1916–17, 1918, manager to Townsend, 16 Mar. 1917.
61 Ibid., Book 3, 18 Jan. 1895–11 Feb. 1898, T.E. to DMP, 15 Dec. 1897.
62 Ibid., Book 1, 14 May 1890–20 Aug. 1892, T.E. to Superintendent, Exchange Court, 5 Aug. 1892.
63 Ibid., Book 2, 21 Aug. 1892–17 Jan. 1895, T.E. to Chief of Detective Unit, Exchange Court, 20 Dec. 1893.
64 Interview with D. Benson, 19 June 1995.
65 Corr. In, Box 9, McAuliffe to D.L., 7 Sept. 1896.
66 Corr. Out, 28 May 1903–21 Dec. 1905, T.E. to Thompson, 28 May 1903.
67 Ibid., 2 Feb. 1895–26 Apr. 1900, T.E. to Dr Usher, 16 Feb. 1895.
68 Corr. In, Box 12, T.E. to Colman, 18 Dec. 1895.
69 Corr. Out, Book 5, 11 Nov. 1902–7 Oct. 1905, T.E. to Cahill, 29 Dec. 1902.
70 Corr. In, Box 28, Brown to R.B. (n.d.), filed under ' Urban District'.
71 Ibid., Fawcett to D.L., 23 Aug. 1909.
72 Ibid., 17 Aug. 1908.
73 GSIR/218(6), 219(2,3,4), 220(c8, c22), 224(1) .
74 Martindale, Hilda, *From One Generation to Another* (London: Allen and Unwin, 1944), p. 94.
75 Costelloe, Mary, 'The Sisterhood of Sorrow', No.2, 'The Magdalens', ibid. (15 Mar. 1897), p. 8.
76 *Thom's Directory*, 1897.
77 *List of religious and charitable institutions in which laundries are carried on*, pp. 93–4, 97 [Cd 2741], HC 1905, XCVIII, 85.
78 Corr. In, Box 5, Letter from Dublin Mercantile Association Ltd to D.L., 29 July 1895, ref. No. 69572, re-Shank: Mercantile to Hely Hutchinson, 26 July 1896. Many letters from the Mercantile to the D.L. in, for example, 1897.
79 Corr. Out, Book 5, 21 Mar. 1900–11 Nov. 1902, D.L. to Earl of Clancarty, 21 May, 4 Nov. 1901: Private Letter Book (6), 7 Dec. 1921–6 Nov. 1922, secretary, D.L. to Russell, 13 July 1922.
80 Corr. In, Box 9, MUP–MUZ, Wynnfield House, Rathmines to D. L., 8 Mar. 1897: G.B. Edmondson to D.L., 16 Jan. 1899.
81 Corr. Out, 2 Feb. 1895–26 Apr. 1900, T.E. to Marjorie, 8 Feb. 1899.
82 Ibid., Dub.56, V19, Private Letter Book (2), 1916–17, 1918, Foster to Benson, 24 Aug. 1917.
83 Ibid., Book 5, 11 Nov. 1902–7 Oct. 1905, D.L. to Reilly, 14 Sept. 1905.
84 Ibid., 28 May 1903–21 Dec. 1905, p. 157, Account of Whelan, sacked from D.L. and T.E. to Whelan, 21 Dec. 1904.
85 Ibid., T.E. to Superintendent, 25 Apr. 1904.
86 Ibid., Private Letter Book (2), 1913–15, D.L. to Healy, 20 Oct. 1913.
87 Ibid., Book 4, 2 Dec. 1898–16 Mar. 1900, T.E. to Johnston, 8 Mar., 11, 28 Oct. 1898; R.B. to Johnston, 27 Sept. 1898.
88 Ibid., 2 Feb. 1895–26 Apr. 1900, T.E. to Henshaw, 13 June 1899.
89 Ibid., Private Letter Book (6), 7 Dec. 1921–6 Nov. 1922, R.B. to Manchester Steam Users Association, 30 Oct. 1922.

90 Ibid., Book 5, 11 Nov. 1902–7 Oct. 1905, T.E. to Murphy, 3 Aug. 1904, 4, 15, 28 Aug. 1905, 7 Oct. 1905.
91 Corr. In, Box 9, Murphy to T.E, June 1901.
92 *Dictionary of Quaker Biography*, Friends House, London.
93 Interview with D. Benson, 19 June 1995.
94 Corr. In, Box 8, BEN–BEQ, 1895–99, D.E. Benson to Cousin Thomas, 16 Jan. 1896.
95 Ibid., R.B. to T.E., 10 Feb. 1897.
96 Dublin Laundry, 'Success', pp. 7, 9–11.
97 Ibid., p. 2.
98 Corr. Out, Book 5, 21 Mar. 1900–11 Nov. 1902, R.B. to Patriotic Assurance Co., 17 June 1901.
99 Interview with G. Benson, 8 May 1996.
100 Corr. In, Box 5, Drury to T.E., 14 June 1895.
101 Dublin Laundry, 'Success', p. 5: Corr. Out, Book 3, 18 Jan. 1895–11 Feb. 1898, T.E. to Mayhew, 27 Dec. 1895.
102 Ibid., Book 2, 21 Aug. 1892–17 Jan. 1895, T.E. to Spicer, 18, 27 Dec. 1894.
103 NAI, Dub. 56. 'History of the Dublin Laundry Co. Ltd', p. 3.
104 Corr. Out, Book 3, 18 Jan. 1895–11 Feb. 1898, T.E. to West, 6 June 1896.
105 *Thom's Directory*, 1897.
106 Corr. In, Box 8, BEN–BEQ, Benson to T.E., 3 Nov. 1896.
107 Corr. In, Box 3, Porte and Sykes to T.E., 10 June 1896.
108 Corr. Out, Book 4, 2 Dec. 1898–16 Mar. 1900, T.E. to Egan and Tatlow, 11 Oct. 1898.
109 Ibid., Transferred from Private Letter Book, Dub.57/2, 13 Jan. 1916–24 Nov. 1916, R.B. to Alliance and Dublin Consumer Gas Co., 2 Feb. 1916.
110 Ibid., 2 Feb. 1895–26 Apr. 1900, T.E. to Mosse, 11 Jan. 1896.
111 Michael McCarthy, *Five Years in Ireland, 1895–1900* (Dublin: Hodges Figgis, 1901), pp. 106–7: Denis Johnston, 'The Dublin Trams', *Dublin Historical Record*, 12.
112 Dub.56, Minute Book, Seventh and Eighth AGMs, 20 Apr. 1895 and 27 Apr. 1896.
113 Ibid., Tenth and Thirteenth AGMs, 4 Aug. 1898 and 12 Aug. 1901.
114 Dub.56, 28 May 1901, Dublin Laundry Co. Ltd, 'Case for Counsel and Opinion', Goodbody and Tisdall.
115 Minute Book, Dublin Laundry Co. Ltd, EGMs, 12, 27 Aug. 1901, 'Scheme of Reconstruction'.
116 Corr. Out, 21 July 1900–26 May 1903, T.E. to Wood, 21 Aug. 1901; T.E. to Goodbody and Tisdall, 25 Oct. 1901.
117 Minute Book, EGM, 27 Aug. 1901, 'Memorandum by MD, at 11.45 a.m. on that date'.
118 Audited accounts, 30 June 1897: Tenth AGM, p.13.
119 Dub. 56, Minute Book, First AGM of the new company.
120 Ibid., Fifth AGM, 15 Mar. 1906.
121 Ibid., Sixth AGM, 20 Mar. 1907.
122 EGM, 24 Apr. 1907.

### 6. *The Factory Acts and the Laundry Industry*

1 'Law and the Laundry,' *Nineteenth Century* (Feb. 1897), p. 224.
2 Corr. Out, Book 1, 14 May 1890–20 Aug. 1892, T.E. to O'Brien, 2 June 1890; T.E. to Webb, 16 June 1891.

3 'Law and the Laundry', p. 244.
4 Corr. Out, Book 2, 21 Aug. 1892–17 Jan. 1895, T.E. to D.E. Benson, 23 Aug. 1893.
5 Ibid., T.E. to Hamilton, 4, 15 Nov. 1893, see also pp. 524–9.
6 *Reports of inspectors of factories as to hours of work etc.* [C 7418], HC 1894, XXI, 709, p. 715.
7 Corr. Out, Book 2, 21 Aug. 1892–17 Jan. 1895, T.E. to Hamilton, 15 Nov. 1893 and pp. 524–9.
8 Ibid., T.E. to Webb, 3 May 1894.
9 Ibid., 10 May 1894.
10 Ibid., T.E. to D.E.. Benson, 10 May 1894.
11 Ibid., Book 5, 21 Mar. 1900–11 Nov. 1902, R.B. to Brittain, 10 June 1901.
12 Corr. In, Box 8, BEN–BEQ, R.B. to T.E., 11 Mar. 1896.
13 Ibid., NLTPA [National Laundry Trade Protection Association] to D.L., 10 June 1899.
14 Corr. Out, Inside Letter Book, 3 Sept. 1909–3 July 1912, D.L. to Coats, 26 July 1911; Corr. In, Box 30, Fed. of Laundries Assocs., to R.B., 22 Feb. 1910.
15 Ibid., Book 2, 21 Aug. 1892–17 Jan. 1895, T.E. to NLA, 10 and 15 May 1894.
16 Ibid., T.E. to O'Brien, 18 May 1894.
17 Ibid., 22 June 1894.
18 Ibid., Book 3, 18 Jan. 1895–11 Feb. 1898, T.E. to R.B., 17 Apr. 1895.
19 Ibid., 1, 7 May 1895.
20 Ibid., T.E. to D.E. Benson, 18 May 1895.
21 Ibid., 4 Apr. 1895.
22 Robert Ensor, *Oxford History of England, 1870–1914* (Oxford: Oxford University Press, 1988), pp. 209–11, 221.
23 'Law and the Laundry', p. 225.
24 Frances Finnegan, *Do Penance or Perish* (Piltown, Co. Kilkenny: Congrave Press Ireland, 2001), p. 224.
25 'Law and the Laundry', pp. 225–6.
26 Ibid., pp. 226–9.
27 Corr. Out, Book 3, 18 Jan. 1895–11 Feb. 1898, T.E. to Carr, 31 Dec. 1895.
28 Ibid., T.E. to D.E. Benson, 14 Dec. 1895.
29 'Law and the Laundry', p. 228.
30 Corr. In, Box 8, BEN–BEQ, Benson to T.E., 23 Jan. 1896.
31 Corr. Out, Book 3, 18 Jan. 1895–11 Feb. 1898, T.E. to D.E. Benson, 14 Dec. 1895.
32 Fabian Society, 'Life in the Laundry', *Tract No. 112* (London: 1902), p. 6.
33 Ibid., pp. 5–6.
34 Mona Wilson, *Our Industrial Laws: Working Women in Factories, Workshops, Shops & Laundries and How to Help Them* (London: Duckworth, 1899), pp. 25–6, 46–7.
35 Corr. In, FAA–FAN, Bellhouse to T.E., 27 Mar. 1896.
36 Ibid., 13 July 1896.
37 Ibid., Home Office to T.E., 1 Feb. 1897.
38 *Annual report of the chief inspector of factories and workshops for the year ending 31 Oct. 1897* [C 8965], HC 1898, XIV, 1, p. 107.
39 Corr. In, Box 3, Laundry Assoc. to R.B., 2 Apr. 1900.
40 Ibid., Box 4, FOZ–FRA, O'Brien to T.E., 24 July 1901.
41 Ibid., Box 3, NLTPA to T.E., 31 July 1901.
42 Lords Londonderry, Downshire and Shaftsbury, *T.L. Corbett, William Moore,* Arnold Foster, *J.M. McCalmont, Col. Saunderson and others.* From several of these, especially those whose names are italicised, they had sympathetic replies and

promises of support. Moore told them what was being done in the matter and the probable decision of the Cabinet before the Bill would be reported to the House.

43 Corr. In, Box 4, FOZ–FRA, O'Brien to R.B., 13 Sept. 1901.

44 Fabian Society, 'Life in the Laundry', p. 9.

45 'Law and the Laundry', p. 231.

46 Fabian Society, 'Life in the Laundry', pp. 5, 12.

47 *List of Religious and Charitable Institutions in which Laundries are carried on* [Cd. 2741], HC 1905, XCVIII, 85, pp. 87–9, 93–4, 97.

48 Rothery, G. Cadogan and Edmonds, H.O., *The Modern Laundry, Its Construction, Equipment and Management* (London: Gresham Publishing, 1909), Appendix II, p.247.

49 GSIR 222(4).

50 Interview with Sr. de Lourdes at the House of Mercy, Baggot Street, 21 Apr. 1980.

51 GSIR, 222(4), 'Modification by Order of the Secretary of State'.

52 GSIR, 222(5).

53 GSIR, 222(4). Home Office, Whitehall, 31 Dec. 1907, 'General Requirements of the Act'.

54 Fabian Society, 'Life in the Laundry', p. 14.

55 'Law and the Laundry', p. 230.

56 *Report of inspectors of factories as to hours of work, etc.* [C 7418], H.C. 1894, XXI, 709, p. 715.

57 Fabian Society, 'Life in the Laundry', p. 14.

58 'Law and the Laundry', pp. 230–1.

59 Hearn, Mona, *Below Stairs* (Dublin: Lilliput Press, 1993), pp. 1–2.

60 'Law and the Laundry', pp. 230–1.

61 Fabian Society, 'Life in the Laundry', pp. 14–15.

62 Ibid., p. 9.

63 Ibid., pp. 12, 15.

64 Ibid., p. 11.

65 *Report of the commissioners appointed to inquire into the working of the factory and workshop acts* [C. 1443–1], HC 1876, XXX, vol. II, p. 898.

66 Ibid., p. 891.

67 Ibid., p. 899.

68 Finnegan, *Do Penance or Perish*, p. 224.

69 Joseph Robins, *The Lost Children* (Dublin: Institute of Public Administration, 1890), p. 303.

70 Interview with Sr. de Lourdes, 21 Apr. 1980: GSIR, 222(3).

71 *Royal Commission on Labour. Report on the employment of women by Misses Orme,. Collet, Abraham and Irwin* [C 6894–XXIII], HC 1893–4, XXXVII, Pt I, 545, p. 846.

72 GSIR, 222(3).

73 Mary Costello, 'The Sisterhood of Sorrow', No.1, 'The Magdalens', *The Lady of the House* (15 Feb. 1897), p. 8.

74 Ibid., 'The Sisterhood of Sorrow', No.2, 'The Magdalens', *The Lady of the House* (15 Mar. 1897), p. 7.

75 Catriona Clear, *Nuns in Nineteenth-Century Ireland* (Dublin: Gill and Macmillan, 1987), p. 106.

76 'The Care of the Magdalens', *Freeman's Journal* (21 Oct. 1916).

77 'A Woman's Crime', IT (30 Oct. 1995); Finnegan, *Do Penance or Perish*, p. 104.

78 GSIR, 222(3).
79 GSIR, 241(3).
80 Costello, 'Sisterhood of Sorrow', No.1, 'The Magdalens', *Lady of the House* (15 Feb. 1897), p. 8.
81 Ibid., 'The Sisterhood of Sorrow', No.2, 'The Magdalens', ibid. (15 Mar. 1897), p. 7.
82 Association of Dublin Charities, *Dublin Charities* (Dublin, n.d.), pp. 153–6, 160: Finnegan, *Do Penance or Perish*, p. 158.
83 Costello, 'Sisterhood of Sorrow', No.1, 'The Magdalens', *Lady of the House* (15 Feb. 1897), p. 8.
84 Maria Luddy (ed.), 'Magdalen Asylums, Doc. 20, Guide for the Religious Called Sisters of Mercy (London, 1866)', *Women in Ireland, 1800–1918* (Cork: Cork University Press, 1995), p. 58.
85 Finnegan, *Do Penance or Perish*, p. 103.
86 Costello, 'The Sisterhood of Sorrow', No.4, 'Conclusion of Magdalens', *Lady of the House* (15 May 1897), p. 15.
87 Ibid., 'Sisterhood of Sorrow', No.1, 'The Magdalens', *Lady of the House* (15 Feb. 1897), p. 8.
88 Ibid., p. 7.
89 Finnegan, *Do Penance or Perish*, pp. 65, 109, 154.
90 Ibid., pp. 35, 197, 228–9.
91 Costello, 'Sisterhood of Sorrow', No.1, 'The Magdalens', *Lady of the House* (15 Feb. 1897), p. 8.
92 Finnegan, *Do Penance or Perish*, p. 136.
93 Luddy (ed.), 'Magdalen Asylums, Doc. 20', p.59.
94 Finnegan, *Do Penance or Perish*, p. 26.
95 Luddy (ed.), 'Magdalen Asylums, Doc. 20', pp. 58, 60.
96 Finnegan, *Do Penance or Perish*, pp. 87–8.
97 Clear, *Nuns in Nineteenth-Century Ireland*, p. 134.
98 Ibid., p. 76.
99 Ibid., p. 75.
100 Ibid., p. 70.
101 Caitriona Clear, 'Walls within Walls—Nuns in 19th–Century Ireland', Chris Curtin, Pauline Jackson, Barbara O'Connor (eds), *Gender in Irish Society* (Galway: Galway University Press, 1987), p. 134.
102 Ibid., pp. 141–2.
103 Robins, *The Lost Children*, pp. 160–1, 297, 301–2.
104 Clear, *Nuns in Nineteenth-Century Ireland*, p. 106.
105 Finnegan, *Do Penance or Perish*, p. 239.
106 Costello, 'The Sisterhood of Sorrow', No.1, 'The Magdalens', *Lady of the House* (15 Feb. 1897), p. 7.
107 Finnegan, *Do Penance or Perish*, p. 35.
108 Costello, 'The Sisterhood of Sorrow', No.4, 'Conclusion of Magdalens', ibid. (15 May 1897), p. 15.
109 GSIR 214–217.
110 Census, 1901, Limerick, Form B 1.
111 Ibid.
112 Finnegan, *Do Penance or Perish*, pp. 123–5.
113 Ibid., pp. 230–1.
114 GSIR 222 (3), 'Parrish to the Hon. the Commons of Great Britain and Ireland'.

115 Costello, 'The Sisterhood of Sorrow', No.1, 'The Magdalens', *Lady of the House* (15 Feb. 1897), p. 8.
116 GSIR 222(3).
117 Costelloe, 'The Sisterhood of Sorrow', No.3, 'The Magdalens', *The Lady of the House* (15 Apr., 1897), p. 8.
118 Martindale, Hilda, *From One Generation to Another* (London: Allen and Unwin, 1944), pp. 94–5.
119 'New Laundry and Magdalen Asylum', *Irish Builder* (1 June 1878), p. 163.
120 Royal Commission on Labour [C6894–XXIII], HC 1893–4, XXXVII, Pt I, 545, p. 846.
121 GSIR 224(1, 2, 3, 4).
122 GSIR 224(1, 6).
123 GSIR 222(3).
124 GSIR 221(5), 'Institutional and Commercial Laundries'.
125 Fabian Society, 'Life in the Laundry', p. 9.
126 Martindale, *From One Generation to Another*, p. 95.
127 Fabian Society, 'Life in the Laundry', p. 10.
128 Ibid., p. 13.
129 'Law and the Laundry', p. 225.

## 7. The Quaker Influence

1 Dub.56, Corr. Out, Book 3, 18 Jan. 1895–11 Feb. 1898, T.E. to Simon, 11 Dec. 1895.
2 *The Friend*, 48 (New Series, 1908), p. 118.
3 Corr. Out, 21 July 1900–26 May 1903, T.E. to Barker-Welles, 4 Dec. 1901.
4 Ibid., 2 Feb. 1895–26 Apr. 1900, T.E. to Ellie, 27 Dec. 1895.
5 *The Friend*, 48 (New Series, 1908), p.118; Maurice J. Wigham, *The Irish Quakers* (Dublin: Historical Committee of the Religious Society of Friends in Ireland, 1992), p. 109.
6 Corr. Out, 2 Feb. 1895–26 Apr. 1900, T.E. to Alexander, 21 June 1896.
7 Ibid., Book 2, 21 Aug. 1892–17 Jan. 1895, T.E. to Grubb, 12 Sept. 1893.
8 Corr. In, Box 2, Webb to T.E., 1 July 1896.
9 Rathmines and Rathgar Urban District Council, Council Minutes, 5 Feb. 1902–3 Mar. 1917, p.214.
10 'A Leinster Friend', *Society of Friends in Ireland in 1896* (Dublin: William McGee, 1896), p. 4.
11 N.L., *Christian Discipline in the Society of Friends, Ireland 1881. Revised rules of the Society to come into force on the First of the Ninth month 1881*, p. 51.
12 Maurice J. Wigham, *The Irish Quakers* (Dublin: Historical Committee of the Religious Society of Friends in Ireland, 1992), p. 107.
13 JB, *From the Lune to the Neva* (London: Saml. Harris, 1879), 'Opinions of the Press', p. 4.
14 Wigham, *The Irish Quakers*, p. 105.
15 Ibid., p. 58.
16 Corr. In, Box 2, Waring to T.E., 24 Jan. 1898.
17 Interview with D. Benson, 19 June 1995.
18 Corr. Out, 2 Feb. 1895–26 Apr. 1900, T.E. to Hayes and Sons, 25 Feb. 1898, 6 Apr. 1898: T.E. to Anderson, Stanford and Ridgeway, Apr./May 1898.

19 Ibid., T.E. to Hayes, 30 June 1898.
20 Interviews with D. Benson, 19 June 1995 and former worker Essie Nolan, 10 May 1996.
21 Census, 1901, Form A, No.726.
22 Corr. Out, Book 3, 18 Jan. 1895–11 Feb. 1898, T.E. to D. E. Benson, 6 May 1896.
23 Ibid., 2 Feb. 1895–26 Apr. 1900, T.E. to manager, Grand Hotel, Malahide, 8 Aug. 1895.
24 Anne Vernon, *A Quaker Business Man: The Life of Joseph Rowntree, 1836–1925* (London: Allen and Unwin, 1958), p.120.
25 Dublin Laundry, 'The Side the Sun's Upon' (Dublin, 1894), p.12.
26 Corr. Out, Book 2, 21 Aug. 1892–17 Jan. 1895, T.E. to Grubb, 12 Sept. 1893; T.E. to D.E. Benson, 18 May 1893.
27 Ibid., T.E. to D.E. Benson, 22 Jan. 1894.
28 Ibid., Book 3, 18 Jan. 1895–11 Feb. 1898, T.E. to Simon, 3 July 1895; 2 Feb. 1895–26 Apr. 1900, T.E. to G. Edmondson, Ohio, 3 Dec. 1895; to Mosse, Toronto, 11 Jan. 1896.
29 Ibid., 2 Feb. 1895–26 Apr. 1900, T.E. to Bentley, 6 May 1897.
30 Ibid., Book 4, 12 Feb. 1898–16 Mar. 1900, T.E. to Chambers, 23 Mar. 1899.
31 Wigham, *The Irish Quakers*, pp. 47–8.
32 Dublin Laundry, 'The Side the Sun's Upon', p. 18.
33 Corr. Out, Book 3, 18 Jan. 1895–11 Feb. 1898, ref. for Anne M'Cardle, 7 Feb. 1898, p. 986; Book 4, 2 Dec. 1898–16 Mar. 1900, ref. for Eliza Moor, 11 Jan 1899, p. 530.
34 Ibid., 21 July 1900–26 May 1903, T.E. to Hill, 25 Oct. 1900.
35 Ibid., T.E. to Dunlop, 25 Oct. 1901.
36 Ibid., 2 Feb. 1895–26 Apr. 1900, T.E. to Sullivan, 27 Apr. 1899.
37 Ibid., 17 June 1880–5 Nov. 1883, T.E. to Dietrich, 6 Dec. 1882.
38 Ibid., Book 2, 21 Aug. 1892–17 Jan. 1895, T.E. to Matthew, 13 Aug. 1893.
39 Ibid., Book 3, 18 Jan. 1895–11 Feb. 1898, T.E. to Doyle, 6 Apr. 1897.
40 Corr. In, Box 8, BEN–BEQ, D.E. Benson to T.E., 13 Dec. 1895.
41 Wigham, *The Irish Quakers*, p. 59.
42 *Christian Discipline in the Society of Friends*, p. 86.
43 Corr. Out, 2 Feb. 1895–26 Apr. 1900, T.E. to editor, *IT*, 26 Dec. 1895.
44 *IT*, 26 Dec. 1895.
45 Corr. Out, 2 Feb. 1895–26 Apr. 1900, T.E. to editor, *IT*, 26 Dec. 1895.
46 Wigham, *The Irish Quakers*, pp. 98, 111.
47 Corr. Out, 2 Feb. 1895–26 Apr. 1900, T.E. to Grace, 14 Jan. 1896; T.E. to Evens, 27 Jan. 1896.
48 Ibid., T.E. to Brookes, 14 Aug. 1896.
49 Ibid., T.E. to Harris, 4 Jan. 1897; T.E. to Mellinger, Feb. 1897; T.E. to Marshall, 24 Feb. 1897.
50 Corr. Out, 21 July 1900–26 May 1903, T.E. to Usher, n.d. (last quarter 1901).
51 Corr. Out, 2 Feb. 1895–26 Apr. 1900, T.E. to Beale, 26 Aug. 1897.
52 Ibid., T.E. to doctor, 2 Feb. 1900.
53 Ibid., Book 5, 21 Mar. 1900–11 Nov. 1902, T.E. to Controller, Savings Bank Department, 20 July 1900; T.E. to Hearn, 20 Feb. 1901.
54 Dub. 56, 96, Cash Book, 1907–1908.
55 Corr. Out, 28 May 1903–21 Dec. 1905, T.E. to Hon. Sec., 'Herbert Presentation', Town Hall, Ballsbridge, 7 Jan. 1904.
56 Corr. In, Box 2, Wilkenson to T.E., 2 Jan. 1896.

57 Corr. Out, 2 Feb. 1895–26 Apr. 1900, T.E. to Wilkenson, end Nov. 1896.
58 Corr. In, Box 2, Wilkenson to T.E., 16 Apr. 1897.
59 Corr. Out, Book 3, 18 Jan. 1895–11 Feb. 1898, T.E. to Wilkenson, 20 Apr. 1897.
60 Corr. In, Box 2, Wilkenson to T.E., 26 Jan. 1898.
61 Ibid., 31 Jan. 1898.
62 Ibid., 15, 18 July 1898.
63 Ibid., 11 Oct. 1898.
64 Ibid., 15 Aug. 1899.
65 Corr. Out, Book 4, 12 Feb., 1898–16 Mar. 1900, T.E. to Wilkenson, 16 Aug. 1899.
66 Corr. In, Box 2, George Wilkenson to T.E., 29 Aug. 1899.
67 Corr. Out, Book 4, 12 Feb. 1898–16 Mar. 1900, T.E. to Bennett, 2 Sept. 1899.
68 Ibid., T.E. to Wilkenson, 2 Sept. 1899.
69 Corr. In, Box 2, Wilkenson to T.E., 2 Sept. 1899.
70 Corr. Out, Book 4, 12 Feb. 1898–16 Mar. 1900, T.E. to Wilkenson, 4 Sept. 1899.
71 Ibid., Book 5, 11 Nov. 1902–7 Oct. 1905, T.E. to Wilkenson, 3 July 1905.
72 Ibid., Book 3, 18 Jan. 1895–11 Feb. 1898, T.E. to West, 6 June 1896.
73 Ibid., Book 4, 12 Feb. 1898–16 Mar. 1900, T.E. to Bennett, 26 Nov. 1898.
74 Ibid., 2 Feb. 1895–26 Apr. 1900, T.E. to Sullivan, 27 Apr. 1899.
75 Ibid., Book 4, 12 Feb. 1898–16 Mar. 1900, T.E. to Duff, 2 Sept. 1899.
76 Corr. Out, 21 July 1900–20 May 1903, T.E. to business associate, 8 Apr. 1903.
77 Ibid., T.E. to Hayes, 8 Dec. 1902.
78 Ibid., T.E. to trustees of Henshaw's estate, 1 Apr. 1903; T.E. to Murphy, 9 Mar. 1903.
79 Corr. In, Box 28, T.E. to painter and decorator, 18 Feb. 1905.
80 Corr. Out, 28 May 1903–21 Dec. 1905, T.E. to Roberts, 6 Aug. 1903.
81 Ibid., T.E. to Roberts, 16 Mar. 1904, 31 Mar. 1904.
82 Corr. In, Box 28, Roberts to T.E., 15 Sept. 1904.
83 Corr. Out, 28 May 1903–21 Dec. 1905, T.E. to Murphy, 8 Sept. 1903.
84 Ibid., T.E. to Murphy, 2 Dec. 1905; T.E. to Dublin United Tramway Co., 6 Dec. 1905.
85 Ibid., T.E. to McGetrick, 17 Jan. 1905.
86 Ibid., T.E. to National Telephone Co., 5 May 1904.
87 Ibid., Book 6, 9 Oct. 1905–15 Nov. 1907, R.B. to Adam and Son, 23 Mar. 1908.
88 Ibid., 21 July 1900–26 May 1903, T.E. to MacCarthy, 22 Apr. 1902.
89 Ibid., T.E. to Charlie, 27 Aug. 1902.
90 Ibid., T.E. to Batchelor, 23 Feb., 11 May 1903.
91 Ibid., Book 4, 12 Feb. 1898–16 Mar. 1900 (about twenty letters to Haughton in this book, including this one), T.E. to Haughton, 6 Mar. 1896.
92 Ibid., 2 Feb. 1895–26 Apr. 1900, T.E. to Haughton, 8 Nov. 1897.
93 Corr. In, Box 12, COR–COS, Haughton to T.E., 29 Jan., 12 Mar., 8, 13 Apr. 1898, 19 Jan. 1899.
94 Corr. Out, Book 4, 12 Feb. 1898–16 Mar. 1900, T.E. to Haughton, 26 May 1898.
95 Corr. In, Box 12, Haughton to T.E., 14 June 1898.
96 Ibid., 28 May 1898, 2 June 1898: Corr. Out, Book 4, 12 Feb. 1898–16 Mar. 1900, T.E. to Haughton, 6 May 1898. xx
97 Ibid., Box 2, Wakefield to D.L.., 6 Sept. 1898.
98 Ibid., Box 12, Haughton to T.E., 20, 23 Dec. 1898.
99 Ibid., Box 12, Haughton to T.E., 28 Jan. 1899; Corr. Out, Book 4, 12 Feb. 1898–16 Mar. 1900, Webb to Dixon, 17 Feb. 1899; Book 5, 21 Mar. 1900–11 Nov. 1902, T.E. to Wakefield, 21 Feb. 1901.

100 Corr. Out, Book 5, T.E. to Wakefield, 21 Feb. 1901.
101 Ibid., Book 4, 12 Feb. 1898–16 Mar. 1900, T.E. to Chernside, 25 Nov. 1899.
102 Ibid., T.E. to Haughton, 8 Dec. 1899.
103 Ibid., Book 5, 21 Mar. 1900–11 Nov. 1902, T.E. to Haughton, 21 Apr. 1900, 14 June 1900, 17 July 1900.
104 Corr. In, Box 9, Munster Steam Laundry to T.E., 5 Dec. 1900.
105 Corr. Out, Book 5, 21 Mar. 1900–11 Nov. 1902, T.E. to Haughton, 17 Dec. 1901.
106 Ibid., Book 4, 12 Feb. 1898–16 Mar. 1900, T.E. to Haughton, 11 Jan. 1899.
107 Ibid., 3 May, 26 July 1898.
108 Corr. In, Box 3, Orr to T.E., 13 June 1898.
109 Corr. Out, Book 4, 12 Feb. 1898–16 Mar. 1900, T.E. to O'Brien, 22 Aug. 1898.
110 Corr. In, Box 12, Haughton to T.E., 28 Jan. 1899.
111 Ibid., Cook to T.E., 15 June 1896.
112 Corr. Out, 21 Nov. 1887–11 May 1890, T.E. to Armstrong, 1 Jan. 1890.
113 Wigham, *The Irish Quakers*, pp. 91, 122.
114 Ibid., p. 101.
115 Corr. Out, 17 June 1880–5 Nov. 1883, T.E. to O'Brien, 2 Dec. 1880.
116 Ibid., T.E. to friend, 23 May 1883.
117 Connolly, S.J. (ed.), *The Oxford Companion to Irish History* (Oxford: Oxford University Press, 1998), pp. 262, 440.
118 R.F. Foster, *Modern Ireland 1600–1972* (London: Allen Lane, The Penguin Press, 1988), pp. 406, 408.
119 Corr. Out, 17 June 1880–5 Nov. 1883, T.E. to friend in Canada, 4 Apr. 1883.
120 Michael McCarthy, *Five Years in Ireland, 1895–1900* (Dublin: Hodges Figgis, 1901), p. 463.
121 Ibid., pp. 467–501.
122 Corr. Out, Book 5, 21 Mar. 1900–11 Nov. 1902, R.B. to Bellhouse, 22 Mar. 1900.
123 McCarthy, *Five Years in Ireland*, p. 469.
124 Ibid., pp. 482–7, 533–7.
125 Corr. In, Box 12, Cro–Cry, Crossley to T.E., 28 Mar. 1900.
126 Corr. Out, Book 5, 21 Mar. 1900–11 Nov. 1902, T.E. to Crossley, 29 Mar. 1900.
127 Ibid., T.E. to Courroux, 2 Apr. 1901.
128 Dub.56, Deeds and Leases, V19, Hammond to D.L., 25 Apr. 1900; Mannington to D.L., Apr. 1900.
129 Ibid., T.E. to Courroux, 19 May, 5, 22 June 1900.
130 Ibid., 12 July 1900; n.d., p. 199.
131 Dublin Laundry, 'Success: A Story of Twelve Years' (Dublin, 1900), pp. 19–20.
132 Corr. Out, Book 5, 21 Mar. 1900–11 Nov. 1902, T.E. to Courroux, 2 Apr. 1901, 2 July 1901.
133 Ibid., Book 5, 11 Nov. 1902–7 Oct. 1905, T.E. to Webster, 11 May 1903: T.E. to Courroux, 6 June 1904.
134 Ibid., Book 2, 21 Aug. 1892–17 Jan. 1895, T.E. to Thom's, Jan. 1895.
135 Séamus Ó Maitiú, *Rathmines Township, 1847–1930* (Dublin: Rathmines Senior College, Rathmines, 1997), p. 24.
136 Civic Museum, Rathmines and Rathgar, UDC 1/Mins. I/7a, 23 Jan. 1903, p. 38.
137 Corr. Out, 21 July 1900–26 May 1903, T.E. to Todd, 13 Dec. 1901, 10 Feb. 1902.
138 Ibid., T.E. to Breslan, 22 Apr. 1902; T.E. to Oldham, 18 Mar. 1902.
139 Ibid., 28 May 1903–21 Dec. 1905, T.E. to Oldham, 3 Sept. 1903.
140 UDC 1/Mins. 1/7a, Council Meeting, 5 Feb. 1902, 23 Jan. 1903, 23 Jan. 1905.

141 UDC 1/1/Mins. 1/7a, Council Meeting, 1 May 1907, p. 186.
142 Corr. In, Box 4, GOR–GOZ, Day, GPO to T.E., 28 Aug. 1895.
143 Corr. Out, 28 May 1903–21 Dec. 1905, T.E. to Reid, DWW R, 21 July 1905.
144 Ibid., T.E. to Reid, 22 June 1903.
145 Ibid., Book 2, 21 Aug. 1892–17 Jan. 1895, T.E. to Thom's, 21 Feb. 1893, Jan. 1895.
146 Corr. In, Box 5, Annie Edmondson to T.E., 12 Sept. 1897, 13 Jan. 1900: Edmundson to T.E., 4 June 1902.
147 Corr. Out, 21 July 1900–26 May 1903, T.E. to unknown, 7 Apr. 1903.
148 Ibid., 28 May 1903–21 Dec. 1905, T.E. to friend, 1 July 1903.
149 Ibid., 2 Feb. 1895–26 Apr. 1900, T.E. to Shipworth, n.d., 1896.
150 Friends House, London, *Annual Monitor*, p. 65.
151 Ibid., p. 73.
152 Corr. Out, 2 Feb. 1895–26 Apr. 1900, T.E. to McKenna, 24 Aug. 1896.
153 Ibid., T.E. to Redford, MD, 2 Feb. 1895.
154 Ibid., 28 May 1903–21 Dec. 1905, T.E. to Kelly, 17 Nov. 1903.
155 Ibid., 21 July 1900–26 May 1903, T.E. to Roberts, 4 May 1903.
156 Friends House, *Annual Monitor*, pp. 59, 66.
157 Ibid., p. 71.
158 The Friend, 48, New Series (1908), p. 118.
159 Ibid., 47, New Series (1907), p. 790.
160 Friends House, *Annual Monitor*, p. 20: *The Friend*, 48, New Series (1908), p. 118.
161 UDC 1/Min 1/7a, pp. 207, 212.
162 Margaret Forster, *Rich Desserts and Captain's Thin: A Family and Their Times, 1831–1931* (London: Chatto & Windus, 1997), p. 44.
163 Ibid., p. 55.
164 Ibid., p. 44.
165 Ibid., p. 72.
166 Vernon, *The Life of Joseph Rowntree*, pp. 125–6.
167 NAI, R 07–3007, File No. 953/08.
168 NAI, T 7550, will probated 26 July 1907.
169 Corr. In, Box 30, Goodbody to R.B., Aug. 1909.
170 NAI, Wills and Admon. 1908, Thomas Edmondson [228] 31 March. Probate of Will and Codicil of Thomas Edmondson, late of Creevagh, Orwell Park. Effects £11,611.9s.5d. Re-sworn at £12,601.0s.8d.
171 Dub.56, 'History of the Dublin Laundry', pp. 2–3.
172 Dub.56, 260 Private Ledger, 1909–70.
173 Dub.56, 'History of The Dublin Laundry', p. 3.
174 Dub.56, 96 Cash Book, 1907–1908.

## 8. The Dublin Laundry after Thomas Edmondson

1 Dub.56, Dublin Laundry and Co. Ltd, Balance Sheets 1888–1936, Balance Sheet for 1907.
2 Ibid., Minutes of the Eighth AGM.
3 Ibid., Ninth AGM.
4 Ibid., First and Fifth AGMs, held on 21 Mar. 1902 and 15 Mar. 1906.
5 Ibid., Sixth AGM, held of 20 Mar. 1907.
6 Inventory and Valuation, 1908, pp. 1–6.

7 Minute Book, Eleventh AGM, held on 13 Mar. 1912.
8 Ibid. Twelfth and Thirteenth AGMs, held on 18 Mar. 1913 and 26 Mar. 1914.
9 Ibid., Fifteenth AGM.
10 Ibid., Nineteenth, Twentieth, Twenty-First AGMs, held on 18 Mar. 1920, 16 Mar. 1921, 22 Mar. 1922.
11 Balance Sheets 1888–1936, Balance Sheet, 31 Dec. 1923.
12 Corr. In, Box 28, RAP–RAU, RRUSA to T.E., 2 Sept. 1904, 20 Jan. 1905.
13 Ibid., RRUSA to D.L., 26 Nov. 1906.
14 Ibid., ROA–ROB, Roberts to R.B., 28 Apr. 1908, 27 Jan., 10 Feb., 15 Apr., 17 June 1910, 21 Sept. 1911, 22 Apr., 9 Sept., 5 Oct. 1912.
15 Minute Book, Twelfth AGM, held on 18 Mar. 1913.
16 Ibid., Thirteenth AGM, held on 26 Mar. 1914.
17 *Thom's Directory*, 1909 and 1914.
18 Minute Book, Thirteenth AGM.
19 Corr. Out, Private Book, No. 3, 23 Oct. 1919–17 Aug. 1920, p.132, R.B. to secretary, Meath Hospital, 29 Mar. 1920
20 Minute Book, Eleventh AGM, held on 13 Mar. 1912.
21 Ibid., Thirteenth AGM.
22 Minutes of Evidence of the IWWU to the Commission on Vocational Organisation (NL, Mss 922–4, vol.4, 925, p. 1309, para, 8277).
23 Dermot Keogh, *The Rise of the Irish Working Class: the Dublin Trade Union Movement and Labour Leadership, 1890–1914* (Belfast: Appletree Press, 1982), p. 180.
24 Corr. Out, Private Letter Book, 1916–17, 1918, Foster to D.E. Benson, 24 Aug. 1917.
25 Mary Jones, *The Obstreperous Lassies* (Dublin: Gill and Macmillan, 1988), p.3.
26 Ibid., p. 4.
27 Ibid., pp. 41–2.
28 R.M. Fox, *Louie Bennett* (Dublin: Talbot Press, 1957), pp. 66, 114.
29 Jones, *Obstreperous Lassies*, p. 42.
30 Fox, *Louie Bennett*, pp. 114–15.
31 Corr. Out, Book for 10 June 1918–31 Dec. 1918, p. 247, Foster to Musgrave, 29 Oct. 1918.
32 Jones, *Obstreperous Lassies*, p. 79.
33 Fox, *Louie Bennett*, pp. 114–15.
34 Daly, Mary E., *Dublin the Deposed Capital* (Cork: Cork University Press, 1984), pp. 70–2.
35 Jones, *Obstreperous Lassies*, p. 9.
36 Daly, *Dublin, the Deposed Capital*, p. 73.
37 Minute Book, Twelfth AGM.
38 Corr. In, Box 29, DEO–DEZ, Dey Time Registers to D.L., 20 Sept. 1911.
39 Ibid., ED–EK, Edinburgh Roperie and Sailcloth Co. Ltd to D.L., 3 Oct. 1913.
40 Ibid., DAA–DAN, Plonk Davis to D. L., 20 Oct. 1913.
41 Jones, *Obstreperous Lassies*, p. 10.
42 S.J. Connolly (ed.), *The Oxford Companion to Irish History* (Oxford: Oxford University Press, 1998), pp. 163, 274.
43 Joseph V. O'Brien, *Dear Dirty Dublin* (London: University of California Press, 1982), pp. 214–15.
44 Ibid., p. 219.
45 Corr. In, Box 29, DUA–DUC, Coghlan to D.L., 5 Nov. 1913.

46 Ibid., The Dublin Employers' Federation, Ltd Incorporated under the Companies (Consolidation) Act, 1908. Memorandum and Articles of Association.
47 Minute Book, Fourteenth AGM, held on 24 Mar. 1915.
48 Ibid., Fifteenth, AGM, held on 29 Mar. 1916.
49 Ibid., Sixteenth AGM, held on 28 Mar. 1917.
50 Ibid., Seventeenth AGM, held on 20 Mar. 1918.
51 Eighteenth AGM.
52 Corr. In, Box 30, FE–FEN, Federation of Laundry Associations to D.L., 20 Nov. 1914.
53 Ibid., Box 29, DUA–DUC, Dublin Employers' Federation to D.L., 3 Sept. 1914.
54 Corr. Out, Private Letter Book, 1913–1915 (2), D.L. to Whitham, 15 Dec. 1914.
55 Ibid., D.L. to Editor, *Laundry Record*, 21 Dec. 1914.
56 Corr. In, Box 35, C–CU, City and County of Dublin Recruiting Committee to R.B., 22 Sept. 1915.
57 Pauline Gregg, *A Social and Economic History of Britain 1760–1955* (London: Harrap, 1960), p.417.
58 *The Starchroom Laundry Journal* (15 Dec. 1919).
59 Corr. Out, Private Letter Book, 1913–1915 (2), D.L. to Hon. Sec. Rathmines Committee for the Prevention and Relief of Distress, 13 Oct. 1914.
60 Ibid., Transferred from Private Letter Book, 1915–1916 (2), D.L. to Green, 22 Jan. 1916.
61 Ibid., D.L. to secretary, Auxiliary Hospital, Bray, 6 Mar. 1916.
62 Ibid., R.B. to Nugent, 24 Aug. 1916.
63 Ibid., D.L. to Messrs Dawson and Mason, 24 Aug. 1916.
64 Ibid., Book for 10 June 1918–31 Dec. 1918, D.L. to Petrol Control Department, 14 Oct. 1918.
65 Ibid., D.L. to Coal Controller, 7 Sept. 1918.
66 Ibid., Foster to Alliance Gas Co., 25 July 1918.
67 Ibid., Foster to Goodall, 26 July 1918.
68 Ibid., D.L. to Appleby, Ministry of Munitions, 17 June 1918.
69 Ibid., D.L. to Ministry of Munitions, 11 July 1918; D.L. to Match Control Office, 17 June 1917.
70 Ibid., Private Letter Book, 1916–1917, 1918, D.L. to Petrol Control Committee, Board of Trade, 18 May 1917.
71 Ibid., manager, D.L. to Petrol Control Committee, 29 May 1917.
72 Ibid., Foster to Fallon, Petrol Control Committee, Dublin, 25 July 1917.
73 Ibid., Foster to Petrol Control Committee, London, 20 Dec. 1917.
74 Ibid., Book for 10 June 1918–31 Dec. 1918, Foster to Petrol Control Department, Dublin Castle, 14 Dec. 1918.
75 Ibid., Transferred from Private Letter Book (2), 13 Jan. 1916–24 Nov. 1916, D.L. to Edmondson, 4 Oct. 1916.
76 Ibid., Private Letter Book (2), 1916–17, 1918, D.L. to Manor Mill, 13, 19 Apr. 1917.
77 Elizabeth Butler, *Women and the Trades: The Pittsburgh Survey* (New York: Charities Publication Committee, 1909), p.164.
78 Corr. Out, Book for 10 June 1918–31 Dec. 1918, Foster to Steele, 15, 21 June 1918.
79 Corr. In, Box 29, Dublin Fire and Property Losses to D.L., 3 June 1916; Dublin Corporation, Electricity Supply Committee to D.L., 6 July 1916.
80 Corr. Out, Book for 10 June 1918–31 Dec. 1918, D.L. to Musgrave, 29 Oct. 1918.
81 Ibid., Private Letter Book, 8 Jan. 1919–21 Oct. 1919, manager, D.L. to Armitage, 28 Aug. 1919.

82 Ibid., Private Book, No. 3, 23 Oct. 1919–17 Aug. 1920, R.B. to D.E. Benson, 13 Jan. 1920.

83 Ibid., Printed Letter Books (4), 18 Aug. 1920–11 May 1921, R.B. to Crabree, 18 Mar. 1921.

84 Ibid., Private Letter Book (2), 1916–17, 1918, Foster to D.E. Benson, 24 Aug. 1917.

85 Gregg, *Social and Economic History of Britain*, pp. 470–2.

86 Corr. Out, Private Book, 23 Oct. 1919–17 Aug. 1920, D.L. to Lowes, 21, 29 Nov. 1919.

87 Ibid., Foster to Stark, 10 June 1920.

88 Ibid., 15 June 1920.

89 Ibid., 21 July 1920.

90 Ibid., 11 Aug. 1920.

91 Ibid., Printed Letter Book 1920–1 (4), 18 Aug. 1920–11 May 1921, Foster to Stark, 3 Sept. 1920.

92 Ibid., Private Letter Book (6), 7 Dec. 1921–6 Nov. 1922, Sec., D.L. to Mellon, 7 Sept. 1922.

93 Ibid., Transferred from Private Letter Book 1915–16, 13 Jan. 1916–24 Nov. 1916, R.B. to Milligan, 28 Mar. 1916.

94 Ibid., Private Book, 1919–20, No. 3, 23 Oct. 1919–17 Aug. 1920, R.B. to Mellon, 9 Feb. 1920.

95 Ibid., Book for 10 June 1918–31 Dec. 1918, R.B. to Mason, 8 Aug. 1918.

96 Ibid., Private Letter Book 1919–20, 8 Jan. 1919–21 Oct. 1919, R.B. to Fletcher, 30 Jan. 1919.

97 Ibid., R.B. to Maddock, 20 Feb. 1919.

98 Ibid., R.B. to Stark, 12 Aug. 1919.

99 Ibid., R.B. to Goodall, 13 Aug. 1919.

100 Ibid., Private Letter Book,1921–3, (6–7) Book 6, 7 Dec. 1921–6 Nov. 1922, R.B. to Stark, 15 Nov. 1921.

101 Interview with D. Benson, 19 June 1995.

102 Corr. Out, Transferred from Private Letter Book, 1915–16, 13 Jan. 1916–24 Nov. 1916, R.B. to editor, *Power Laundry*, London, 24 Oct. 1916.

103 Ibid., Private Book, 23 Oct. 1919–17 Aug. 1920, D.L. to Musgrave, 22 Nov. 1919.

104 Ibid., 10 June 1918–31 Dec. 1918, Foster to Musgrave, 29 Oct. 1918.

105 Ibid., Printed Letter Books (4), Book 4, 18 Aug. 1920–11 May 1921, R.B. to Goodall, 20 Aug. 1920.

106 Ibid., Private Letter Book, 8 Jan. 1919–21 Oct. 1919, R.B. to Kellett, 8 Aug. 1919; manager to Kellett, 19 Aug. 1919.

107 Twenty-Second AGM, held on 21 Mar. 1923.

108 Twenty-First AGM, held on 22 Mar. 1922.

109 Twenty-Second AGM; Dub. 56, Balance Sheets 1888–1936. Balance Sheet, 31 Dec. 1907.

110 Dub.56, Wages Book, 1921–23, week commencing 24 June 1922.

111 Corr. Out, Private Book, 23 Oct. 1919–17 Aug. 1920, D.L. to Bloomfield, Terenure, White Heather, Blackrock, Phoenix, Dunlop, Mirror Laundries, 15 Mar. 1920.

112 Ibid., manager to Osborne, 2 June 1920.

113 Ibid., R.B. to Stark, 11 May 1920.

114 Twenty-Second AGM.

115 Twenty-Seventh AGM.

116 *Thom's Directory*, 1924 and 1951.
117 Jim Nolan, *The Changing Face of Dundrum* (Dublin: Dundrum Books, 1993). p.59.
118 Dub.56, Deeds and Leases.
119 Twenty-Sixth and Twenty-Seventh AGMs, held on 31 Mar. 1927 and 22 Mar.
     1928.
120 Twenty-Sixth, Twenty-Seventh and Twenty-Eighth AGMs.
121 Interview with D. Benson, 19 June 1995.
122 Thirty-Ninth AGM, held on 2 Apr. 1940.
123 Twenty-Second and Twenty-Third AGMs.
124 Twenty-Eighth AGM, held on 21 Mar. 1929.
125 Twenty-Ninth AGM, held on 13 Mar. 1930
126 Thirtieth AGM , held on 19 Mar. 1931.
127 Corr. Out, Private Book 1921, No. 5, 12 May 1921–6 Dec. 1921, R.B. to Stark,
     18 Oct. 1921.
128 Ibid., R.B. to editor, *Laundry Record*, 6 Dec. 1921.
129 Ibid., Book 2, 21 Aug. 1892–17 Jan. 1895, T.E. to Jones, 20 Sept. 1892.
130 Twenty-Eighth AGM.
131 Forty-Seventh AGM, held on 24 Mar. 1948.
132 Forty-Ninth AGM, held on 21 Mar. 1950.

# Bibliography

## Parliamentary Papers

*Report of the commissioners appointed to inquire into the working of the factory and workshop acts with a view to their consolidation and amendment* [C 1443–1], HC 1876, XXX, Vol.II.

*Royal Commission on Labour. Report on the employment of women by Misses Orme, Collet, Abraham and Irwin* [C 6894–XXIII], HC 1893–4, XXXVII, Pt. I, 545.

*Reports of Inspectors of factories as to hours of work and dangerous machinery in laundries and to their sanitary condition* [C 7418], HC 1894, XXI, 709.

*Annual report of the chief inspector of factories and workshops for the year ending 31 Oct. 1897* [C 8965], HC 1898, XIV, 1.

*List of Religious and Charitable Institutions in which Laundries are carried on* [Cd. 2741], HC 1905, XCVIII, 85.

## Books

Adams, Samuel and Sarah, *The Complete Servant* (Lewes: Southover Press, 1989).

Archer, Joseph, *Statistical Survey of the County Dublin* (Dublin, 1801).

Arlen, F.H.A., 'The Working Class Housing Movement', in Michael J. Bannon (ed.), *The Emergence of Irish Planning* (Dublin: Turoe Press, 1975).

Ball, Francis Elrington, *History of the County Dublin*, Vol.2 (Dublin: Alex. Thom, 1903).

Beeton, Isabella, *Mrs. Beeton's Cookery Book* (London/Melbourne: Ward, Lock, 1912).

Beeton, Isabella, *The Book of Household Management* (London: Ward, n.d.).

Bennett, Douglas, *Encyclopaedia of Dublin* (Dublin: Gill and Macmillan, 1991).

Benson, Jane, *Quaker Pioneers in Russia* (London: Headley Brothers, 1902).

Bourke, Joanna, *Husbandry to Housewifery* (New York: Oxford University Press, 1993).

Burke, Helen, *The People and the Poor Law* (Women's Education Bureau, 1987).

Butler, Elizabeth, *Women and the Trades: The Pittsburgh Survey* (New York: Charities Publication Committee, 1909).

Clear, Caitriona, 'Walls within Walls—Nuns in 19th-Century Ireland', Chris Curtin, Pauline Jackson and Barbara O'Connor (eds), *Gender in Irish Society* (Galway: Galway University Press, 1987).

Clear, Caitriona, *Nuns in Nineteenth-Century Ireland* (Dublin: Gill and Macmillan, 1987).

Connolly, S.J. (ed.), *The Oxford Companion to Irish History* (Oxford: Oxford University Press, 1998).

Costello, Peter, *Dublin Churches* (Dublin: Gill and Macmillan, 1989).

Cunnington, C. Willet and Phillis, and Charles Beard, *A Dictionary of English Costume 900–1900* (London: A. & C. Black, 1976).

Daly, Mary E., *Dublin the Deposed Capital* (Cork: Cork University Press, 1984).

*Dictionary of National Biography*, Vol.16 (Oxford: Oxford University Press, 1888).

Ensor, Robert, *Oxford History of England, 1870–1914* (Oxford: Oxford University Press, 1988).

Farmar, Tony, *Ordinary Lives* (Dublin: A. & A. Farmar, 1995).

Finnegan, Frances, *Do Penance or Perish* (Piltown, Co. Kilkenny: Congrave Press Ireland, 2001).

Forster, Margaret, *Hidden Lives: a Family Memoir* (London: Viking, 1995).

Forster, Margaret, *Rich Desserts and Captain's Thin: A Family and Their Times, 1831–1931* (London: Chatto & Windus, 1997).

Foster, R.F., *Modern Ireland 1600–1972* (London: Allen Lane, The Penguin Press, 1988).

Fox, R.M., *Louie Bennett* (Dublin: Talbot Press, 1957).

Girouard, Mark, *Life in the English Country House* (Harmondsworth: Penguin Books, 1980).

Gregg, Pauline, *A Social and Economic History of Britain 1760–1955* (London: Harrap, 1960).

Hearn, Mona, *Below Stairs* (Dublin: Lilliput Press, 1993).

JB, *From the Lune to the Neva* (London: Saml. Harris, 1879).

Jeremy, David J. (ed.), *Dictionary of Business Biography* ( London: Butterworth, 2 vols, 1984).

Johnston, Mairin, *Around the Banks of Pimlico* (Dublin: Attic Press, 1985).

Jones, Mary, *The Obstreperous Lassies* (Dublin: Gill and Macmillan, 1988).

Kearns, Kevin C., *Dublin Tenement Life* (Dublin: Gill and Macmillan, 1994).

Keogh, Dermot, *The Rise of the Irish Working Class: the Dublin Trade Union Movement and Labour Leadership, 1890–1914* (Belfast: Appletree Press, 1982).

Luddy, Maria (ed.), 'Magdalen Asylums, Doc. 20, Guide for the Religious Called Sisters of Mercy (London, 1866)', *Women in Ireland, 1800–1918* (Cork: Cork University Press, 1995).

M'Cready, Revd C.J., *Dublin Street Names, Dated and Explained* (Blackrock: Carrig Books, 1998).

Martindale, Hilda, *From One Generation to Another* (London: Allen and Unwin, 1944).

McCarthy, Michael, *Five Years in Ireland, 1895–1900* (Dublin: Hodges Figgis, 1901).

Nolan, Jim, *The Changing Face of Dundrum* (Dublin: Dundrum Books, 1993).

O'Brien, Joseph V., *Dear Dirty Dublin* (London: University of California Press, 1982).

Pearson, Peter, *Between the Mountains and the Sea* (Dublin: O'Brien Press, 1998).

Pepys, Samuel, *Diary*.

Robins, Joseph, *The Lost Children* (Dublin: Institute of Public Administration, 1980).

Ronan, Revd Myles V., *An Apostle of Catholic Dublin* (Dublin: Richview Press, 1944).

Rothery, G. Cadogan and Edmonds, H.O., *The Modern Laundry, Its Construction, Equipment and Management* (London: Gresham Publishing, 2 vols, 1909).

Taylor, John, *Map of the Environs of Dublin . . . by Actual Survey* (Dublin, 1816).

Vernon, Anne, *A Quaker Business Man: The Life of Joseph Rowntree, 1836–1925* (London: Allen and Unwin, 1958).

Wigham, Maurice J., *The Irish Quakers* (Dublin: Historical Committee of the Religious Society of Friends in Ireland, 1992).

Wilken, Paul H., *Entrepreneurialship, A Comparative and Historical Study* (Norwood, NJ: Ablex Publishing, 1979).

Wilson, Mona, *Our Industrial Laws: Working Women in Factories, Workshops, Shops and Laundries and How to Help Them* (London: Duckworth, 1899).

Woods, Audrey, *Dublin Outsiders* (Dublin: A. & A. Farmar, 1998).
Zola, É., *L'Assommoir* (Penguin Books).


## Directories

Kelly's *Post Office London Directory*.
*Thom's Directory*.


## Periodicals

'Thomas Edmondson', *The Friend*, 1908, New Series, 48, p. 1182.
Bayley-Butler, Beatrice, 'Lady Arabella Denny', *Dublin Historical Record*,
    9 (1946–48), pp. 9–10.
Butler, Sr. Katherine, 'Friends in Dublin', *Dublin Historical Record*, 44, p. 34.
Costello, Mary, 'The Sisterhood of Sorrow', No.1, 'The Magdalens',
    *Lady of the House* (15 Feb. 1897), p. 8.
Costelloe, Mary, 'The Sisterhood of Sorrow', No.2, 'The Magdalens',
    ibid. (15 Mar. 1897), p. 7.
Costelloe, Mary, 'The Sisterhood of Sorrow', No.3, 'The Magdalens',
    ibid. (15 Apr. 1897), p. 8.
Costello, Mary, 'The Sisterhood of Sorrow', No.4, 'Conclusion of
    Magdalens', ibid. (15 May 1897), p. 15.
Johnston, Denis, 'The Dublin Trams', *Dublin Historical Record*, 12.
*Lady of the House* (13 Feb. 1893).
Malcolmson, Patricia P., 'Laundresses and the Laundry Trade in
    Victorian England', *Social Studies*, 24 (1980–81), pp. 440–1.
Martineau, Harriet, 'The English Passport System', *Household Words*, 131
    (25 Sept. 1852).
Mason, T.H., 'Dublin Opticians and Instrument Makers', *Dublin
    Historical Record*, 6 (1943–44), p. 148.
*The Friend*, 1907, New Series, 47, p. 790.
*The Starchroom Laundry Journal*, 15 Dec. 1919.
Thomais, Eamonn Mac, 'Seven Hills of Dublin', *Dublin Historical Record*, 23.


## Newspapers

*Irish Times* (26 Dec. 1895).
*Rathmines News* (18 Apr. 1896), p. 3.

*Rathmines News* (7 Jan. 1899).

'A Woman's Crime', *Irish Times* (30 Oct. 1995).

Manor Mill Laundry advertisement, *Rathmines News* (30 May 1896).

'The Care of the Magdalens', *The Freeman's Journal* (21 Oct. 1916).

'New Laundry and Magdalen Asylum', *Irish Builder* (1 June 1878), p. 163.

'Pre-Danish Dublin Village Will Vanish Soon', *Irish Times* (1 Sept. 1955).

Dublin Laundry advertisements, *Freeman's Journal and Daily Express* (24 Dec. 1887).

'South Dublin Industries', *Rathmines News and Dublin Lantern* (25 Jan. 1896).


## Pamphlets


'A Leinster Friend', *Society of Friends in Ireland in 1896* (Dublin: William McGee, 1896).

Association of Dublin Charities, *Dublin Charities* (Dublin, n.d.).

*Centenary Year. Short History of Milltown Park. The Irish Province. First Dublin Residence, 1814–1914* (Dublin: O'Brien and Ards, 1914).

*Christian Discipline in the Society of Friends, Ireland 1881:* Rules and Discipline of Dublin Yearly Meeting: Revised Rules of the Society—to come into force First of Ninth Month 1881.

Coote, Michael H. (ed.), *A Short History of Taney Parish* (Dublin: Select Vestry, Taney Parish, 1968).

Dublin Laundry, 'The Side the Sun's Upon' (Dublin, 1894).

Dublin Laundry, 'Success: A Story of Twelve Years' (Dublin, 1900).

Fabian Society, 'Life in the Laundry', *Tract No. 112* (London: 1902).

*Gratis, Dublin, Wicklow and Wexford Railway, Arrangements of Trains*, 1 Aug. 1870.

MacDonald, Margaret, 'Report on Enquiries into Conditions of Work in Laundries', in Ellen Mappen, *Helping Women at Work. The Women's Industrial Council, 1889–1914* (London: Hutchinson/The Explorations in Feminism Collective, 1985).

Séamus Ó Maitiú, *Rathmines Township, 1847–1930* (Dublin: Rathmines Senior College, Rathmines, 1997).

Murphy, Revd Michael G., 'The Story of Milltown', 'A Section of Many Parishes' in *Blessing and Dedication of the Church of the Immaculate Virgin Mary of the Miraculous Medal, Clonskeagh, 8 September 1957.*

National Trust, *The Laundry at Castleward.*

# Appendix

The Side ..THE.. Sun's Upon

Illustrated.

Figure 1. Pamphlet issued by the Dublin Laundry in 1894.

# NOTICE.

## The following Schedule of Minimum Wages for Female Workers will be paid from the 2nd October, 1916.

### With some Experience.

| | | |
|---|---|---|
| Over 16 Years of Age 6/- per week. | | |
| 17 " " 7/- " | | |
| 18 " " 8/6 " | | |
| 19 " " 10/- " | | |
| 20 " " 11/- " | | |
| 21 " " 12/- " | | |

### Learners.

| Age | Wage | Rising |
|---|---|---|
| Over 14 Years of Age 4/- per week. | | |
| 15 " " 5/- | | |
| 16 " " 5/6 | Rising to 6/- in 6 months. |
| 17 " " 6/- | Rising to 7/- in 6 months. |
| 18 " " 7/- | Rising to 8/- in 6 months and 8/6 in 12 months. |
| 19 " " 8/6 | Rising to 9/6 in 6 months and 10/- in 12 months. |
| 20 " " 9/- | Rising to 10/6 in 6 months and 11/- in 12 months. |
| 21 " " 10/- | Rising to 11/- in 6 months and 12 in 12 months. |

Signed :—Blackrock Laundry Co., Limited; Bloomfield Laundry Co., Limited; Court Laundry; Dublin Laundry Co., Limited; Dunlop Laundry and Dye Works, Limited; Harold's Cross Laundry Co., Ltd.; Kelso Laundry; Kenilworth Laundry; Metropolitan Laundry; Mirror Laundry (Dublin) Limited; Phœnix Laundry; Swastika Laundry, Limited; Terenure Laundry; Whitechurch Laundry, Ltd.; White Heather Laundry, Ltd.

Figure 2. Schedule of minimum wages signed by fifteen Dublin laundries, including the Dublin Laundry, in 1916.

# THE IRISH WOMEN WORKERS' UNION

(Affiliated with the Trades Council and Irish Trades Union Congress),

## 18 DAME ST., DUBLIN.

THE Irish Women Workers' Union is organised to improve the wages and conditions of the Women Workers of Ireland, and to help the Men Workers to raise the whole status of labour and industry.

The I.W.W.U. is out for more independence, more leisure, and more comfort for the Working Classes.

All Women Workers are invited to join, either in the Special Trade Sections (such as Printers, Laundresses etc.), or with the Central Body. Come to the office at 18 DAME STREET (second floor) and get further information. The office is open every evening from 7.30 to 9.30.

The Union has already secured an increase in wages for a large number of workers, and has a splendid programme of activities for the coming months.

Join up and help to make the world a better place to live in. We can do that if we stand together and help one another.

Hard times lie ahead of us: we must be ready to meet them. Organisation is the workers' safeguard. Therefore don't hesitate—

# JOIN Our Union NOW !

WEST, PRINTER, CAPEL ST.

Figure 3. The I.W.W.U. had a special section for laundresses.

DUBLIN LAUNDRY CO. LTD.
MILLTOWN,
Tel. 257.                          Co. DUBLIN

Servants'

Special appliances are
in use for the delicate
handling of servants'
aprons and similar
goods, to prevent in-
jury during the wash-
ing process, and these
articles are ironed by
hand by skilled work-
women.

| | | |
|---|---|---|
| Aprons, Plain ... ... | | 1d |
| „ Frilled, Embroidered, or other Fancy ... from | | 1½d |
| Caps ... ... ... „ | | 1d |
| Chemises ... .. ... | | 1d |
| Collars ... ... ... | | ¼d |
| Cuffs ... ... ... | | 1d |
| Drawers ... ... ... | | 1d |
| Dresses ... ... ... from | | 4d |
| Night Dresses ... ... | | 1½d |
| Petticoats ... ... | | 3d |
| „ Flannel ... ... | | 1½d |

N.B.—These prices are only for "bona fide"
Servants' Washing, and that of the plainest
description. Any fancy or trimmed articles included in a servants' list will be charged full
price.

Figure 4. The price list issued by the Dublin Laundry in the 1920s. It was usual
to charge less for servants' washing.

DUBLIN LAUNDRY CO., LTD.
MILLTOWN,
Tel. 257. Co. DUBLIN.

## Gentlemen's.

Our system of starching collars and shirts imparts a beautiful gloss to the linen and gives stiffness, but at the same time flexibility, so that they do not easily crack.

We iron the edges of collars as well as the sides, so as to give greater comfort in wear.

We shape double collars with a space for the tie to slip in when putting on, first damping the seam to prevent cracking when turning over.

Figure 5. Men's shirts and the stiffly starched collars fashionable at the time were a very important part of the work of the laundry.

DUBLIN LAUNDRY CO., LTD.
MILLTOWN,
Tel. 257. Co. DUBLIN.

## Ladies'

All Flannels, Laces, Silks, Blouses and delicate coloured goods are carefully washed separately by hand by women of great experience in such matters. They are also ironed by hand by experts. Each ironer only irons one class of goods all the year round, and so becomes exceptionally skilled in her particular line.

| | | | | | |
|---|---|---|---|---|---|
| Aprons | ... | ... | ... | from | 1d |
| Blouses | ... | ... | ... | ,, | 4d |
| Bodices | ... | ... | ... | each | 1d |
| ,, Web | ... | ... | ... | ,, | $1\frac{1}{2}$d |
| Chemises | ... | ... | ... | from | 2d |
| ,, Silk | ... | ... | ... | ,, | 6d |
| Collars | ... | ... | ... | each | 1d |
| Collarettes | ... | ... | ... | from | $1\frac{1}{2}$d |
| Combinations | ... | ... | ... | ,, | 3d |
| ,, Woollen | ... | ... | ... | ,, | 3d |
| ,, Silk | ... | ... | ... | ,, | 4d |

Figure 6. Note the articles priced 'from'; higher prices were charged for delicate fabrics, lacework and so on.

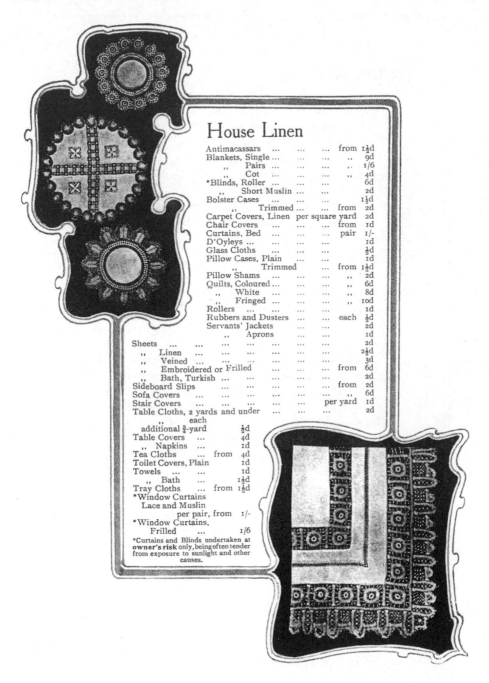

## House Linen

| | | |
|---|---|---|
| Antimacassars ... ... ... | from | $1\frac{1}{2}$d |
| Blankets, Single ... ... ... | ,, | 9d |
| ,, Pairs ... ... ... | ,, | 1/6 |
| ,, Cot ... ... ... | ,, | 4d |
| *Blinds, Roller ... ... ... | | 6d |
| ,, Short Muslin ... ... | | 2d |
| Bolster Cases ... ... ... | | $1\frac{1}{2}$d |
| ,, Trimmed ... ... | from | 2d |
| Carpet Covers, Linen | per square yard | 2d |
| Chair Covers ... ... ... | from | 1d |
| Curtains, Bed ... ... ... | pair | 1/- |
| D'Oyleys ... ... ... ... | | 1d |
| Glass Cloths ... ... ... | | $\frac{1}{2}$d |
| Pillow Cases, Plain ... ... | | 1d |
| ,, Trimmed ... | from | $1\frac{1}{2}$d |
| Pillow Shams ... ... ... | ,, | 2d |
| Quilts, Coloured ... ... ... | ,, | 6d |
| ,, White ... ... | ,, | 8d |
| ,, Fringed ... ... | ,, | 10d |
| Rollers ... ... ... | | 1d |
| Rubbers and Dusters ... ... | each | $\frac{1}{2}$d |
| Servants' Jackets ... ... | | 2d |
| ,, Aprons ... ... | | 1d |
| Sheets ... ... ... ... ... | | 2d |
| ,, Linen ... ... ... ... | | $2\frac{1}{2}$d |
| ,, Veined ... ... ... ... | | 3d |
| ,, Embroidered or Frilled ... | from | 6d |
| ,, Bath, Turkish ... ... ... | | 2d |
| Sideboard Slips ... ... ... | from | 2d |
| Sofa Covers ... ... ... | ,, | 6d |
| Stair Covers ... ... ... | per yard | 1d |
| Table Cloths, 2 yards and under ... | | 2d |
| ,, each additional $\frac{3}{4}$-yard | | $\frac{1}{2}$d |
| Table Covers ... | | 4d |
| ,, Napkins ... | | 1d |
| Tea Cloths ... from | | 4d |
| Toilet Covers, Plain | | 1d |
| Towels ... ... | | 1d |
| ,, Bath ... | | $1\frac{1}{2}$d |
| Tray Cloths ... from | | $1\frac{1}{2}$d |
| *Window Curtains Lace and Muslin per pair, from | | 1/- |
| *Window Curtains, Frilled ... | | 1/6 |

*Curtains and Blinds undertaken at **owner's risk** only, being often tender from exposure to sunlight and other causes.

Figure 7. In the small print at the bottom, the management warned customers that curtains and blinds were washed at 'owner's risk'.

# Regulations.

Our minimum charge for any one washing is 6d. We cannot allow any deduction from, or alteration of, the prices charged by us.

Unless our attention is specially called to valuable articles when sent in, only the value of plain articles of similar description will be allowed for in case of injury or loss. Valuable articles will be charged extra, according to the risk.

We cannot be responsible for articles on which we are not allowed to place a distinguishing mark.

Goods wanted out of the usual course, or unusually soiled, will be charged extra.

Curtains, blinds, articles dyed in fugitive colours, or frail articles, are undertaken at customer's risk only.

Although not legally liable, we insure to a reasonable amount **customers' goods against loss by fire** while on the Dublin Laundry Co.'s premises at Milltown, and hold ourselves responsible for such amount as we may receive from the Insurance Company and no more.

Please note our address is **DUBLIN LAUNDRY CO., Ltd., Milltown, Co. Dublin.**

Our Telephone Number is 257.

We have receiving Offices at **2 Upper Sackville Street, 64 South Richmond Street**, and **Eyre Street, Newbridge.**

Figure 8. The laundry used the price list to bring laundry policy and regulations to the notice of its customers.

DUBLIN LAUNDRY CO., LTD.
MILLTOWN,
Tel. 257. Co. DUBLIN.

## Please Read the
## following carefully,

As it will greatly assist us in maintaining an efficient system if these suggestions are observed.

WRITE distinctly in the Washing Book, and send it with your linen each week. Be sure that your full name and address are on it, or on your list if you do not send a book. We supply books free on application.

Write special instructions on a separate note, and not on the list of articles, and give to Vanman for delivery in the office, or send per post. Do not send it in the basket or bundle, or it may be found too late for attention. Verbal messages are frequently incorrectly carried, and we, therefore, pay no attention to them.

Do not use pins in your bundle, or fasten the linen in table-cloths, either in the basket or not. Injury to your own, or other people's clothes may result from these practices.

Have your linen ready, and do not delay the Vanman. He has a great many calls to make, and cannot get round if delayed.

Return your baskets, etc., promptly. We will obtain a basket for you, marked with your name, at cost price, if you desire it, but cannot allow our own baskets (marked D. L. C.) to be detained.

Make enquiries for any article short at once (by post preferred), to enable us to investigate the matter. We cannot acknowledge any claim unless made within *ten days*.

**Pay our Vanman weekly,** as we do not give credit unless special arrangements are made at the office. Obtain a printed receipt for all money paid.

**INFECTED LINEN.—Under no circumstances whatever do we undertake the cleaning of infected articles, nor will we receive linen (whether it be disinfected or not) from any house in which there is, or has recently been, illness of an infectious character.**

Figure 9. The important warning about 'infected linen' is in bold type.

**DUBLIN LAUNDRY CO., LTD.**
MILLTOWN,
Tel. 257.                                          Co. DUBLIN.

# Van Collections and Deliveries.

| DISTRICT. | COLLECTED. | DELIVERED. |
|---|---|---|
|  | Monday or | Friday or |
| Dublin City (North and South) ... | Tuesday | Saturday |
| Clonskeagh, Donnybrook, Ranelagh... | ,, | ,, |
| Rathgar, Rathmines ... ... | ,, | ,, |
| Sandymount ... ... ... | ,, | ,, |
| Kingstown ... ... ... | ,, | ,, |
| Ball's Bridge ... ... ... | Monday | Friday |
| Rathfarnham ... ... ... | ,, | ,, |
| Inchicore, Island Bridge and Kilmainham ... ... ... | ,, | ,, |
| Newbridge, Curragh and Kildare ... | ,, | ,, |
| Harold's Cross and Terenure ... | Monday | Saturday |
| Blackrock, Booterstown ... ... | Tuesday | Saturday |
| Merrion, Monkstown, Williamstown | ,, | ,, |
| Dalkey ... ... ... ... | ,, | ,, |
| Carrickmines, Foxrock and Stillorgan | ,, | ,, |
| Dundrum ... ... ... | ,, | ,, |
| Drumcondra and Phibsboro' ... | ,, | ,, |
| Clontarf, Dollymount and Fairview... | ,, | ,, |
| Naas ... ... ... ... | ,, | ,, |
| Ballybrack and Killiney ... ... | Wednesday | Wednesday |
| Shankill and Bray ... ... | ,, | ,, |
| Greystones ... ... ... | ,, | ,, |
| Howth and Sutton ... ... | ,, | ,, |
| Wicklow, Rathnew, Delgany, &c. ... | Thursday | Thursday |
| Malahide ... ... ... | Wednesday | Wednesday |

Figure 10. The extent of the laundry service in the 1920s.

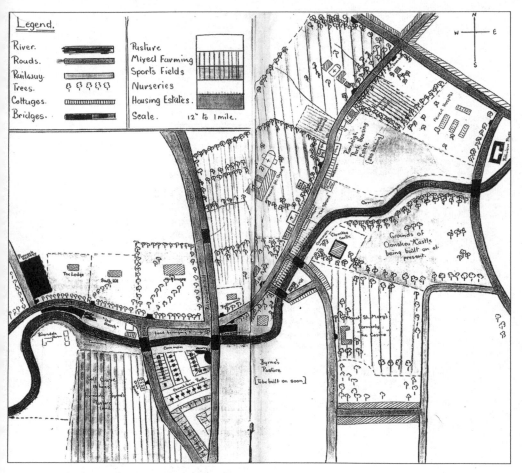

Figure 11. Milltown at the beginning of the twentieth century (courtesy of St. Anne's Primary School, Milltown, Dublin).

IN LOVING MEMORY

OF

# THOMAS EDMONDSON,

WHO DEPARTED THIS LIFE AT

THE ENGLISH HOSPITAL, RIO DE JANEIRO,

ON THE 11TH OF SECOND-MONTH, 1908,

IN HIS 71ST YEAR.

Oh ! call it not death, 'tis a holy sleep,
And the precious dust the Lord will keep ;
He shall wake again, and how satisfied,
With the likeness of Him who for him died.

ENGLISH CEMETERY.        RIO DE JANEIRO,        SECOND-MONTH, 12TH, 1908.

Figure 12.

# Index

231